The Many Voyages
of Arthur Wellington Clah

Arthur Wellington Clah

The Many Voyages of Arthur Wellington Clah

A Tsimshian Man on the Pacific Northwest Coast

Peggy Brock

UBCPress · Vancouver · Toronto

LIBRARY AND ARCHIVES CANADA CATALOGUING IN PUBLICATION

Brock, Peggy
The many voyages of Arthur Wellington Clah :
a Tsimshian man on the Pacific Northwest Coast / Peggy Brock.

Includes bibliographical references and index.
ISBN 978-0-7748-2005-9 (bound); 978-0-7748-2006-6 (pbk.)

1. Clah, Arthur Wellington, 1831-1916. 2. Clah, Arthur Wellington,
1831-1916 – Diaries. 3. Clah, Arthur Wellington, 1831-1916 – Travel –
Northwest Coast of North America. 4. Tsimshian Indians – British Columbia –
Government relations. 5. Tsimshian Indians – First contact with Europeans.
6. Tsimshian Indians – Biography. I. Title.

E99.T8B76 2011   971.1004'974128092   C2011-900994-3

e-book ISBNs: 978-0-7748-2007-3 (PDF); 978-0-7748-2008-0 (e-pub)

Canadä

UBC Press gratefully acknowledges the financial support
for our publishing program of the Government of Canada
(through the Canada Book Fund), the Canada Council for the Arts,
and the British Columbia Arts Council.

This book has been published with the help of a grant from the
Canadian Federation for the Humanities and Social Sciences, through the
Aid to Scholarly Publications Program, using funds provided by the
Social Sciences and Humanities Research Council of Canada.

UBC Press
The University of British Columbia
2029 West Mall
Vancouver, BC V6T 1Z2
www.ubcpress.ca

*C*ontents

Conclusion / 224

Appendices:

Illustrations

MAPS

Acknowledgments

This project could never have been completed without financial support from the Australian Research Council, which provided a small exploratory grant in 1997 and a Discovery Grant that enabled me to travel to London to transcribe the diary and make several research trips to British Columbia between 2005 and 2007. I would also like to thank the staff at the libraries and archives I have worked at over the years, including the Wellcome Library, the BC Archives, the Royal BC Museum, and Special Collections at the University of British Columbia. Darcy Cullen, acquisitions editor at UBC Press, has been a pleasure to work with, and the text of the book has benefitted from a careful copy-edit by the Press' editorial staff, for which I thank them.

Many friends and colleagues have supported and shown interest in this project. I will mention only a few. I would like to thank John Barker, for sharing his research on the Wellcome Papers, which helped me trace the diary's path to the Wellcome Library; Jennifer Haynes, who tracked the diary's accession through the Wellcome Library's records; Bob Galois, for enjoyable conversations about our joint obsession with the Clah diary; Burlington Wellington, for showing me around on my visit to New Metlakatla, Alaska; Sylvia Van Kirk, for making time to show me the McNeill land at Shoal Bay in Victoria and the graves of William Henry and Martha McNeill (Nisakx); Andrew Martindale for sharing his scholarship on Tsimshian history with me; and Adele Perry, for her interest in the project and invitation to present a paper on the missionaries in Clah's life. I am greatly indebted to Christopher Roth, who deserves special thanks for his generous advice and assistance in identifying and transcribing many of the Tsimshian names in the diary. His deep anthropological knowledge of Tsimshian kinship systems and his willingness to grapple with some of the ambiguities in Clah's text helped me enormously. He also translated my data on Clah's family connections (supplemented with other sources, such as Viola Garfield's *Tsimshian Clan and Society* [1939] and Barbeau's field notes) into a genealogical chart that clarified family links.

Three of the four maps that appear in this book are courtesy of Robert Galois and *BC Studies*. They appeared in R.M. Galois, "Colonial Encounters: The Worlds of Arthur Wellington Clah, 1855-1881," *BC Studies* 115-16 (1997-98): 105-47 (cartography by Eric Leinberger). They have been slightly adapted for use in this book.

In Australia, my husband, Norman Etherington, has been amazingly patient and helpful over the years of this project. My sons, Nat and Ben, have spent half their lives listening to and participating in conversations about Clah's diary. I would also like to thank Sherry Saggers, Ed Jaggard, Jacqueline Van Gent, and Anne Atkinson for their friendship and ongoing interest in this research.

Chronology

1778	Captain James Cook visits Nootka Sound on the Pacific Northwest Coast.
1821	British Parliament gives the Hudson's Bay Company (HBC) sole trading rights west of the Rocky Mountains.
1831	The HBC establishes the first trading post, Fort Simpson, on the upper Northwest Coast at the mouth of the Nass River. Clah is born.
1834	Fort Simpson is relocated to Lax Kw'alaams on the Tsimshian Peninsula.
1836	Smallpox epidemic.
1838	Clah's father, Krytin, is killed.
1846	Clah's uncle is killed.
1851	William Henry McNeill stationed at Fort Simpson as chief trader. He is chief factor in 1856-59 and 1861-63.
1851	James Douglas appointed governor of Vancouver Island.
1853	Clah works at the Fort Simpson trading post.
1855	Clah goes to Victoria in Harry McNeill's boat.
1857	William Duncan, Church Missionary Society (CMS) missionary, arrives at Fort Simpson in October.
1858	Fraser River gold rush.

James Douglas appointed governor of British Columbia.

1859   Clah embarks on an extended trip to Victoria and New Westminster from February 1859 to December 1860.

1860   Clah's brother Wallace is killed.

1861   Clah makes several fur-trading trips between May and October, up the Nass River and along the grease trail to the upper Skeena River.

1862   Clah makes a fur-trading trip to Victoria from February to April.

Smallpox epidemic starts in Victoria in March (after Clah has left).

Clah goes on a fur-trading trip up the Skeena River as a member of Legaic's party in May and returns 12 June. He visits Metlakatla on the way home.

Smallpox epidemic arrives at Fort Simpson in May (after the fur-trading party has left).

William Duncan and some Tsimshian establish the Metlakatla Mission in May.

Paul Legaic moves to Metlakatla in June.

Three white miners are murdered. Duncan accuses Clah of the killings.

HMS *Devastation* arrives in September to stop liquor traders. Clah brings Nisga'a chiefs to Fort Simpson for a meeting with Captain Pike.

Clah makes a fur-trading trip with Nisakx in October.

Clah goes to Metlakatla in December to invite Paul Legaic to his feast at Fort Simpson, where he parades four hundred men in military uniforms.

1863   Paul Legaic is baptized on 20 April at Metlakatla.

Robert Cunningham arrives at Metlakatla as a lay CMS missionary.

Clah accompanies Nisakx up the Nass River in April, trading for the HBC.

HMS *Devastation* confiscates two liquor-trading schooners, *Petrel* and *Langley,* in April.

Clah makes a fur-trading trip up the Nass River and across to the upper Skeena River in May–June.

Clah's daughter, Martha (Wellington), is born on 18 May.

Clah goes to Victoria on 25 June and returns 23 August.

William Duncan buys mission schooner *Carolina.*

Clah and Nisakx go on trading trip up the Nass River in October and meet HBC official, Hamilton Moffatt.

Clah hosts feast on the Nass River after Niy'skinwaatk's death.

1864   Clah returns with furs to trade from Nass River on 23 January.

Trading trip to the Nass River in February–March.

Trading trip up the Skeena River.

Clah leaves on 30 May by canoe for a trading trip to Victoria; he returns 15 July.

Clah accompanies Robert Cunningham to Nass River, where he establishes a mission with Arthur Doolan.

Clah makes a trading trip up the Skeena River in August, followed immediately by a hunting trip up the Nass River.

Hamilton Moffatt is appointed chief trader at Fort Simpson until 1866.

1865   Clah's daughter Rebecca (Wellington) is born on 23 April.

Clah makes four trading trips up the Skeena River, including a mid-winter trip from November 1865 to February 1866.

1866   Clah accompanies Legaic on a trading trip up the Skeena River in April and May.

Clah makes a canoe trip to trade with the Haida on Haida Gwaii in May and June.

Robert Cunningham becomes a HBC official in charge of a store on the Nass River.

Clah trades on the Skeena River in July and August during tensions with the Wet'suwet'en.

Nisakx marries William Henry McNeill.

Clah transports goods to Cunningham on the Nass River in December.

1867   Clah hosts feast on New Year's Day.

Clah goes to Nass River on 4-6 April to bring down furs for the HBC from Cunningham.

Clah makes two trading trips up the Skeena River in May and July.

Arthur Doolan and Robert Tomlinson establish Kincolith (present-day Gingolx) mission on the Nass River.

HMS *Sparrowhawk* with Governor Seymour visits the Northwest Coast.

The United States purchases Alaska.

Clah is briefly married to Habbelekepeen.

Clah brings his wife, Dorcas, and daughters back from the Nass River in September.

Clah makes an unsuccessful trading trip up the Nass and across to the upper Skeena River from November 1867 to January 1868.

1868   Clah builds a new house at Fort Simpson to mark his elevation to head of T'amks house. He holds a feast on 18 February. Duncan raises a black flag when he hears about Clah's feast.

Clah works as HBC trader in February.

Clah trades on the Nass River.

Ligwanh, who murdered Clah's uncle, is killed on the Nass River.

Clah makes a trading trip to the Skeena River via the Nass and grease trail in May.

Duncan divests Clah of his constable's uniform on 10 July.

1869   Clah, in charge of the schooner *Petrel*, trades for the HBC in January and April.

Omineca gold rush (gold first discovered in 1861).

HMS *Sparrowhawk,* with Governor Seymour, visits the Northwest Coast in May.

Paul Legaic dies at Fort Simpson on 7 May.

Paul Legaic II assumes the Ligeex name.

1870   Clah makes a trading trip up the Nass and the grease trail to the Skeena River with Dr. George Chismore.

Clah's son David (Wellington) is born on 3 November. Clah celebrates his birth with a feast on New Year's Day.

1871   British Columbia enters Confederation.

Robert Cunningham becomes an independent trader and store owner with partner Thomas Hankin.

Clah transports goods for Cunningham and Hankin up the Skeena River in May.

1872   Cassiar gold rush.

1873   Clah makes his first trip to the Omineca goldfields from April to August.

Clah makes his first trip up the Stikine River to the Cassiar goldfields in September.

William Duncan at Metlakatla extends a Christmas invitation to the Fort Simpson Tsimshian.

Clah's son Andrew (Wellington) is born on 27 March.

1874   Establishment of Methodist Mission at Fort Simpson. The permanent missionary, Thomas Crosby, arrives in June.

Methodist Rev. William Pollard baptizes four Wellington children in February.

1875   Clah makes his first trip to work at the goldfields in Cassiar; he transports miners and cargo in his own boat.

Clah adopts the name Arthur Wellington.

Clah and Dorcas are married in a Christian ceremony on 1 April.

Clah's daughter Fanny (Wellington) is born on 1 September.

1876	Clah buys land at Laghco.
	First canneries built on the Skeena River.
1877	Clah builds a house at Aiyansh on the Nass River and invites 300-400 people to a celebratory feast on Christmas Day.
	Alfred Green establishes a mission at Laxgalts'ap (Greenville) on the Nass River.
1878	Stephen Redgrave pre-empts the land on which Clah's Aiyansh house was built.
	Clah builds a house at Laxk'a'ata (Canaan) on the Nass River.
	Clah's daughter Mary Elizabeth (Wellington) is born on 28 August.
1878-79	Tomlinson leaves Kincolith mission.
1879	William Ridley is appointed bishop of Caledonia at Metlakatla.
1881	Clah and Dorcas are baptized on 23 January.
	Clah's last trip to Cassiar goldfields.
	Juneau gold rush.
	First cannery on the Nass River (Croasdaile).
	Indian Reserve Commissioner Peter O'Reilly visits the Northwest Coast in October to determine the boundaries of reserves.
	Clah's son Albert (Wellington) is born on 26 December, the same day his sister Martha marries William West.
1882	Clah's first visit to the Juneau–Douglas Island goldfields in Alaska.
	Andrew Wellington dies on 13 September on the Nass River.
1883	David Wellington dies at Port Simpson.
	Nisakx dies.
	Clah's daughters Ida and Maggie die.
1884	Parliament passes a law banning the potlatch.
	Paul Legaic returns to Port Simpson from Metlakatla.

1885   Wellington family moves back to Port Simpson. Clah's land dispute with the HBC begins.

1885-87   Temporarily no canneries on the Nass River.

1887   Clah meets Governor Alfred P. Swineford of Alaska in Douglas.

William Duncan and eight hundred Tsimshian relocate to New Metlakatla on Annette Island, Alaska, in August.

1888   Dominion government introduces new regulations to control fishing activities.

William West, Martha's husband, dies.

Clah's last trip to Juneau goldfields.

The Salvation Army arrives in Port Simpson.

1889   Dr. Albert Edward Bolton arrives at Port Simpson as medical missionary and becomes a justice of the peace.

1891   Wellington family starts clearing land at Laghco for agriculture.

Wellington family travels to the hop fields at Snoqualmie in Washington State.

On the death of her brother George Niy'skinwaatk, Dorcas Wellington is in line to inherit some of Nisakx's property at Shoal Bay.

Paul Legaic II dies on 8 January.

Martha Legaic becomes the Gispaxlo'ots' Chief Ligeex.

1894   Martha Wellington (West) marries Henry Wesley on 18 December.

Fanny Wellington dies.

1895   A house is built at Laghco.

1897   Thomas Crosby leaves Port Simpson.

1899   Wellington family goes to the hop fields at White River Valley, Washington State.

1902   Martha Legaic dies.

1903   Albert Wellington hosts a feast on the way to adopting the Gwisk'aayn chieftainship.

1905	Henry Wesley, Martha's second husband, dies.
1907	Dorcas Wellington receives her inheritance from Martha McNeill on 22 August.
	Clah visits William Duncan at New Metlakatla.
	George Kelly becomes Chief Ligeex.
1913-15	McKenna-McBride Royal Commission on Indian Affairs.
1913	Albert Wellington dies.
1915	Clah interviewed by anthropologist Marius Barbeau.
1916	Clah dies.
1918	William Duncan dies.

*The Many Voyages
of Arthur Wellington Clah*

steamed up in break/or I can see
the man are men call me one steam they
sheared me everything on steamer
ships all kinds guns big shot 9 miles
stay one hour an go back home

16. Monday. Very rough day. Clouds
But still raining. S E. Blow.
Sardony shiping freight to day.
promising will start tomorrow 17 of
December 1889. I went cross the Bridge
to see Sainada McDonald about 9 oclok.
went in his house. Just the time. have
Breakfast. an all his family with him
he ask. If I had Breakfast. I say. I
have my Breakfast. one hour ago.
he ask If I gat land. I said no Sir
he ask why. I Speaks to him about Judge
O Reily. that Mr O Reily wishing to help
me about the land Nasshiver and Fort
Simpson. I explaint him about the agen
the agent he Promise to have meeting
at Fort Simpson. to ask the Chiefes. If they
give me land. an ask Kingalog Council
If they give me land.
I told him I don't know who Belongs
the land. I come down here to ask
government about my land at north.
some I told him about our places
an war destroy every year

Page from Arthur Clah's diary, 16 December 1889. Wellcome Library, London.

Introduction

This is the story of one man's many voyages of discovery, both figuratively and literally, in the latter half of the nineteenth and the early twentieth century. Arthur Wellington Clah, a Tsimshian man who lived on the Pacific Northwest Coast, kept a diary for fifty years between 1859 and 1909. The diary's daily entries reflect the minutiae of life in an Aboriginal community and the many journeys into the colonial world undertaken by its inhabitants. Clah travelled hundreds of kilometres by canoe (and later by steamer) from his home at Fort Simpson. He travelled south to Victoria and Washington State; north as far as Juneau and Sitka, Alaska; west to Haida Gwaii (the Queen Charlotte Islands); and inland to the goldfields at Omineca, Cassiar, and Yukon.

> NWC History reported [by] arthur Welliington or indian named Sadle Clah. writed [written] when he travel[led] amongs[t] the heathen [in the] interior[,] where in land where heads [of] the rivers Skeenah [Skeena], nass[,] Stickeen [Stikine], Dyea of Alaska U.S.A. one time in Omineca. 6 years in Caisar [Cassiar] and alround the Coast amongs[t] the heathern from Victoria, Seattle U.S.A., Vancouver BC, Nanaimo, Comox, Bek-calar, Weekenoh, Bala Bala [Bella Bella] and Queen Charlot[te] island, Masuth [Massett], Skategats [Skidegate] where I travel amongs[t] them[,] preach them some times about our Saviour Jesus Christ the lord. Besid[e]s make myself good do[c]tor to them[.] But God help me for that work.[1]

Clah's voyages of religious and intellectual discovery were also wide ranging. As he boasted in his diary, he was "the first man [among the

Tsimshian to] believe the gospel of Jesus Christ in the mouth of William Duncan[.] he came from England from mission society[.] arrived Clah Callams [Lax Kw'alaams or Fort Simpson] October 1857[.] [H]e calling me to interpreted [interpret] amongs[t] the heathen people who keep all kind Dances every years and Big potleche [potlatch] amongs[t] themselves, thee not want King or Queen stop them."[2] The missionary William Duncan not only introduced Clah to Christianity but also taught him to read and write in English, enabling Clah to record his observations and thoughts in a diary that is a unique record of Tsimshian life and one man's responses to the opportunities, constraints, and restrictions of colonialism as it came to envelop his world. Such a first-hand account of colonialism from the inside is rare. It reveals the complexities of personal interactions between colonizers and the colonized and the shift from discovery of new knowledge, skills, and possibilities to the realities of land dispossession, interference by the colonial state in cultural and political matters, and diminishing economic opportunities: "Clquah Collams [Lax Kw'alaams][,] British Columbia[,] north west coast history[.] Arthur Wellington write report ... about the indian country that whit[e] people cliame [claim] that makes the indians crying for Gods Power and Kings Edwards power." Clah, the colonial subject, did not have to travel far to encounter new intellectual, spiritual, and cultural challenges because they were imported into his community, forcing him and his people to navigate the waves of change buffeting their own society. At the same time, economic changes encouraged the Tsimshian and their neighbours to extend their physical voyages beyond the bounds of their previous seasonal rounds of hunting, fishing, gathering, and trading. New worlds opened up as established modes of thought and interaction were constricted or were made redundant by changing circumstances.

Clah's diary is housed at the Wellcome Library in London, and microfilm copies are available. As the extracts quoted above reveal, however, there are many puzzles in the more than 650,000 words Clah wrote over fifty years. Because of the difficulties of working with Clah's text, scholars have made little use of it. Robert Galois wrote an important article in 1997 based on the diary. More recently, Susan Neylan has written two book chapters about Clah, and I have written several articles and a chapter that use the diary as a major source.[3] Many other historians and anthropologists have dipped into the diary, and Tsimshian communities have extracted information for communal and family histories. *The Many Voyages of Arthur Wellington Clah* is the first full-length book based on Clah's diary.

Rather than presenting a truncated version of Clah's diary, I supplement his text with other archival sources to investigate Clah's life in the context of the imposition of colonial rule in British Columbia. This book follows Clah on long arduous journeys along coastal waters and fast-flowing rivers as he fulfills his curiosity about distant places and chases the wealth, often illusive, of the fur trade and the gold rushes. Other activities – fishing, hunting, and gardening – kept the Tsimshian closer to home. Clah also took many rather quixotic trips to Victoria, the centre of the provincial government, in an attempt to reassert his rights to land. Clah's spiritual and cultural journeys towards an increasingly strong commitment to Christianity are equally fascinating, for his attitude towards Tsimshian cultural and social practices and political activities reflect a certain ambivalence and pragmatism in a changing world.

Clah began writing entries in his diary after only a few months' tuition in English, as is discussed in Chapter 2. As a result of this superficial grounding in English grammar and spelling, the diary poses great challenges for the reader. Punctuation is almost non-existent. I realized how important and useful punctuation was as I read the diary. A text without full stops obscures meaning. Discussing diary entries with other scholars, puzzling over which words form a sentence or phrase, has highlighted the extent of the text's ambiguity. Clah's spelling is haphazard. Sometimes the same word is spelled differently in one entry. If Clah was not sure how to spell a word, he wrote it phonetically. The names of English and Tsimshian people and places are particularly difficult to decipher because Clah spelled them out as they sounded to him. As a result, a name might be spelled many different ways throughout the diary. The problem of the spelling of Tsimshian personal and place names is compounded by the many different spellings used by anthropologists, linguists, and Tsimshian scholars throughout the nineteenth and twentieth centuries as they developed a range of different orthographies to accurately represent Sm'algyax, the Tsimshian language.

The task of reading and transcribing the diary has been immense. I have transcribed about 1,770 pages of single-spaced A4 pages, and the work is still not quite complete. Dealing with a document this size presents great challenges because there is no coherent narrative but rather a series of finite daily entries. Clah describes what he is doing with no explanation or context. Despite problems with the text, Clah has taken me on a stimulating and rewarding journey. I admire his extraordinary endeavour and his lifelong commitment to his writing. Clah, the man, was a complex character – admirable and infuriating, smart and self-serving, inventive and open to new experiences and ideas – yet firmly anchored in his own community. He was ambitious and dogged in the pursuit of his own and his family's interests but sympathetic towards the struggles of other Tsimshian. And he found the poverty of the old and infirm upsetting.

I hope this book partially fulfills the elderly Clah's fervent desire to tell the history of the Northwest Coast and its people to a wide audience. Tsimshian and other scholars will in future, I am sure, find a wealth of information that I can only touch on in this first book-length foray into the life of Arthur Wellington Clah.

1

The Life and Times
of Arthur Wellington Clah

The many voyages of Arthur Wellington Clah took him to distant places along the waterways that dominate Canada's Pacific Northwest. Rivers and coastal waters were the Tsimshian's highways, and their main means of transport was canoes that ranged from small canoes for gathering food on the upper reaches of the rivers to large cargo transporters for long-distance trade. The latter were superseded by steamships.[1] Clah lived close to the elements during his travels by open canoe. He was buffeted by rain, wind, and unexpected storms, which were even more dangerous during the long nights of the winter months. His life was also a voyage of revelation shaped by the devastations of epidemic diseases, the wealth generated by the fur trade, the disappointments of the gold rushes, and the tragedy of losing his lands. He encountered many foreigners on the Coast, from fur traders of the Hudson's Bay Company fort in his home village to miners from China, Europe, Canada, and the United States, from colonial officials in the goldfields to judges and politicians in the halls of government buildings in Victoria. Clah's spiritual voyage, however, was the most sustained journey of his life. He became a committed Christian and grappled with the implications of reconciling this new religion with the beliefs and values of his childhood. He lived in a society dominated by the wealth and violence of the fur trade, a society in which powerful chiefs predominated and status was celebrated by dances, magnificent feasts, and the distribution of property. But he lived to see much of that power and prosperity dissipate. He and many of his people were reduced to poverty as their lands were alienated, and the power of the chiefs was undermined by Christianity and the colonial process. Clah had to map a path through a changing social and cultural landscape, a landscape in which powerful chiefs became supplicant Christians and Tsimshian women served as liaisons with newcomer traders and miners. Clah negotiated his way through a developing colonial society that had its own social mores and political hierarchies.

As a young and middle-aged man, Clah found these voyages of material, spiritual, and intellectual discovery stimulating and challenging. He grasped opportunities to learn new skills such as reading and writing, sailing schooners, and mining for gold. But, ultimately, he became disillusioned as he realized that these journeys of exploration and discovery did not lead to a richer (in both senses) life. Although Clah became a disappointed old man, the skills and experiences he accumulated over his long life are reflected in his lifelong project – his diary. Clah's diary was the crowning achievement of his life. Although Clah never gained the recognition he sought for this prodigious work during his lifetime, the diary ensured that his life and his achievements would live on.

THE COLONIAL SETTING

The Aboriginal societies of the Northwest Coast were maritime societies. As in the South Pacific and Hawaii, coastal food resources and transport systems were water based. People clung to coastal strips and river valleys hemmed in by rugged mountain ranges. Although the region experienced heavy rainfall, it was not ideal for agricultural development because there was little flat land. The Coast was, however, rich in food and timber. Fish (both deep-sea and anadromous, that is, fish that migrate up the rivers to spawn), fish roe, seaweed, and shellfish were abundant, and Aboriginal people supplemented their diet with berries, other vegetable foods, and game. The main communication and trading routes followed the protected waters of the Inside Passage, the rivers, and the trails connecting the upper reaches of the rivers and their inland communities.

These geographic and environmental factors shaped the history of the peoples of the Northwest Coast, including the Tsimshian, Nisga'a, Haida, Heiltsuk (Bella Bella), Kwakwa̱ka̱'wakw (Kwakiutl), and Tlingit. Although oral and archaeological records suggest that people might have migrated from the north and east, these migrations were limited in scope, occurring from within the region.[2] Strangers from Europe and the eastern United

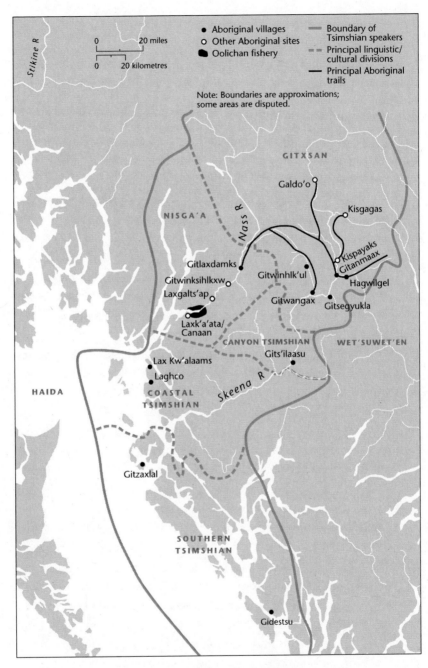

Clah's world. From R.M. Galois, "Colonial Encounters," 107.

States tended to approach the region north of the Columbia River from the sea rather than overland. The Spanish were the first to visit the Coast, but it was Captain James Cook's visit to Nootka Sound in 1778 that had the most profound impact. Cook's crew found a market for sea otter furs in China, a country with which Europeans had long wished to trade, in 1779. Demand for the exotic pelts ensured that ships from Britain and the United States would soon follow Cook to the Pacific Northwest Coast. Russian traders also competed for the Chinese market.[3]

Large sailing vessels became a common sight along the Coast at the turn of the nineteenth century. Aboriginal traders became adept at negotiating with Europeans and Americans, most of whom were independent merchants. But the large fur-trading companies of eastern North America positioned themselves to take over the trade. The North West Company sent explorers over the Rockies with Alexander Mackenzie, who reached the mouth of the Bella Coola River in 1793. Because the difficult terrain made communication and transportation between the region, which became the province of British Columbia, and the rest of the continent impractical and expensive, the ocean continued to be the most effective and efficient way to access the region. In 1821, the British Parliament passed legislation that gave the Hudson's Bay Company (HBC), which had amalgamated with the North West Company, the sole right to trade west of the Rocky Mountains, the so-called Indian Territory, for twenty-one years.[4] A few years later, in 1825, the HBC reached a boundary agreement with the Russian American Company to the north. By this time, the sea otter trade had come to an end because of the virtual extinction of the animals, and land-based fur animals had become the main target of trade.

The HBC established its first trading post in the upper Northwest Coast, near the mouth of the Nass River, in 1831. Three years later, the company moved the fort south to a coastal location, Lax Kw'alaams, which came to be known as Fort Simpson.[5] Although the HBC was a private company, its charter gave it special privileges and a monopoly on trade. The company was part of the British mercantile system of trade that sprang up in the sixteenth century and continued through the nineteenth. Although British Columbia did not become part of the formal empire until 1858, the establishment of HBC posts along the Coast ensured the region a place in the informal British Empire by the 1830s.

The HBC initially established trading posts along the Coast to undermine private traders, particularly Americans, who outnumbered the British. American ships sailed between Hawaii (the Sandwich Islands), the Dutch East Indies, Russian Alaska, and China and traded arms, ammunition, and liquor for furs in violation of British monopoly rights and international agreements. The HBC broke its own regulations by entering the liquor and arms trade in competition with these so-called Boston traders. The company introduced the first steamship, the *Beaver,* on the Coast in 1835 to enable its traders to access inlets that the less manoeuvrable American sailing ships could not negotiate. The HBC also poached one of the most experienced American captains, William Henry McNeill, when they purchased his brig, the *Lama,* in Honolulu in 1832.[6] Five years later, McNeill was commanding the *Beaver.* By the mid-1840s, he was in charge of various HBC forts, and in 1851 he was posted at Fort Simpson, where he remained until 1859, returning to Fort Simpson briefly from 1861 until 1863, after which he retired to Victoria.[7]

In 1846, Britain and the United States signed the Oregon Boundary Treaty, which formalized the international boundary between the United States and Britain on the Coast. Britain retained Vancouver Island, where the HBC's chief factor, James Douglas, had established a trading post, Fort Victoria, in 1843, and territory to the north of the forty-ninth parallel.[8] The quasi-governmental status of the HBC was evident when Douglas succeeded Richard Blanshard as the second governor of Vancouver Island in 1851.

As a colonial township started to emerge around Fort Victoria, it attracted Aboriginal people from other parts of Vancouver Island and mainland coastal communities, causing consternation among the newcomer community. Governor Douglas wrote to the British secretary of state in 1856, advising him that he was raising a militia of thirty men to control the people travelling to the town from the north and noting that thirty-eight canoes with three hundred people had already arrived in Victoria.[9] By 1860, the number of Aboriginal people converging on Victoria in the spring had greatly increased, resulting in tensions and conflict. Tsimshian, Haida, Tlingit, and other northerners were all living cheek by jowl. Violence erupted, and the colonial administration was unable to keep it under control. Douglas called Aboriginal leaders to a meeting and informed them, using missionary William Duncan as an interpreter, that each tribe would be allocated an area to live in and that they would have to pay a poll tax to fund the police needed to control them.[10] Thus, encampments were reserved for visiting tribes from the north. Douglas also sent three gunboats north as a warning to reduce rampant violence, drinking, and slavery.[11]

Aboriginal people in Victoria were soon vastly outnumbered by the arrival, in 1858, of thousands of miners, mainly from California, in search of gold. This influx forced the British to extend the formal colony to the Mainland. James Douglas became governor of British Columbia that year. The gold rushes on the Fraser River – followed by the Cariboo, Omineca, Cassiar, Yukon, and Alaska gold rushes – changed the dynamic between Aboriginal peoples and newcomers in the province and along the Coast. Although most of the miners were transient, some remained after the gold rushes, as did other migrants who serviced the miners. With formal annexation came gold commissioners to regulate affairs, British courts, a British legislature, and other appurtenances of imperial rule. The British navy was called on to control the illegal liquor trade and the violence that accompanied it.

The HBC hoped that gold would supplement the flagging fur trade. However, the rapid influx of miners and fears that the United States would annex territory west of the Rockies over which the HBC had monopoly trading rights led to a change in the status of the company and presaged government interventions and the dispersal of government officials in regions where HBC traders and factors had been the sole representatives of newcomer authority.

Gold mining had a dramatic impact on Aboriginal communities. Hunting, trapping, and trading were activities that Aboriginal people pursued long before Europeans came to their shores, but gold mining was new. Many Aboriginal nations along the Fraser River and rivers in the Interior, including the Omineca and Dease rivers, had to adjust rapidly to the invasion of thousands of men and a few women whose sole interest in them was as guides to the goldfields. Unlike the fur traders who had depended on the goodwill of their Aboriginal trading partners, miners considered Aboriginal people to be more of a hindrance than a help. Miners ignored Aboriginal peoples' rights to land and resented attempts to regulate their access. They exploited Aboriginal labour to dig and sluice for gold and to transport men and their provisions. Miners did not want to share the transitory benefits of mining with local people. Instead of becoming central to the colonial economy, as they had been to the fur trade, Aboriginal people were marginalized. Some were able to ignore the miners and their activities, but many were sucked into the boom, travelling long distances, only to run up debts or return to their villages with little to show for many weeks' hard labour.

A few miners decided to stay on the Coast, pre-empting land to open stores or establish fishing or agricultural enterprises. These people were a new intrusion on Aboriginal lands, where only the HBC had negotiated access previously. But land could now be claimed under British rather than Aboriginal law. The HBC's agreements with Aboriginal landowners were given new status under colonial rule. The company no longer occupied land at the discretion of Aboriginal peoples but owned the land under the British Crown.

As the rush for gold in northern British Columbia turned to a trickle, fish canneries began to appear on rivers and along the Coast. Thus began the industrialization of the resource that formed the core of Aboriginal subsistence and trade – salmon. As historian Dianne Newell notes, Aboriginal people of the Pacific Northwest "harvested prodigious quantities of local resources, especially salmon, which they processed and used for personal consumption, trade, and ceremony. Such well-managed enterprises allowed them to support a pre-epidemic [smallpox] population numbering in the hundreds of thousands without destroying the fishery resources."[12] The industrialization of the fisheries greatly curtailed Aboriginal people's access to fish and increasingly pushed them into a wage economy. Cannery operations were seasonal and shaped by the spawning season – from late spring through summer – of the various salmon species. These operations irreparably damaged the local population's main source of food and trade and failed to provide local people with enough work to maintain themselves by wage labour.

The colonial system impinged not only on Aboriginal people's economic activities but also on most aspects of life. As industries were established and settlers claimed rights to land, Aboriginal people were relegated to reserves as the rest of their lands were claimed by the Crown and then sold to private interests. The peoples of the Northwest fought unsuccessfully for decades to have their rights to land recognized.

In late 1857, just before the gold rush but long after fur traders were ensconced on the Coast, the first Christian missionary, William Duncan, arrived. The appearance of a missionary was not completely unexpected. A few Tsimshian had encountered missionaries on trips to Vancouver Island, and the appearance of newcomers who would bring a new religion had been predicted by a Wet'suwet'en prophet known as Bini who travelled widely throughout the region. Bini's teachings included Christian elements and promised European innovations in trade and technology. Because many of his predictions came true, it did not surprise coastal people when a proselytizer of a new religion appeared among them.[13]

William Duncan was sponsored by the Anglican Church Missionary Society (CMS). He arrived at Fort Simpson in October and was welcomed into the fort by HBC officials. His first priority was to learn Sm'algyax and then start a school for the few mixed-descent children who lived at the fort. Tsimshian who lived outside the fort could not speak English because the main form of communication between HBC employees and local traders was Chinook trade jargon. Duncan quickly realized that life at the fort, where alcohol was readily available, was not conducive to his mission. In 1862, he and some Tsimshian moved to Metlakatla, the former site of Tsimshian winter villages. Many other Tsimshian joined him over the years. At Metlakatla, Duncan could retain tighter control over the inhabitants. He dictated where and how they lived and who could stay. He built a village with a large church and industries, including a lumber mill and cannery, and he ran his own trading schooner.

Although some Tsimshian followed Duncan to Metlakatla, many stayed at Fort Simpson. In 1874, they invited the Methodists to send a missionary to them. Thomas Crosby took up residence and remained for over twenty years. Many other Anglican and then Methodist missionaries came to the region, establishing mission communities among the Tsimshian and Nisga'a on the Nass and Skeena rivers and among other language groups along the Coast. The Salvation Army soon followed. These denominations competed with one another for adherents, and even within denominations there were rivalries among different factions.

Newcomers who came to the Coast not only brought trade, new technologies and goods, and religious innovations, they also brought infectious diseases that decimated communities up and down the Coast. The Tsimshian and other Northwest Coast peoples were as vulnerable to these microbes as indigenous people throughout the Americas, Australia, and Oceania.[14] The most virulent disease was smallpox, but measles, venereal diseases, tuberculosis, and other infections to which local populations had not acquired immunity killed many people in the latter part of the eighteenth century and throughout the nineteenth century. The impact of smallpox was immediate and devastating, for it indiscriminately killed those in their prime as well as the old and the young. Epidemics occurred periodically at least from the 1830s.[15] The epidemics of 1836 and 1862 are documented and are known to have killed substantial numbers of people along the Coast. The 1862 epidemic began in Victoria, and the disease was carried up the Coast by Tsimshian expelled from the town. They reached Fort Simpson just after Duncan moved to Metlakatla. Fear of the disease encouraged many Tsimshian to follow Duncan to the more isolated location.[16]

During the maritime fur trade and the early decades of the land-based trade, Aboriginal people and traders from outside the area co-existed, each in their own sphere. They largely abided by their own laws and moral codes, but they learned from each other as they adopted and adapted new technologies. But colonization gradually ate away at Aboriginal people's autonomy. Some scholars, viewing this process retrospectively, represent colonization as the inevitable hegemonic imposition of one society on another.[17] But those who lived through it did not see a juggernaut that overwhelmed them. They experienced triumphs and irritations that gradually became major annoyances until they realized that people in distant places were making decisions that affected their lives and over which they had no influence.

THE TSIMSHIAN

The coastal region below the current Alaskan border, including the Nass and Skeena rivers and their tributaries and the rivers and islands of the Douglas Channel to the south, is occupied by the Tsimshian, who comprise four closely related language groups that interacted through trade, intermarriage, cultural exchanges, and warfare. The Tsimshian include the Gitxsan of the upper Skeena River, the Coastal Tsimshian of the lower Skeena River and coastal regions, the Nisga'a of the Nass River and, below the Skeena River, the Southern Tsimshian.[18] The Tlingit reside to the north of the Tsimshian in Alaska, and the Haida live to the west on Haida Gwaii.

Both groups had strong trade and other contacts with the Tsimshian. Wet'suwet'en and other Carrier language groups reside inland with trade links to the Coast. The Kwakwaka'wakw, Haisla, and Heiltsuk (Bella Bella) occupy the lands to the south.

The Tsimshian made the most of available food resources. During periods of plenty in spring and summer, they worked hard to amass food, much of which they preserved through drying, smoking or, in the colonial era, when salt was available, salting. During winter the Tsimshian relied on occasional hunting to supplement the foods they had stored in the previous seasons. The region's heavily forested areas supplied canoe- and house-building materials and wood for weapons, implements, and ceremonial paraphernalia. Between February and October, the Tsimshian moved first to the lower Nass River, where they fished for eulachon (candle fish), from which they made a valued trade item, a highly nutritious oil. They then moved to offshore islands to collect herring eggs and seaweed, hunt sea mammals, and catch deep-sea fish, including halibut. In the summer, they moved to the Skeena River to catch and dry salmon, collect berries, and hunt game. The Tsimshian traded with other peoples (including Europeans) along the Coast, on Haida Gwaii, and inland. They returned to their winter villages (at Metlakatla before 1834 and Fort Simpson after) by November.[19] From November to February, they lived in close proximity in winter villages. The days were occupied with artistic, ritualistic, and intellectual activities centred on winter ceremonials *(halait)*. Alcohol and other exotic goods introduced by fur traders were incorporated into these activities.

Tsimshian social, economic, and political relationships operated within a network of socio-religious units. Tribal affiliation was based on the winter villages, the primary political and economic units. Each tribe included a number of houses *(waap)*. Each house belonged to one of the four clans that formed the basis of Tsimshian social identity. A house took the name of the head of the house *(lik'agigyet)*, who had the highest ranked inherited name.[20] The four matrilineal clans, which intersected with tribal and linguistic boundaries, were Killer Whale (Gispwudwada), Eagle (Laxsgiik), Raven (Ganhada), and Wolf (Laxgibuu). The clans facilitated intermarriage and other alliances and regulated the exogamous marriage system within communities.

Nineteenth-century Tsimshian society was hierarchical. It had the following inherited ranks: royalty, nobility, commoners, and slaves. The highest rank was unique to the Tsimshian and was a product of increased competition among chiefs in response to the wealth generated by the fur trade. After the HBC moved its Fort Simpson trading post from the Nass River to the coastal location at Lax Kw'alaams in the 1830s, the ten Tsimshian tribes wintering at Metlakatla, in separate villages built on inlets on either side of the narrow waterway, moved to the trading post. One tribe became extinct soon after. At Lax Kw'alaams, they lived in one village, but occupied separate locations in immediate proximity to one another. This proximity fuelled competition among the chiefs.[21]

Chiefs *(sm'oogit)* performed both secular and religious functions. As heads of houses – the smallest social, economic, and political unit among the Tsimshian – chiefs held feasts and allocated inherited names.[22] During the winter ceremonials, they fulfilled roles as masked dancers *(naxnox)*, taking on a priestly guise when they donned frontlet, raven rattle, and chilkat robe for the *smhalait*. The *wutahalait*, secret societies in which chiefs played leading roles, were an innovation of the eighteenth and nineteenth centuries, introduced to the Tsimshian from the Heiltsuk to the south.[23] By the nineteenth century, there were four secret societies among the Tsimshian: Dog Eaters *(nulim)*, Cannibals *(xegedem)*, Dancers *(mila)*, and Destroyers *(ludzista)*. Only leading chiefs could become members of the Cannibal Society. Although membership of the other societies was open to all free people, only a few (mainly chiefs) could afford to pay for the ceremonies that were necessary to attain high rank within them.[24]

In the early nineteenth century, the Tsimshian resolved rivalries and intergroup tensions through warfare and a range of competitive feasts, dances, and ceremonies that became known as potlatching.[25] Potlatches gradually came to predominate over warfare as the means to assert superiority over rivals, both within and between tribes. Increased disposable wealth, which had resulted from trade with Europeans, facilitated these peaceful, status-enhancing activities. In such a status-conscious society, rites of passage, particularly those relating to death and inheritance, were crucial. Chiefs, whose standing reflected on the whole tribe, expected and received support to accumulate property from all tribal members. The property was then distributed to other tribal groups at a potlatch. A chief could intimidate or shame a competitor by distributing more property than his or her rival. Potlatches marked and celebrated the completion of a new house. They were the means by which a person acquired a new status within the house or tribe. Missionaries were strongly opposed to these ceremonies that related to rank, status, and wealth and lobbied the Canadian government to ban them. The government responded with a ban in 1884.[26] People, but most particularly chiefs, who converted to Christianity and joined a mission excluded themselves from these status-giving and status-maintaining ceremonies. This exclusion had long-term implications not only for the individuals concerned and their continuing roles in Tsimshian society but also for the society itself, for it depended on these activities to resolve rivalries, determine inheritance, and decide leadership positions.

ARTHUR WELLINGTON CLAH

Arthur Wellington Clah's diary provides a lens through which to view the interactions of the different peoples of the Pacific Northwest. Clah was born in 1831, the same year the HBC established the first land-based fur-trading post at the mouth of the Nass River. He grew up during the prelude to formal colonization and experienced the full impact of the colonial system as an adult. He died in 1916. Clah was born into the hierarchically structured, competitive society of the Tsimshian. He was a member of the Gispaxlo'ots tribe, whose head was Ligeex, and the Killer Whale house of T'amks. Ligeex and the Gispaxlo'ots had used the fur trade to enhance their position among the Tsimshian and their trading partners. Ligeex became the pre-eminent chief, controlling trade between the Coast and the Interior on the Skeena River until the late 1860s, when the incumbent became a Christian and moved to William Duncan's mission at Metlakatla. In the latter part of the nineteenth century, the Gispaxlo'ots found it increasingly difficult to find an appropriate person to inherit the Ligeex name. These difficulties resulted in prolonged negotiations in which Clah, as head of the House of T'amks and a senior Gispaxlo'ots, was involved.

Clah married Datacks, who was also known as Catherine and was later christened Dorcas. This was an unusual arranged marriage. Dorcas, of the Wolf Clan, was a well-connected Nisga'a from the upper Nass River village of Gitlaxdamks. Her mother's sister was Nisakx (Neshaki), a chief who used the fur trade to enhance her position, leaving her Nisga'a husband, Chief Saga'waan, to live with and later marry William Henry McNeill. Her decision to desert Saga'waan led to a series of feasts at which Saga'waan and Nisakx tried to shame each other with extravagant displays of wealth. According to the anthropologist Marius Barbeau, Nisakx outmanoeuvred her ex-husband.[27] Her close ties with the HBC ensured that she and her brother, Niy'skinwaatk, would become the company's chief trading partners. She was baptized as a Christian in 1863.

Dorcas' sons inherited the chiefly name, Gwisk'aayn. This suggests that Dorcas had a higher standing among the Nisga'a than Clah did among the Tsimshian. These tribal and familial affiliations ensured that Clah had strong links to two of the most influential Aboriginal traders in the fur trade: Ligeex, who dominated trade on the Skeena River, and Nisakx, who had powerful contacts on the Nass River.

Clah and Dorcas had nine children.[28] Only three survived to adulthood. Clah had at least three children by other women, including Henry Tate, who was brought up by Dorcas. Clah and Dorcas separated for a few months in 1867, when Clah had a brief marriage with another woman, Habbelekepeen, who left him when Dorcas returned with their daughters, Martha and Rebecca.[29] Of the children who survived into childhood, the oldest was Martha, born in 1863. Rebecca was born in 1865, followed by two sons, David in 1870 and Andrew in 1873, both of whom died in 1882-83 from complications from measles. Two daughters, Fanny and Mary Elizabeth, were born in the 1870s, but both died in their teens. The last child, Albert, was born in 1881 and died in 1914. Clah mentions the deaths of two other daughters, Ida and Maggie, in 1883, but he does not identify their mother, or mothers.

Clah's hereditary names were Hlax (ła'ax) and T'amks. *Clah* is an anglicized and shortened version of his hereditary name Sgała'axł Xsgiigł, which translates as "the eagle holding the salmon in its mouth by biting across it."[30] The first entry in Clah's diary gives his names and his birth:

Clah or Damaks [T'amks]
Number and count by every years[,] and when Clah first born in May 1831 first time[,] and all hudsons bay men Building fort @ Nass River are

in that time ... My Feather [father] an[d] my Mother going [a]shore thee waited another an[d] in the bay[,] this bay also was Name[d] Kaelle-ca-con 7 miles from medlakall [Metlakatla]. That place I was born in the same day and the same Month in May 1831.[31]

Clah's family life was affected deeply by the fur trade. His father was a very successful trader, which provoked his envious brother, Clah's uncle, to kill him. Clah was only eight years old. Seven years later, Clah's uncle was shot dead: "I have seen my uncle die for shot somebody Blame with him for deaths from bad diseases. Says my uncle give bad medicenes."[32] Clah's father, Krytin, had three children: the first son was Wallace, Clah was the second, and there was a daughter, Cclom-S-low.[33] Wallace was shot dead by a Tsimshian chief, Ligwanh, in 1860.[34] Clah waited many years to be compensated and avenged for the deaths of his relatives.

Clah was in his early twenties when he went to work at the HBC fort as a servant to François Quintal, a French Canadian HBC employee who had married a Tsimshian woman. Clah managed to learn some rudimentary English as he worked at the fort, even though Chinook Jargon was the lingua franca among traders and Tsimshian. After three years, he left for Victoria in a canoe captained by McNeill's son, Harry. Although Victoria before the gold rush was a small settlement, Clah quickly found work.

Clah returned to Fort Simpson after several months, and William Duncan came to the fort one year later, 1857. Clah approached Duncan because he wanted to participate in the classes Duncan was running for mixed-descent children. Duncan hired Clah as his language teacher, despite reports that Clah had recently killed an old woman.[35] Clah was an able pupil. He learned to read and write in English, and Duncan believed he was the first Tsimshian to grasp the significance of Christian teaching. Duncan asked Clah to accompany him on his first attempt to preach to Tsimshian outside the fort. He was worried that his knowledge of Sm'algyax might falter when put to the test. Duncan subsequently established a school outside the fort walls. Clah attended for two months before setting off for another long sojourn in Victoria.[36] Duncan noted on 2 June that ten canoes filled with around one hundred people were leaving for Victoria: "One of them is my most forward adult scholar a young man named Clah but a very bad man. He has made amazing progress and would have made more if others of the class could have kept pace with him."[37]

Page from Arthur Clah's diary (undated, 1859). Wellcome Library, London.

Victoria in 1859 was a very different settlement than the one Clah had visited in 1856, for it had been inundated by miners from California and had grown exponentially. Clah immediately found employment. He worked at several stores in Victoria and in the newly established settlement of New Westminster on the Mainland before the police hired him to report on the illegal liquor trade among the Haida in Victoria.[38] Clah returned north in January 1861 in time for the spring fishing. He went on his first fur-trading trip, to Hagwilget, in May.

For the Tsimshian, the most destructive concomitant of the fur trade, far worse than alcohol or firearms, was infectious disease. Clah remembered the smallpox epidemic of 1836 and the many who died from the disease. His account of the epidemic of 1862 is much more detailed. In that year, smallpox, which had been introduced to Victoria via a ship from San Francisco, quickly spread through the Tsimshian Reserve at Rocky Bay and then to other camps. Tsimshian expelled from Victoria took the disease north. Frightened people were given a day's warning to vacate the reserve. They burned their houses and blankets before leaving, and a gunboat in the bay ensured their departure.[39] Although doctors started vaccinating people in Victoria, three hundred Tsimshian had contracted smallpox and twenty had died by late April. Doctors also went up the Coast to vaccinate the Aboriginal population, as did Duncan, who was concerned the vaccinations were not taking. It is impossible from the data available to determine their effectiveness. The epidemic ran its course by December, when Clah wrote to Duncan that there had been 301 deaths and 2,069 survivors among the Fort Simpson tribes.[40] Presumably, Clah had been vaccinated, for he did not get the disease, even though he nursed relatives with smallpox. The Tsimshian also tried treating themselves with remedies such as the "woomasth" plant, which Clah went up the Nass River to collect in July.[41]

This catastrophe ruptured the spiritual cosmos and social fabric of Tsimshian society. Drinking and violence were two symptoms; burning religious paraphernalia and making sacrifices for absolution were others.[42] Clah believed the Tsimshian had angered the Christian God by lying, stealing, committing murder, and engaging in drunken fighting. He prayed for God to forgive them and take away the sickness. This crisis no doubt pushed others towards Christianity. Duncan's mission certainly benefitted, for Paul Legaic, chief of the Gispaxlo'ots and head chief of the Fort Simpson Tsimshian, was not the only Tsimshian to leave Fort Simpson for Metlakatla, which largely escaped the epidemic. The annual migration of thousands of northerners to Victoria ended with the smallpox, suggesting that many were concerned that their lengthy sojourns to the territory of the Songhees of Vancouver Island were contributing to their demise.[43]

Although Clah avoided smallpox, he did become sick with measles but recovered quickly. Several of his children were not so fortunate and succumbed to the disease. Clah suffered from many other unspecified

illnesses throughout his life. He suffered for several years from a chronic-
ally sore throat that at times incapacitated him. He often had colds and
influenza. He tried a range of Tsimshian and European remedies whenever
he or his family became ill and became so adept that he acquired a reputation as a healer. Despite taking a variety of medications, he still relied
heavily on spiritual interventions, whether they were through witchcraft
or, more commonly, the Christian God. When his two daughters from
outside his primary family died, he blamed a witch for their deaths. When
children in his primary family became terminally ill, he prayed relent-
lessly to God for their recovery. Although no one in Clah's immediate
family died of tuberculosis, many of his friends and relatives suffered from
the disease for years before their deaths. Clah often refers to people, particularly women, dying of "bad diseases," by which he means venereal
diseases. Many women were pushed into prostitution to access alcohol
and other commodities, facilitating the spread of venereal diseases.[44]

Legaic, who had so assiduously avoided the smallpox epidemic, died
of tuberculosis in 1869 while visiting Fort Simpson from Metlakatla. He
was one of many Tsimshian at the time who suffered from what Clah
described as "cough speed [spit] blood."[45] Legaic had been a pivotal figure
in Clah's life. When he died, Clah wrote, "O dear Paul I like him very
much.[46] Despite this close relationship and Clah's dependence on Legaic
to assist him in establishing himself as a fur trader up the Skeena River,
Legaic and Clah had had a rocky relationship, as we shall see.

Throughout the 1860s, with wealth accumulated from fur trading, Clah
had been able to hold a series of feasts that enabled him to succeed to the
name of the head of the House of T'amks when his uncle, who held the
name, died. It is not clear from his diary when Clah took the name and
position. Historical geographer Robert Galois suggests that Clah became
T'amks after he hosted a series of feasts in the late 1860s.[47] He notes that
Clah first adds the name to his diary on 22 April 1869.[48] Clah also displayed
his wealth through theatrical displays, including dressing young men in
British and American soldiers' uniforms and marching them around the
streets of Fort Simpson.[49]

The new Ligeex, who also had the name Paul Legaic, was recognized
at a series of feasts that began in October 1869 and ended in February
1871.[50] His accession seems to have been smooth. When he died in 1891,
however, his succession provoked controversy. One of the men who hoped

to take advantage of Paul Legaic II's sudden death and become the next Ligeex was Alfred Dudoward, a man who figures prominently both as a protagonist and antagonist in Clah's diary. Clah resented Dudoward's growing influence at Fort Simpson both in religious and secular matters, particularly his attempts to be both a good Christian (while actively participating in secret society ceremonies) and the head of the Gispaxlóots. Dudoward had inherited the title Sgagweet, head of the Gitando tribe. Dudoward's mother was from a chiefly Tsimshian family, and his father was a French-speaking employee of the HBC. When he was about eight years old, Dudoward became a student at the first school Duncan set up for mixed-descent children of HBC staff. His mother, Elizabeth Lawson (Tsimshian name Diiks or Diex), became an early convert to Methodism in Victoria, where she worked as a servant. On a visit to his mother, Dudoward and his wife, Kate, were converted at a revival in 1873.[51] On his return to Fort Simpson, Dudoward called a meeting at which it was agreed to invite a Methodist missionary to the village. Twelve years after the departure of William Duncan, Fort Simpson was once again the site of a Christian mission. Thomas Crosby became the permanent missionary who lived among the Tsimshian until 1897.

Although the internal politics of the Tsimshian and Christianity were always important aspects of Clah's life, external developments also influenced his day-to-day existence. The gold rushes had a profound affect on him. At first, he was involved in transporting provisions for the miners who were flocking into the northern Interior, but he was soon travelling to the goldfields at Omineca, Cassiar, and Alaska. He hoped to mine, but quickly realized that he could make more money by providing transport for the miners as they moved around the mining regions. Trips to the goldfields during the summer and fall kept him from home and his family for months at a time. The separation must have been difficult for Dorcas and his children, but there is little indication in Clah's diary of how they coped.[52] In the early years of the mining boom, Clah profited from his transport ventures but, as each boom petered out, he found it increasingly difficult to maintain himself and his family.

During this period in the 1870s and 1880s, Clah and his family moved away from Fort Simpson – first, and briefly, to the Skeena River and then to the Nass. With each move, Clah built a new house, which cost him money for materials, wages, and house-warming feasts. He also became

A view of Port Simpson, showing the bridge connecting Rose Island to the mainland village in 1884. BC Archives, A-04180 (photographer: Richard Maynard).

embroiled in conflicts over the land on which he built on the Nass River. The first house near Gitlaxdamks was erected on land to which his wife and children had rights, but this put him in dispute with a white pre-emptor and the local community. He then moved down the Nass River to a place he called Canaan (Laxk'a'ata), where he claimed inherited rights through his father. This move coincided with the federal and provincial governments' allocation of reserves, which galvanized the Nisga'a to make claims to land where the Tsimshian had traditionally fished for eulachon. Clah became enmeshed in these fights over land, returning to Port Simpson only in 1882. A decade later, he and Dorcas spent extended periods at Laghco, to the south of Port Simpson, on land Clah had bought from another Tsimshian. They started a garden and eventually built a house, and they commuted between Laghco and Port Simpson over the ensuing years.

At the time Clah and his family returned to Port Simpson, salmon canneries were sprouting up along the Coast, at the mouths of the rivers

A view of Port Simpson in 1907. BC Archives, B-03764.

and along the Nass River.[53] Although the fur trade and even the gold rushes had created opportunities for Tsimshian and Nisga'a to increase their wealth, the canning industry reduced most Aboriginal people to poverty. It interfered with their long-held fishing rights and forced them to work for wages or to do piecework during the summer. Wages were low and available only for a few weeks a year. Clah and his neighbours tried to supplement their meagre incomes in other ways. Many turned to horticulture, growing potatoes and other vegetables on small garden plots. But cultivable land was limited, and the weather not conducive to agriculture. Crops suffered from frosts and torrential rains. Some people travelled to the hop fields in Washington State during the years the industry survived in coastal areas. Others worked for lumber mills. All tried to supplement their wage labour with subsistence fishing and other food-gathering activities. But when the canneries' heavy demands for salmon reduced stocks, the government passed laws to limit Aboriginal fishing. The aging Clah and his family found it increasingly difficult to maintain themselves. As Clah grew older, he depended increasingly on his sons-in-law to provide for him. But one of his sons-in-laws – married to his daughter, Rebecca

– was a Welsh sea captain, William Beynon, who lived in Victoria and had little to do with his Tsimshian family.[54] In addition, both of the husbands of his other daughter, Martha, died prematurely. The first, William West, died in 1888 under suspicious circumstances – possibly murder. The second, Henry Wesley, died in 1905 after suffering a long illness.

The elderly Clah and Dorcas continued to tend their garden at Laghco, and Clah did a little fishing – he collected seaweed and herring eggs – and hunting, although his failing eyesight and frailty made it difficult for him to be active. Clah also became more socially isolated and politically irrelevant. He sometimes spent days alone at Laghco because he no longer had an active political role at Port Simpson. His commitment to Christianity, however, remained strong.

CLAH THE CHRISTIAN

Clah's adoption of Christianity, which took place before he started his diary, seems to have been gradual. He was introduced to Christianity by William Duncan, and it is possible that he had a sudden conversion experience, but it is unlikely. In Clah's diary, the first entries about faith in God appear when Clah was in dangerous situations on long canoe journeys, situations in which he and his passengers feared drowning. Clah called on God to save them and reprimanded those who did not have faith in God's power to protect them. Clah then began to preach to others as a matter of course as he went about his business, whether it was fur trading, fishing, or gold mining.

What was distinctive about Clah's Christianity was that he treated it as an individual decision and commitment. He did not join Duncan at Metlakatla in 1862 or later, although he was happy to play host to evangelists that Duncan sent to Fort Simpson. When the Methodist, Thomas Crosby, came to Fort Simpson, Clah attended his church and was eventually baptized and married by him, but he never described himself as a Methodist. When Clah preached to others, as he frequently did, it was as an independent Christian. He never attempted to win people over to a particular church – just to the Christian God and Jesus Christ. During his travels, he would attend any church or, occasionally, different churches on the same Sunday. He most often attended the Anglican and Methodist churches, but when Clah visited Victoria, he would also go to the Catholic church. And once the Salvation Army appeared on the Coast,

Clah attended their prayer meetings. Dorcas and Rebecca became members of the Salvation Army.[55] Christianity was perhaps the overriding influence on Clah's life. It provided the moral underpinning of his existence and gave it meaning. As he became older, prayer and preaching took up increasing amounts of his time, sometimes driving his family to distraction, even though they all became practising Christians.

Christianity did not, however, remain a private commitment in Tsimshian and Nisga'a communities. As different factions and tribal groupings aligned with particular denominations, intense rivalries emerged. Dudoward's championing of the Methodists helped his own leadership ambitions. He strongly resisted the introduction of the Salvation Army to Port Simpson because the church posed a direct threat to Methodism. By the 1890s, there were five or six Christian factions active at Port Simpson and other villages in the Pacific Northwest. The Anglican Church retained a presence, as did the Methodist Church. The Salvation Army marched around the streets on Sundays and often during the week. These churches were joined by offshoots of the Methodists – the Christian Band of Workers and the Epworth League – and the Anglican Church Army, all of which had their own marching bands and meeting halls.[56] There were also community groups that did not have religious affiliations – the Riflemen's Company and the Firemen's Company. These groups had uniforms, marching bands, and halls for communal meetings and ceremonies. Clah was closely associated with the Riflemen's Company, which was modelled on his own soldiers, whom he had decked out with uniforms, rifles, and musical instruments in 1862 and on subsequent occasions.

The spread of Christianity was facilitated by both outsider missionaries and local evangelists. Unlike Clah, many of these evangelists had denominational associations. The most prominent evangelist was Clah's nephew, William Henry Pierce. Pierce was used by the Methodists as a missionary vanguard. He set up mission communities that newcomer missionaries then consolidated. He was the first Tsimshian to be ordained, and he established an independent presence through his writings, particularly two books – an autobiography, *From Potlatch to Pulpit,* and a travelogue, *Thirteen Years of Travel and Exploration in Alaska.*[57] Villages up the Nass and, to a lesser extent, on the upper Skeena River came to be associated with the particular denomination that had either created or established a presence in them. These mission communities were modelled on

William Duncan's Anglican mission at Metlakatla or on Thomas Crosby's Methodist mission at Fort Simpson. Both Duncan and Crosby bought boats to facilitate their evangelism. While Duncan's boat was used mainly as a trading vessel, Crosby's boat, the *Glad Tidings,* enabled him to preach at different locations on the coast and rivers. His extended absences from Fort Simpson were one of the many factors that gradually turned the residents against him.

Both Anglican and Methodist missionaries became embroiled in conflicts over land, fulfilling some of the intermediary, non-religious functions that Aboriginal people expected of them. While the colonial authorities tried to sideline missionaries because they believed the missionaries were supporting Aboriginal people against the state, many Tsimshian, including Clah, came to distrust the missionaries because they were ineffectual at protecting land rights. Clah became particularly antagonistic towards Crosby because he believed he was more interested in exploiting the Tsimshian to maintain his church building than helping the Tsimshian to resist state encroachment on their lands. In 1887, after Duncan split from the CMS and the British Columbian Anglican hierarchy, many Tsimshian from Metlakatla followed him to Alaska, where he re-established his mission on Annette Island. The Tsimshian were persuaded that the US government would give them freehold title to the land and treat them as equal citizens, whereas the Canadian government had alienated their land and refused them citizenship rights.

The challenges of Christianity; new transportation technologies that were revolutionizing long-distance travel along the Coast; wage labour in canneries, hop fields, and mines; and, perhaps most importantly, the alienation of Aboriginal land put stress on the fabric of Tsimshian society. Some families tried to reassert the chiefly system as a defence against these emasculating forces; their efforts resulted in the revival of potlatching and negotiations to fill vacant chiefly names. Clah was actively involved in the Gispaxlo'ot's negotiations, and these concerns might have been the deciding factor that determined his return to Port Simpson in the early 1880s after several years' absence.

When Clah wrote the last entry in his diary in 1909, he was an old man of seventy-eight. Over his lifetime he had witnessed dramatic changes to Tsimshian society and the landscape. The young optimist who had voyaged far and wide physically, intellectually, and spiritually, excited by innovations and opportunities, had become an old man whose horizons had narrowed to a difficult day-to-day existence and occasional visits to his daughter's family in Victoria. Clah no longer had access to wealth or political influence; he lived a subsistence existence on his Laghco land and at Port Simpson. His Christian beliefs and strong moral stance against certain aspects of Tsimshian life continued. By the early twentieth century, anthropologists were replacing missionaries as the outsiders who took an interest in the Tsimshian and their neighbours. Clah, as a well-known and accessible Tsimshian elder, was approached for information about Tsimshian social and political formations. He was interviewed by Marius Barbeau in 1915, but he did not take up Franz Boas' invitation to become an informant. He instead recommended his son Henry Tate.[58] Had Clah been a younger man when anthropologists started taking an interest in Tsimshian culture, would he have encouraged or discouraged them? It is likely that he would have fulfilled the roles taken up by his son Henry Tate and grandson William Beynon and been stimulated by the newcomers' interest in his people and the opportunity to parade his expertise to influence how posterity viewed him and his people.

Clah was a man of great physical stamina, an intellectual with a strong commitment to his own and his family's interests. He epitomized Tsimshian curiosity in new ideas and technologies, but he could not anticipate the negative influence of colonialism on both himself and his society. He was very much a man of his time, and the daily entries in his diary allow us to glimpse his time from his perspective.

2

Keeping Account: The Diary

The diary of Arthur Wellington Clah gives us a rarely seen perspective on a colonial society in an outpost of the British Empire. Rather than offering a retrospective view influenced by hindsight, it records the day-to-day musings and observations of an indigenous person as he negotiated his way through a life marked by extraordinary changes.

Before William Duncan's appearance on the Coast, the Tsimshian were a non-literate people; English was a foreign, rarely heard language; and the concept of a personal diary was unknown. Yet Clah managed to maintain the discipline of daily entries in English over a fifty-year period, much longer than most diarists who live in societies in which keeping a daily account of one's life is an accepted mnemonic device and a means to record the minutiae of everyday existence.[1] With only a few role models, Clah took a genre that was evolving in nineteenth-century Britain and North America and adapted it to his own needs. This cross-cultural borrowing was unique to Tsimshian society. It was one man's means of coping with an era of rapid change.

Clah might have been exposed to two models of diary or journal keeping. The first, and the one with which he would have been most familiar, was the Hudson's Bay Company (HBC) trade journal, by which HBC employees recorded activities and transactions. They noted the arrival and departure of fur traders and visitors; daily trade; and conflicts and violence among Aboriginal people at Fort Simpson, including Tsimshian and Haida, Nisga'a from the Nass River, and Tlingit from the Russian-American territory (Alaska) to the north. The post journal tracked the seasonal movements of the Tsimshian, and the recorder observed with alarm the movement of canoes south to trade in Victoria.[3] It recorded high levels of alcohol consumption and resulting violence among Aboriginal people and HBC employees. Clah might have seen William Henry McNeill and other HBC employees making their daily entries. William Duncan also lived at the fort, where Clah helped him to learn Sm'algyax. It is therefore possible that Clah read the HBC journal once he acquired the skills to do so. Clah's daily entries after 1862 begin with the weather, as do each entry in the HBC's journals.[4] Clah's second possible model was Duncan's personal diary. It is unlikely that Duncan showed Clah his diary, although he might well have told him about it or suggested the activity to Clah. Duncan introduced diary writing to at least one other pupil, Thrakalkajik, whom he renamed Edward. Duncan noted twice in his own diary that this young man was making journal entries, including one introspective one in which he recorded he would not live long in this world.[5]

The first two books of Clah's diary are large and well-bound. It took Clah over five years to fill the first book, which he bought in Victoria on 27 September 1859. The second book covers the period from 1 January 1865 to 20 August 1869.[6] Thereafter, the diaries vary in size and shape, but they are much smaller.[7] Some are recycled account books, parts of exercise books, or even loose papers sewn together.

Clah bought himself a dictionary for twenty-five cents in 1863, along with a Bible and a prayer book.[8] He had access to almanacs from time to time from which he gleaned information about a range of subjects, including American Independence Day, Canada's Dominion Day, and the date of Queen Victoria's birthday. Clah used an almanac on one occasion to prove to missionary James McCullagh that he had miscalculated which day of the week was Sunday.[9] Clah often noted the phases of the moon and the shortest and longest days of the year, and he thought he could forecast the weather: "[F]riends ask me in what american almanac says today. I open ayer *[Ayers]* 8 american almanac[.] to them I told the friends to [that] Queen Victoria married[.] they laughing to [at] me. We don't ask about married day[,] we ask you what almanac says about the weather. I told them is all I can [find] in this almanac."[10] Newspapers were another source of information from which Clah found out about the American

Civil War, the Boer War, and other events that had occurred in the wider world.

The mechanics of keeping a diary are straightforward for most diarists: a book is bought each year (or received as a present), it is kept safely in a desk or elsewhere, and it is filled in each day. For Clah, the mechanics were complicated. He lived close to the elements in a very wet and cool environment, and he moved about for much of the year in an open canoe. Amazingly, only one diary shows any damage, possibly water damage, while the rest are well preserved. How did Clah keep these precious objects dry and safe? How did he organize his time to write in them, and how did he ensure that he always had ink and writing implements with him? Unfortunately, Clah leaves only a few clues. He stored completed diaries in a wooden box, presumably in his permanent house at Fort Simpson, where he lived during the winter. Tsimshian kept private and precious possessions in beautifully crafted and decorated cedar bentwood boxes, which were waterproof.[11] A few entries indicate he carried his current diary with him on his travels, although on one occasion he reports that he had lost entries for eleven days because he had written them on a loose piece of paper.[12] In May 1871, while freighting cargo on the Skeena River, Clah noted that he had been observed writing in his diary by others.[13]

Clah does not indicate how much time he devoted to writing each day, although it must have been considerable. His wife complained that his time could be spent more productively: "My wife sometimes telling me about writing. she wants stop me keep writing. she says [it is] no[t] paid. she told me in morning to what come to me writing[,] writing every day lost the time for you[r] work."[14] But the diary was very much part of Clah's persona. It marked him as a man of significance and wisdom, a man with a God-given right to make a record for posterity. Although his sight failed as he grew older, Clah's sense of duty and commitment did not flag, unlike Samuel Pepys, who abandoned his diary when he feared he was going blind.[15] In 1900, Clah complained for the first time that he was half blind, "But my Lord Jesus Christ push my heart to write this History."[16] He continued to have problems with his sight, despite seeking ointments from doctors. Photographs of him show that he acquired glasses at some point, but the date is not recorded in his diary. Clah made his last entry on 31 December 1909 with no warning that it was to be the last.[17]

WRITING THE DIARY

Clah wrote on the inside cover of his first diary:

Tsimshen and Fort Simpson
the Journal of Clah or Damaks [T'amks]
Number by every Years
and county [counting] every months
and every week
and Days and nights
and county [counting] what Doing wrong and do right
But some of men doing Right
An some of doing wrong
of Tsimshen
Sometimes we do better
And sometimes we do wrong
In every year and in this world
But Clah Doing Right Sometimes
And Sometimes doing wrong.
My heart happy sometimes
And sometimes Sorry.

This note sets the tone for Clah's diary keeping. In the first few years, Clah used the diary as a device to remember the European days of the week, the months, and the number of days in each month – a mode of reckoning that differed from the Tsimshian seasons and calculations of available food resources. When he was travelling, which was much of the time, Clah generally recorded the time of his departures and arrivals. In March 1866, he mentioned he always carried his little gold watch with him.[18] In 1888, a "white friend" presented him with a fifteen-dollar silver watch, which he gave away three years later.[19] It is difficult to know whether Clah always had a watch or by what other means he might have judged time.[20] He noted not only the time of his arrivals and departures but also how many days a journey took, and he often recorded the distance travelled. Measuring time and distance was important to all Tsimshian, for they had to locate themselves in time and space as they travelled long distances, often in hazardous conditions. But Clah used British measures for time, distance, and weight in his diary.

Note on inside cover of Clah's first diary. Wellcome Library, London.

The diary's introduction suggests it was more than an exercise in European chronology, for it mentions a moral account – of doing wrong and doing right. Although Clah quickly mastered the Gregorian calendar, the moral accounting went on throughout his life and echoed the tone of Duncan's early sermons, the first of which he delivered in Tsimshian on 13 June 1858. Duncan warned his audiences, "[The] Bible tells us that God sees all what we do and He writes down in His Book all we do bad. The

Bible tells us that if our sins are not wiped out of God's Book when we die He will cast us into a bad place and punish us there."[21] Clah certainly took these admonitions to heart; he judged his fellows in terms of good and bad behaviour and recorded that behaviour, as Duncan suggested God does, in his book.

After setting out the journal's goals, Clah then gives a brief account of his life. He begins by juxtaposing his birth with the establishment of the first HBC trading post and thus links his life to a new source of Tsimshian wealth and power. Several times over the life of the diary, Clah reiterates that his birth and the birth of the HBC were linked. He imbues the moment with a significance that extends beyond mere chronology; he marks himself as a man of a new era of Tsimshian history.

At first, Clah did not follow the conventional diary format, pioneered by Samuel Pepys, of providing a separate entry for each day.[22] His account of his time in Victoria is written as part of an ongoing narrative of his life. Although he sometimes starts an entry with a place and a date, he had not yet devised a systematic means of recording his life. And much of the account seems to have been written after the event. It was only in May 1863 that Clah began to give each day a separate entry that commenced with the date and day of the week and the weather. He used the format for the next forty-six years.

Throughout the 1860s, Clah also used the diary as a means to improve his writing skills. At the beginning of the second book, Clah wrote:

> This is my Poor Journal Book
> I am writing First[;] I learning to Read. But I will liken any one els theaching me more words [I would like anyone else to teach me more words].
>
> I hop[e] somebody Can help me to learning and to teaching me[,] but accept only our Lord God can sent [send] few words upon me. This my account Book to [for] writing what we doing in every year an every months an[d] every days. But if anybody good ways. Keep [illegible] in this book[,] and if any one bad ways an[d] [I] writing in this Book.

By this time, Clah was aware that his diary keeping had an audience. He showed his diary to a local trader in July 1866, and in September 1870 he noted the astonishment of a man who had seen him writing in his journal.[23]

During one of Clah's trips to Juneau during the gold rush, Governor Alfred P. Swineford of Alaska walked into his tent while he was writing.[24]

In February 1872, Clah indicated for the first time that he was keeping a record for posterity: "[A]lso when We die[.] the children comes[.] New people Can read this book an[d] See what Old people doing[:] murders, stealing, Liars [lying][,] Drunkeness, fighting[,] Quarling [quarrelling,] chete [cheating.] someone steal wifes[,] mak[e] Gods angry."[25] The following year, a storekeeper told Clah that Duncan had written a book about his arrival among the Tsimshian.[26] Clah did not see Duncan's book himself until 1882.[27] By this time, Clah was well aware of the power of the written word. In 1886, he asked Duncan to write about what he, Clah, had done for him, for he wanted his children to be able to read about him after his death. By 1891, Clah had conceived the idea of publishing his diary.[28]

By that time, Clah had already indicated he wanted to write a history of his people. And entries throughout the last twenty years of the diary have a common refrain. Clah claims that he is writing a history of the Northwest Coast, that he is writing a history of the old people for the new people based on knowledge from his extensive travels throughout the region, and that he is reporting on people's moral state: "[N]orth west coast History[.] Arthur Wellington Clah written report in the name of Jesus. [He] Gave me power and authority to wrote all peoples name[s] who not obey the law of God Father."[29] Clah is God's amanuensis, keeping an account of people doing right and wrong, the role Duncan had claimed for God.

Although the idea of diary as moral ledger dominates the end of Clah's diary, it was already in Clah's mind when he began writing. Although the desire to write a document that would become public was only gradually realized, it might well have been stimulated by Clah's knowledge that Duncan's book was so widely known and read.[30]

A Tsimshian Diarist in a Colonial Setting

Clah was always interested in innovation and novel experiences, and his diary represents an innovation in his life. Many first-generation Christians have recorded their lives through autobiographies, pious tracts, or oral testimony that were closely monitored and edited by the missionaries with whom they worked.[31] Clah told missionaries and government officials about his diary and wanted their approbation and support, but he did not reveal the contents, in which he judged them by the same standards he applied to others.[32] He similarly rebuffed Tsimshian individuals who asked to see the diary.[33] Clah accused an unidentified person of stealing his diary over ten days in November 1876 because he believed people did not like Clah writing about them.

The Tsimshian and neighbouring peoples, although non-literate, had their own means of recording the past, a highly developed and structured form of oral history known as *adawx* in Tsimshian.[34] Susan Marsden has worked for many years documenting various adawx against archaeological and documentary sources. She and the archaeologist Andrew Martindale investigated Tsimshian history between 3,500 and 1,500 BP by comparing archaeological data against oral accounts recorded by anthropologists who used Tsimshian informants. They found that adawx record a history over thousands of years that can be verified by other sources.[35] The idea of recording human activities was, therefore, not new to Clah, but his means of doing so – not only the diary format but also his insistence on secrecy – was a radical break from Tsimshian forms.[36] Adawx are official versions of history, and they must be verified over and over again through public performances to carefully selected audiences.[37] Clah's record was made without oversight from anyone (other than God!). He was conscious of the potential power this gave him, particularly if his history became *the* history of the Tsimshian. As R.M. Galois observes, it is no coincidence that Clah's grandson William Beynon became an ethnographer of the Tsimshian who worked for Franz Boas and Marius Barbeau, among others, as well as in his own right.[38] Beynon, who grew up in Victoria, stayed with his grandfather in Fort Simpson from time to time, and his grandfather stayed with the Beynon family whenever he visited the city, sometimes for extended periods.[39] William Beynon would have been aware not only of his grandfather's strong preoccupation with keeping a record of his community but also of his disapproval of many aspects of Tsimshian life that Beynon later recorded as an ethnographer.[40] Beynon's strong interest in Tsimshian culture might have been a response to Clah's ambivalence. The strong Christian ideology that underpins Clah's diary does not represent a rejection of Tsimshian culture but rather a wish to influence it for the better.[41] Although he was never an ethnographer in the same sense as Beynon, Clah's son Henry W. Tate was an informant to Boas over several years. He sent Boas written accounts of Tsimshian adawx that he had collected and written down in secret. He worried that his friends and relatives would disapprove if they knew what he was doing. It is possible that this secrecy was influenced by his father's diary, which contained observations and judgments of people with whom Clah interacted.[42]

The extensive literature on European diary writing shows how diaries have changed in content and style over time.[43] The literature on diarists who lived in societies without a tradition of diary writing is, however, meagre.[44] It is therefore difficult to place Clah the diarist in a comparative context. Lloyd Rudolph, who has studied the diary of Amar Singh, a Sikh who lived in British India, describes Singh inhabiting a liminal space between princely and British India that allowed him to distance himself from the familiar.[45] Clah's diary entries do not reflect a man caught between two worlds or a man who has lost his cultural roots but someone who is forward looking and engaged with innovations. Clah never tries to distance himself from his physical and cultural environment; he is much too combative for that. He is often at loggerheads with Tsimshian and settlers, but he never dissociates from them. Singh, Lloyd suggests, "constructed himself in a variety of contexts, who he had been, who he meant to be, who he might become."[46] Clah used his diary in a similar way, both in his daily accounting and when he reminisced, which he did increasingly as he got older. He constructed himself retrospectively as the first Tsimshian Christian, the man who risked his life to stop potlatches and other ceremonial activities; by contrast, his Christian persona in the early diaries is not so strongly articulated or formed.[47] In the last ten years of the diary, Clah often refers to himself as General Wellington and Saint Clah. He gives himself a status outside Tsimshian hierarchies and hails himself as the man who writes the history of the north, the history of the old people for the new generation and those to come.

Despite this retrospective commentary, it is the daily entries that define Clah. A diary, as Stuart Sherman observes of Samuel Pepys', "gives the impression of grabbing hold of everything the diarist encounters," but it is actually selective in what it records. The regular daily entries or serial measure introduced by Pepys replaced the sporadic, signal occasions of previous diarists. These regular entries give the impression of a systematic endeavour, but the diarist has decided who and what has be recorded.[48] The diarist is central to the narrative, and Clah the Tsimshian diarist promotes himself and his interests throughout his diary. The Tsimshian and Euro-Canadians he mentions are of high standing in his world. The diary presents a man who is an integral part of the Tsimshian community but who, at the same time, has a keen eye for his own individual advantage. This is best illustrated by his long-running battle to realize his wife's inheritance of land, not in Tsimshian territory, but in the city of Victoria.

The diary reflects Clah's faith in prayer and gradual disillusionment with missionaries, particularly Thomas Crosby. His Christian God was a God of the Tsimshian who did not appear with William Duncan but had always existed, overseeing the older generations as they made their canoes, stone axes, knives from mussel shells, and spears from bone.[49] Clah does not present spiritual and material innovations, even those with negative consequences such as the poisonous liquor sold by traders, as foreign imports but as naturalized aspects of Tsimshian life.

The world encapsulated in Clah's diary is a Tsimshian world, upon which colonial interests and innovations have settled. The man who deemed a governor, a senator, missionaries, judges, lawyers, and bureaucrats his friends, who saw opportunities for advancement materially and spiritually, came to regret the presence of these people who had changed his status from an independent entrepreneur and man of standing into a wage slave who had had his land stolen without compensation by the Queen and her colonial successors, that is, Canadians: "[S]o Mr Robinson [a Methodist missionary] open his mouth about english government in Victoria Canada ... the english government take away our Land. I think If I die [I] go into Heaven[,] or if the government die[,] they all in Hell. Because they steal our land ... I Believe the whit[e] people make us slave. Because[,] when we have work to them[,] they paid us piece of papers we call tickets. I have seen about whit[e] people on [in] Alaska paid good. [They] paid the indians in mon[e]y."[50] This observation reveals Clah's evolving view of colonial power. He did not distinguish between Britain and Canada; in his view, they both participated in the control being imposed on the Tsimshian to divest them of their land by stealing it rather than buying it. Thus both had reduced the Tsimshian to landless slaves. Tsimshian labour was not being properly remunerated with cash but rather tickets or vouchers that had to be exchanged for goods at the company store. Slavery had very real connotations for the Tsimshian, a slave-owning society. Slaves had no property, no land, no personhood; they were property that, before the advent of missionaries and colonial regimes, could be killed or sold.[51] When Clah refers to himself as a slave, he means he has lost everything. The young man of the early years of the diary is full of optimism and hope; the older man looks back to a time when he was a general fighting bad ways and a saint promoting Christian values. If the diary is viewed as an extended narrative, it is a tragedy and, with hindsight, we can see the tragedy unfold. Arthur Wellington Clah, however, lived his life from day to day.

3

The Fur Trade Era

Clah grew up in the era of the fur trade, but he did not become a trader until the trade was in abeyance in the 1860s. Clah's birth, childhood, and early adult life were all deeply influenced by the trade and its consequences, including the location of the winter village at Fort Simpson, employment opportunities, the liquor trade, and high levels of violence among the peoples of the Northwest Coast. As a mature man, Clah became involved in buying and selling pelts, which required long and dangerous canoe voyages up the rivers and into the Interior. As a result of this trade, Clah was able to establish himself as an influential Gispaxlo'ots elder and head of the House of T'amks.

Clah learned that his birth coincided with the establishment of the Hudson's Bay Company's (HBC) fort on the Nass River from chief trader and later chief factor William Henry McNeill: "There was Capt W.H. McNeill telling me about that HBC Built Fort at Nass in May 1831 the time I was born."[1] Clah remembered himself as an unsophisticated child, a "naked boy[,] no shoe[,] no panshs [pants] accept [except] cotton shirt," who swept the houses, occasionally helped out with hunting, and was paid with a few tobacco leaves. Although Clah spoke "very small English" at the time, McNeill employed Clah in the mid-1850s to help out the HBC's steward, Peter Quintal.[2] This job gave him entry to the fortified complex, which was denied to most Tsimshian. The fort was about eighty yards (seventy-three metres) square and surrounded by a double palisade fence that was so high that only the roofs of the buildings inside peaked above it. At each corner was a tower with openings for eight guns. Even the entrance door was fortified. In 1857, there were twenty-one men, their wives, and five children who lived at the fort.[3]

In December 1855, Clah left Fort Simpson for Victoria, a fledgling town on Vancouver Island, with McNeill's son Harry. Harry had persuaded a number of Tsimshian to paddle him a thousand kilometres south. Clah's memories of this sojourn were dominated by a street fight that he and his brother became embroiled in after they broke an evening curfew imposed by colonists who felt threatened by the hundreds of Aboriginal people arriving from the north to trade and experience the excitements of urban life. Clah arrived as Governor James Douglas was raising a militia to defend the persons and property of the colonial society from what they viewed as invading hoards.

In this atmosphere of fear and distrust, Clah and his brother Wallace finished work one Saturday evening in May and walked to Yates Street in the centre of town, where they were attacked by a Metis man, Baptiste Bottineau, who ordered them back to their lodgings. In the ensuing fight, Clah knocked out Bottineau, who was older but much bigger than Clah. Bottineau recovered and struck Clah with a rock, causing much bleeding and a head wound that left a prominent indentation on his forehead, which is still visible in photographs taken of Clah as an old man.[4]

It was not until 1859, when he returned to Victoria and began working in privately run stores, that Clah learned about trading. His first employer ran a legitimate (molasses, rice, and bread) business alongside an illegal trade in liquor. When the white staff were arrested and jailed, the unsuspecting Clah turned up to work one day, only to find the place empty until the police arrived to arrest him. The magistrate released him the next day.[5] Clah then worked at P.J. Roche's general store, which sold clothing, food, and dry goods. By keeping his own detailed inventory of prices, he prepared for his own entry into the fur trade after he returned to Fort Simpson.[6] By this time, many more northern people were travelling to Victoria and the southern Mainland.[7] On 3 April 1860, for instance, sixty-five canoes with six hundred people arrived from Fort Simpson, while on 7 June another seventeen canoes with two hundred Tsimshian were reported as being in Victoria.

GUNS, LIQUOR, AND FURS
Guns were easily obtained at this time. They were needed for hunting and were often procured through trade transactions up and down the Coast and inland. Traders, however, were not the only source of weapons: Clah

bought guns from soldiers on a number of occasions. He often went armed, and not simply when hunting. During the fight with Baptiste Bottineau, both Clah and Wallace had pistols, although they did not fire them during the altercation. In 1857, Clah used his pistol to shoot an old woman, whom he blamed for the death of a friend. Although Clah makes no mention of this incident in his diary, the HBC's Fort Simpson journal states, "A poor old woman was deliberately shot dead by a young scamp by name Clah." William Duncan, who arrived at Fort Simpson a few weeks later, noted that Clah expected to be killed in retribution, even though he had paid thirty blankets in compensation for the death.[8] Clah had already lost several family members to violent deaths.

The alcohol traded on the Coast was sometimes called rum and sometimes whisky. Clah always referred to it as whisky. It was a poisonous brew diluted with dangerous additives. In 1861, the *Nonpareil* was intercepted on the Nass River while trading pure alcohol and camphine (rectified turpentine) for furs.[9] D.W. Higgins described the whisky as "alcohol, diluted with water, toned up with extract of hot pepper, and coloured so as to resemble the real thing."[10] By the time the HBC set up its trading post on the Nass River, alcohol was already available on the Coast. William Tolmie's description of the relocation of the HBC fort from the Nass River to the Tsimshian Peninsula in 1834 graphically portrays the early impact of alcohol: "On Saturday morning rum had been sold to the Indians & some of them getting intoxicated were very turbulent & from noon til sunset when we embarked we were all under arms & in momentary expectation of having to fight our way on board or being butchered on the spot."[11]

In 1839, the HBC and the Russian American Company, an early competitor, agreed to stop trading liquor for furs because of its detrimental effect on the trade. Yet the destructive effects of alcohol continued to be felt in the 1850s and 1860s. Tsimshian and other Aboriginal traders brought liquor back from the south.[12] One day in October 1856, the HBC reported that more than five hundred men, women, and children were drunk. A year later, in his first diary entry after arriving at Fort Simpson, William Duncan observed that "intercourse with whites and rum" were the "bane of the Indians," thanks to the Americans. He later helped curb the trade by calling in British gunboats to confiscate whisky-trading vessels and to arrest traders. Two of these vessels, the *Petrel* and the *Langley,* were trading quite openly in December 1862 and January 1863. McNeill had to pay more for his furs to compete with Captain Taylor of the *Petrel,* who was offering fifty pounds of rice or two gallons of molasses for a marten skin. McNeill was forced to offer seven gallons of rice or four gallons of molasses for the same item.[13] On a trip to the Nass River in April 1863, the HMS *Devastation* confiscated the *Petrel* and *Langley* and broke up three liquor-trading outlets onshore, forcing Aboriginal traders to go further afield to obtain liquor.[14] As a magistrate, Duncan continued to police the sale of spirits, but after the United States purchased Alaska in 1867, his vigilance could extend only to the international border, just a few kilometres to the north.[15] Whisky traders out of reach of British authorities supplied customers who took liquor back in their canoes. Spirits were also available in Victoria and across the US border, where Tsimshian, Nisga'a, and Haida, among others, went to trade and often returned with gallons of spirits. The impounding of whisky traders' boats not only reduced the availability of liquor, it also reduced the Tsimshian's trading opportunities, to the benefit of the HBC.

Clah maintained a double standard when it came to the consumption of alcohol. He was critical of the liquor trade and was concerned about the awful impact it was having on his society, yet he both bought and drank alcohol. He worked at the police barracks in Victoria for two months, spying on the illegal liquor trade, and his investigation led to the arrest of Haida and Tsimshian.[16] In 1862, Clah was sent to the Nass River by McNeill and Duncan to escort chiefs to Fort Simpson. John Pike, the captain of HMS *Devastation,* interrogated the twenty chiefs about the *Nonpareil's* illegal trading.[17] Nine years later, Clah appeared as a witness against two whisky traders arraigned before Magistrate Duncan. One of them, John Collins, had paid Clah soap, tobacco, a pipe, matches, powder, shot, and several gallons of whisky to collect his wife from a Nass River village and bring her to Fort Simpson.[18] These forays into law enforcement did not reflect any moralistic attitude on Clah's part. He was always eager to make a buck (or a bottle) when he could. Duncan paid him twenty dollars for informing on Collins. Clah, however, was not at all happy with the sum, for he believed he had a right to a third of the fine of $250 imposed on Collins. The money would be split with two other informants.[19] Collins, not surprisingly, held a strong grudge against Clah and threatened him both verbally and physically for ruining him.[20]

During this period, Clah did occasionally carouse with whisky drinkers. In September 1861, after accompanying McNeill up the Nass River, he "went trunking [drinking] on Thursday 27 inst morning[,] and I has [have] been Quarling [quarreling] to every body because I trinking bad spirit[s] and whisky." Later in his life, however, after Clah became an evangelizing Christian, he gave up drinking and took a consistent moral stance against alcohol.

Before their schooners were confiscated, the whisky traders took advantage of every trade opportunity, whatever the circumstances. In December 1862, during the smallpox epidemic, when everyone was traumatized by the devastation to their families and communities, Captain Taylor of the *Petrel* sold "bad spirits" to the Tsimshian: "Poor Tsimshens lie it down and[,] when Drunkness[,] Some fighting & some Quarrlin[g,] an[d] those all foolishness[.] an[d] some of the Indians hath Some few things an[d] Soling [sell them] for whisky[,] and thee [they] had no clothes for themselves[.] and Capt Taylor been soling whisky 3 days an[d] nights with water an[d] mixed an[d] little alcohol. 2 Martens [skins] for one gall[on] full water an[d] little alcohol."[21]

A few months later, Clah witnessed people on the Nass River drinking one hundred gallons of bad spirits.[22] There was social pressure to drink. After 1862, Aboriginal people who wanted an escape route could become Christian and move to Duncan's mission at Metlakatla, where alcohol was banned. But for those who remained at Fort Simpson, where liquor came to be incorporated into the feasting system, there were competitive obligations to fulfill.[23] Chiefs and others who participated in these feasts were expected to drink the liquor offered to them or be humiliated by their inability to consume it. Whisky feasts became occasions for outrageous behaviour that often resulted in violence between family and clan members.

Clah held a number of whisky feasts in his house. On New Year's Day, 1870, he feasted his newborn son, who took his mother's uncle's name – Gwisk'aayn (Kuskin). He invited fifty Tsimshian chiefs, who drank two-and-a-half gallons of liquor (which they themselves provided). Two days later, at another whisky feast, thirty to forty gallons of grog was consumed.[24]

A whisky feast was held in 1868 on the Nass River to celebrate the marriage of a Tsimshian chief, Nislaganos of the Gitlan, to the daughter of a Nisga'a chief. Both Nisga'a and Tsimshian people participated. During the drunken festivities, a Tsimshian's gun accidentally discharged and injured

a Nisga'a, precipitating reprisals in which two Tsimshian chiefs and sev-
eral Nisga'a died, including three people from the Anglican mission at
Kincolith (present-day Gingolx). Among those killed were Tsimshian chiefs
Ligwanh and Nisnawa.[25] Ligwanh was a notorious murderer who had killed
Clah's brother Wallace and three other relatives. In 1867, when Governor
Seymour had visited the Northwest Coast on the HMS *Sparrowhawk*, Clah
had approached him to make a complaint about Ligwanh's failure to ad-
equately compensate him for his relatives' deaths. Seymour promised to
give Duncan the authority to send ten constables out to arrest Ligwanh.
Whether Duncan received or acted on this directive is unknown, but when
Ligwanh and his relative were shot dead on the Nass, Clah believed God
had finally intervened.[26]

In May 1869, Governor Seymour again visited the Coast aboard the
Sparrowhawk, this time to negotiate a peace between the Tsimshian and
the Nisga'a. The two sides met on board at Fort Simpson and agreed on
compensation. Seymour warned the chiefs that in future they would be
answerable to British law for their criminal behaviour. According to Clah
and another account recorded by the anthropologist Marius Barbeau, this
intervention was unnecessary, for peace had already been restored and
compensation had been paid for the murders in June 1868, almost a year
before the arrival of the British navy vessel.[27] Ironically, as the *Sparrowhawk*
returned to Victoria, Governor Seymour died from an alcohol-induced
illness.[28] During subsequent visits, the *Sparrowhawk*'s crew destroyed large
amounts of liquor and arrested those in possession of it. These seizures
and arrests succeeded in drastically reducing, if not eradicating, the amount
of liquor available to coastal societies.[29] Duncan reported in 1871 that between two and three hundred gallons of liquor had been destroyed and
that forty people had been taken prisoner, twenty of whom were fined
between twelve and twenty blankets each.[30]

TRADING FURS

Alcohol and guns were only one aspect of the fur trade. Slaves were also
bought and sold. Clah sold a slave to a man he called Sokun in 1862. The
newly acquired slave, however, died of smallpox. When Sokun encountered
Clah on the Stikine River eleven years later, he demanded recompense in
the form of half the price of the slave. Clah refused to acknowledge such
an old debt, arguing that the slave had belonged to Sokun's tribe and that

Sokun had sold the young slave's remains to his relatives, who paid him well.[31] It is quite possible that Clah owned other slaves, but this is the only mention in the diary of his involvement. Slavery was a pre-colonial institution in Pacific Northwest Coast societies, one that signalled wealth and prestige. Anthropologist Viola Garfield claims that the nine tribal chiefs at Fort Simpson in the mid-nineteenth century each had between ten and twenty slaves, while lineage heads, such as Clah, were reported to have between two and ten.[32] Some estimates suggest that at the height of the fur trade boom, 15 to 20 percent of Northwest Coast village populations could have been slaves.[33] As Clah's wealth peaked in the 1860s, he might well have enhanced his status by acquiring slaves.

Clah's records show that a great diversity of goods was traded. The most common currency used for procuring furs was blankets manufactured for the HBC in England that had markings or points woven into the side to denote their size and value.[34] For much of the fur trade era, the HBC traded through intermediaries such as Clah. As a result, blankets, firearms, tobacco, clothes and many other items manufactured in distant parts of the British Empire – as well as goods produced by Northwest Coast peoples such as eulachon oil, dried fish and berries, canoes, and carved boxes – moved through a complex system of trade and exchange.

The Nass River to the north of Fort Simpson and the Skeena River to the south served as the region's main transportation routes. Both gave access to the Interior. Many of Clah's trips up the Nass were to trade with villagers along the river, but he also went as far as Gitlaxdamks by canoe and then proceeded overland on routes known as grease trails (they had been used for centuries to trade eulachon grease from the Nass fisheries) that connected to the upper Skeena and beyond. The alternative route to the inland region was via the Skeena River. These routes were not open highways: they were controlled by geopolitical interests. While it had its dangers, the journey to Victoria, which Clah made three times as a fur trader, was not a traditional trade route. It was open to anyone who had the resources to negotiate the long passage.[35]

When Clah became a trader in 1861, the land-based fur trade had been in operation for thirty years. At the time that the HBC established Fort Simpson, the Tsimshian chief Ligeex controlled access to much of the trade. Ligeex's daughter had married an HBC official, Dr. John Kennedy, in the early 1830s, and Ligeex further consolidated his links with the HBC when he allowed the company to move its fort from the Nass River to Lax Kw'alaams.[36] Ligeex controlled access to the Interior, a rich source of furs, via the Skeena River through his alliance with another Tsimshian tribe, the Gits'ilaasu, who held jurisdiction over the Kitselas Canyon. Because the Skeena is narrow and fast flowing at this point, villagers could regulate passage through the canyon. When Clah entered the fur trade, Paul Legaic, a baptized Christian, had succeeded the Ligeex who had negotiated the close relationship with the HBC. Legaic tried to maintain his and the Gispaxlo'ot's control over the Interior, but ready access to alcohol often reduced him to a drunken bully. The first time Clah ventured up the Skeena River as a trader with a party led by Paul Legaic, the members were well stocked with liquor, which Legaic dispensed freely at every stop along the way. Clah reported that everyone, including Legaic, was drunk day after day. En route, Legaic was determined to seek compensation from the Gits'ilaasu (spelled *Cathgelashe* by Clah) for the death of his uncle, who had been shot by a young man a year earlier. All the protagonists were armed. Clah warned them not to fire their guns, but his advice was ignored. Shots were exchanged, and a man was wounded.

A few days later, Legaic was drinking again. He beat his wife so badly that she could not see out of her swollen eyes. Some members of the party returned to Fort Simpson, while others continued up the Skeena, walking into Gitxsan country to Hagwilget, to trade. As they returned down the Skeena, they heard that many Tsimshian were dying of smallpox at Fort Simpson.[37]

Despite the smallpox epidemic, Clah continued his trading expeditions, perhaps because he realized there might be new opportunities as competitors died. The year prior to his trip with Legaic, Clah had made a brief, unsuccessful foray up the Nass River: he acquired only six marten and two beaver skins from the Nisga'a. He had also made two disappointing trips along the Nass to visit the Gitxsan in the Interior. His fortunes improved in 1862 under the patronage of his wife's relative Nisakx, with whom he engaged in joint trading expeditions for several years.

Nisakx was a successful trader on the Nass. Her name appears frequently in HBC records, which make it clear that the company depended on her family to maintain the flow of furs to the fort at a time when business was suffering from competition from American whisky traders.[38] In March 1863, HBC personnel reported that nine large canoes had arrived

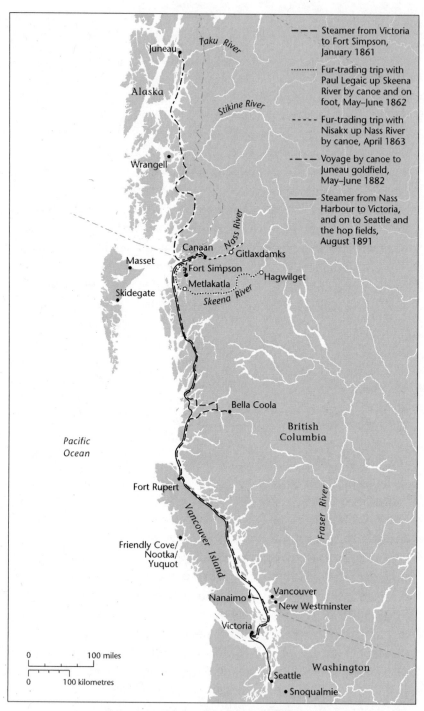

Some of Clah's long-distance voyages, 1861-91

from the Nass. They feared the new arrivals, probably Nisgaʼa, would trade with the *Petrel,* which would pay them four times as much in rum as they would receive from the company. Two weeks later, Nisakx, accompanied by Clah, left for the Nass River to pre-empt liquor traders before they could further undercut the HBC. When they reached the mouth of the river, however, they discovered the *Langley,* trading whisky, and many drunken Tsimshian.[39] Nisakx continued upriver to her home village, Ankida, where she greeted Captain John Pike of the gunboat HMS *Devastation* and his passenger, Bishop George Hills, who was visiting from Victoria. The HBC supported Nisakx's trade with provisions sent from Fort Simpson. She and Clah returned with 402 skins.[40]

In September, Nisakx returned to the Nass. She was accompanied by Clah and Lucy Moffatt, William Henry McNeill's daughter by his first marriage. She was the wife of HBC trader Hamilton Moffatt, who had arrived triumphantly on the *Petrel* and set up a temporary HBC trading post in Niskax's house.[41] This ad hoc arrangement was formalized three years later when the HBC established a permanent post on the Nass River under the management of Thomas Hankin and, later, Robert Cunningham.[42] Clah's links to two of the most effective traders on the Coast, Ligeex and Nisakx, therefore helped him to establish himself as an entrepreneurial trader. Once he collected pelts, Clah had the option of selling them to the HBC or taking them south to Victoria.

Victoria was a lucrative if long journey for northern people. The thousand-kilometre voyage took about three weeks by canoe.[43] Nevertheless, Victoria offered trade and shopping opportunities not available at Fort Simpson. In 1864, Clah traded 128 marten, 29 beaver, 13 bear, 49 muskrat, and some mink skins before returning home with $500, of which $130 was his personal return.[44] William Duncan also entered the trade in 1863. By purchasing the schooner *Carolina,* he could buy furs and transport them directly to Victoria rather than dealing with the HBC at Fort Simpson.[45] Tsimshian traders therefore had a variety of outlets for their furs.

Collecting furs, however, could be a hazardous business. In 1865-66, Clah made one of his longest fur-buying journeys. His provisions included 1 pair of boots, 150 pounds of rice, 2 dozen small square-headed axes, 10 gallons of molasses, 2 bars of yellow soap, and 50 pounds of flour.[46] He set out with three other men late in the year – on 23 November. It snowed and the river was frozen for much of the trip. As it made its way up the Skeena, the party faced a headwind, and because the days were very short, the men often travelled in the dark. By the end of the first week, Clah admitted he was ready to turn around and go home. But because it would be too humiliating to admit defeat, the men battled on. When they approached Kitselas Canyon, their canoe was so full of ice and the cold was so extreme that it burned like fire.[47] When they arrived at Gits'ilaasu (Kitselas) village on 1 December, their clothes were frozen to them.

In Gits'ilaasu, they witnessed an extraordinary scene that distracted them from the cold. A young man of the village had died, and the villagers were determined to identify who was responsible for this premature death. When he was cremated, a pistol was placed in the corpse. As the body burned, the gun exploded, and flesh flew in all directions. The villagers hoped this would reveal who was culpable for his death. Clah does not record whether this dramatic cremation exposed the killer.[48] He certainly thought it a novel way to identify the culprit.

Clah's small trading party continued up the river on snowshoes, hauling the canoe over the ice. They only managed to travel two miles (3.2 kilometres) a day and slept outside under the trees. By this time, they were weak and exhausted, but they continued to haul the canoe a few miles a day for the next five days. They then hid the canoe and continued on foot. After nine days, Clah established his men in a Gitxsan village, Gitwangax (*Kitcunahk* in Clah's diary), and sent his men out to trade. Clah's account book gives details of some of this trade (see Appendix 1).

On 10 January, Clah and his men began the difficult journey home. Short of food, Clah felt weak and was in pain. At Gits'ilaasu, he hired ten men to haul his canoe across the snow. The weather was so bad that he sheltered in the village for eight days. The party then continued on, pulling the canoe down the frozen river. Walking on snowshoes, Clah fell through thin ice into the water. But he managed to swim for half an hour in the freezing temperatures until his men rescued him. A few days later, as the men were hauling the canoe overland, a strong wind upended and broke the canoe, injuring Clah and one of his party.[49] After twenty-seven days travelling from the Interior, Clah stumbled back to Metlakatla, only to be subjected to a two-hour harangue from Duncan over some (unspecified) misdemeanour.[50]

The following day, Clah took a cargo of two hundred skins to Fort Simpson. He paid the HBC thirty-six marten, eleven mink, and two beaver skins to cover his debts and had many good furs to trade elsewhere.[51] He traded eighty marten skins to a couple of visiting fur traders. A few days later, Clah paid fifteen inferior white blankets for a canoe for his brother-in-law, and he helped an old man pay a debt of two blankets. Most of Clah's resources were invested in a feast at which he gave away seven hundred blankets. The next day, he bought a gold watch from a HBC official for thirty dollars.[52] Another feast was held the following day in Clah's house, to which he no doubt contributed.

Clah's day-to-day account rarely provides a context for his busy life. Although most of his fur-trading trips were undertaken in summer or fall, Clah did complete a late season journey to Hagwilget via the Skeena River in 1865.[53] He was home for only three days before he set out on the longer trip to Gitwangax. Did Clah return to the Interior because he knew there were a lot of furs available or because he needed funds to hold a feast? The details of the 1865-66 journey not only reveal the trade's difficult physical conditions but also its complexities. Clah needed a good stock of tradable provisions. If he was caught short, he would miss out on profits; if he overestimated, he would have to haul his provisions back home again. On the day Clah left for Fort Simpson on his long journey, he disposed of unsold goods by extending credit to those who could not pay him in full. He noted in his debit book how many furs were owed to him – for instance, he gave Duask one pair of three-point blue blankets worth four marten skins, but he was only paid two. Duask was in debt for two skins. Clah would chase these debts for many years, using threats and the British legal system to recoup his losses.

Traders needed a good understanding of the pricing system – which was based on the size, quality, and type of fur – and the return they hoped to make. As Clah's records for late December 1865 show, traders had to carry a variety of goods to satisfy the requirements of people in the Interior. Because Clah's trip was in the winter, he could only take dry provisions: blankets, cotton, gunpowder, tobacco, rice, and molasses. In summer, he had eulachon oil and other locally acquired foodstuffs to take, such as seaweed, which was prized as a source of salt. Clah came back empty-handed from one expedition because people had asked more for their furs than Clah had been willing or able to pay.[54] Once traders returned with a cargo of furs, they needed to sell them at a profit. Although the HBC strove to maintain a monopoly so that it could dictate prices, it rarely achieved its goal. The company was prepared to extend credit to traders to create obligations to trade, but it could not force a trader such as Clah to do more than repay a debt. Whisky traders had lower overheads because they could buy doctored liquor cheaply. Their trade undermined the HBC, which had to employ a large staff that spent much of its time maintaining the fort and producing and buying food. Historian Helen Meilleur points out that HBC employees spent time and much energy on maintenance work and cutting wood for palings to protect the fort and for firewood. HBC staff grew potatoes and other fresh foods to vary their monotonous diet of salted meat and fish and to guard against scurvy. The company's blacksmith made and repaired many of their tools and firearms, and staff were on constant alert for possible attacks by disgruntled or drunk Aboriginal people.[55]

Clah ran up debts with the HBC, and he employed men to help him with transport and trade who had to be fed during the journey and paid at the end of it. He also tried to recover debts owed to him. In 1869, when the Gitxsan broke the embargo Ligeex and the Gispaxlo'ots had imposed on them, they came down the Skeena River below Kitselas Canyon to trade directly at Fort Simpson. This development had an adverse effect on the trading activities of Clah and the Gispaxlo'ots. In the short term, however, Clah seized the opportunity to kidnap a woman whose father owed him six furs from his trade in 1864-65. Duncan heard of Clah's action and ordered him down to Metlakatla. Clah claimed the Gitxsan owed him two hundred marten skins from trade six years previously. Duncan, or as Clah referred to him on this occasion, "dear Duncan," confiscated the Gitxsan's goods and held them as security against the debt he owed Clah. The following year, Clah went up the Nass River to collect other outstanding debts. Some people paid him, but others prevaricated until they were confronted by twenty so-called constables Clah had hired to recoup his losses. The strategy worked, and Clah paid off the constables at fifty cents a day.[56] Although missionaries criticized Clah for taking the law into his own hands, his satisfaction over acquiring eleven boxes of eulachon oil was not spoiled.[57] Clah, still seeking payment for debts in 1872, sought the advice of Chief Justice Matthew Baillie Begbie when he passed through Fort Simpson. Begbie advised Clah to write to Governor Joseph Trutch in Victoria.[58]

By the end of 1866, life as an individual entrepreneur was more difficult. The Gitxsan no longer waited in the Interior for Gispaxlo'ots middlemen.

At the same time, the HBC was establishing outposts up the Nass and Skeena rivers.[59] Resourceful as ever, Clah began working for the HBC. He appreciated the status that he felt was attached to working in a responsible position for the company. In the latter part of 1866, he made several small trading trips for the company. In early April 1867, he transported furs from the HBC post on the Nass River to Fort Simpson, and later in the month he took charge of two canoes and four men to transport goods to the new post on the Skeena River. The Skeena in spring posed different problems than in winter, but it was equally dangerous. Clah and the men risked life and cargo as they took heavily laden canoes up the fast-flowing river, through rapids, and through narrow canyons. The canoes almost capsized several times as Clah and his crew poled, hauled, and portaged the boats up the river. Clah had to hire additional labour – as many as thirty-three men – to help carry the cargo on certain days.[60] Clah and his crew were paid seventy-five cents a day for thirty-two days of work.[61] Clah then worked in the HBC store, trading furs with Haida from Haida Gwaii. Over two days, Clah and another HBC trader processed 502 sealskins. Clah alternated between working for the HBC and trading furs on his own account over the next couple of months.

During this period, Clah's troubled marriage seems to have ended. In November 1866 he reported that his wife, like many wives, wanted to run away, so Clah sent her back to her own people on the Nass River and took a new wife, Habbelekepeen, whose trade he recorded in his account book.[62] The new marriage ended when Clah went up the Nass to reclaim Dorcas (Datacks) and his two daughters.[63] A few weeks later, he noted that his wife had brought ninety-eight gallons of eulachon oil, five bushels of potatoes, a case of dried berries, and a case of other goods with her from the Nass.[64] This is one of the few occasions when Clah recorded Dorcas' economic contributions. The entry suggests that his reason for reconciling with his wife was both economic and personal, despite the humiliation of capitulation.[65]

In January 1869, after helping with the annual inventory of goods at the HBC, Clah was delighted to be put in charge of the *Petrel* and trade with Gitxaala and Gidestsu. Never before had Clah commanded such a large sailing vessel, bound for waters and a coastline with which he was not familiar: "I was in a bed ... [although] I never fall sleep Because I never on a Board [boat] before my Live [in my life]. I always afraid."[66] The company does not seem to have supplied Clah and his crew with provisions, for they spent much of their time out hunting. Because Clah was excited and apprehensive about sailing in what were unfamiliar waters, he hired pilots to help navigate treacherous stretches. Despite his inexperience as a maritime trader, Clah returned to Fort Simpson after only thirty-eight days of sailing with a cargo of 257 skins.[67] A week later, the *Petrel* headed out on a trip farther south to Gidestsu (spelled *Kitasoo* by Clah) and returned on 14 April with a large haul of skins: 545 mink, 112 deer, 4 otter, 2 wolf, 7 beaver, 23 seal, and 1 fur seal.[68]

Clah enjoyed the anonymity of travelling through communities he did not know: "Some people I have seen not the single word against me because I never been there before [in] my Live[,] since I was borne in May 1831."[69] This throw-away line suggests that even a combative person such as Clah could find communal life wearing. Although Clah often took pride in challenging people who did not live by his moral and religious standards, his self-appointed role earned the resentment of those he reprimanded. Nevertheless, Clah was a man who sought approbation and recognition, as is indicated by the dreams he recorded while on board the *Petrel*. Most of the dreams featured HBC officials and missionaries. In one dream, William Henry McNeill, William Manson, and Roderick Finlayson, all HBC officials, accuse Clah of having no shame because he wanted to be a white man. These dreams reflected Clah's ambivalent attitude towards officials and missionaries, including Robert Cunningham, a failed missionary who had become a company employee. Clah was one of them, yet he was not completely accepted by them. He tried to emulate them, but he was not part of their society. As captain of the *Petrel*, Clah was removed from his everyday life; he was operating in the white man's world of trade, far from his own Tsimshian community.[70]

George Chismore's Voyage

The following year, Clah served as a guide for George Chismore, who wanted to explore the coastal hinterland. Chismore, a medical doctor, had accompanied the work parties constructing the Western Union Telegraph and then found employment with the United States Army based at Fort Tongass, Alaska. Clah first mentions meeting him in 1866, when Clah paid him three black marten skins for medicine.[71] In June 1870, Chismore had a few weeks' leave, which allowed him to journey up the Nass River, along the grease trail, to the head of the Skeena River. He published an account of the journey in the *Overland Monthly* in 1885. Chismore's observations of Clah confirm that the Tsimshian man had a liminal position among colonists:

> Two Chimp-se-ans [Tsimshian], Clah and George, volunteered to go with me for the opportunity of trading with the interior. The first was a very bright Indian, who not only spoke English, but read and wrote it well. He had been a leading convert at a missionary station, but innate depravity proving in his case too much for saving grace, he backslid, and became one of the most consummate rascals that ever wore copper skin. Nevertheless, he was good-natured, and his ready tongue and subtle wit made him a useful man to have on such a journey as I contemplated.[72]

Chismore's impression of Clah did not change over the ensuing three weeks: "And Clah, sly Clah, how calmly did he lie, and how unblushingly deny it when detected. What ingenious schemes he devised to transfer coin or equivalent from my pouch to his, and how he did cheat those whom he traded with! Still, Clah was a good man – for a backslider."[73] According to Chismore, Clah had all the positive attributes of a white man – he was literate, smart, witty, good natured, and a sharp trader – *but* he was a copper-skinned Indian, which meant he was sly and a cheat. Most damning of all, having found grace in religion, Clah had backslid. His Tsimshian companion, George, however, "was an Indian, nothing more nor less."[74]

 Clah was neither an Indian like George nor a white man. In the increasingly racialized world of the late nineteenth century, Clah would never attain equal standing in colonial society. Chismore was fascinated by the landscape and people that Clah took for granted, but he was oblivious to the protocols Clah negotiated for the party. This ignorance coloured his view of Clah. Clah was certainly capable of trickery and hard bargaining, but Chismore probably mistook some of Clah's motives as the guide ensured the party's smooth passage through Nisga'a and Gitxsan territory.

Chismore prided himself on travelling light. He carried a hatchet, a blanket, a poncho, a change of underwear, a few provisions and cooking implements, and a rifle and ammunition. He also carried tobacco, beads, and fishhooks as presents for the "Natives." By contrast, Clah and George were burdened with goods they planned to trade.[75] When they reached the

HBC store on the Nass River, heavy rain held them up for three days. They then spent nine hours paddling and poling up the river through a heavily timbered valley, only to spend an evening plagued by mosquitoes and midges. The next day, they spent ten hours making their way slowly up the river; the surrounding mountains became higher and the valley more heavily timbered before they reached the village of Gitwinksihlkxw.

Clah was gratified by the kind invitation of the chief who fed and accommodated them, and Chismore recognized that the chief's invitation had been mediated through Clah. Chismore was also amazed by how quickly the chief's "followers" secured the canoe and moved their cargo into the house, which had been decorated in honour of the American. "The Boston man's crest," an enlarged copy of the reverse side of a half-dollar, had been painted in black and white on a screen opposite the entrance door. The house was square and had sides of thick plank: "Around the walls were guns, paddles, skins, salmon, and other articles of Indian property." Chismore's party was fed boiled and roasted salmon, potatoes, rice, berries, stick-skin (inner bark of the hemlock), bear meat, and mountain goat, all accompanied by eulachon grease. The chief expressed hope that more white men would visit but warned that people farther along the route might not be so hospitable. Chismore did not take the warning seriously. After the meal, the men were entertained with dancing and a speech "delivered in a semi-ventriloquial tone – the voice seeming to come from a short distance without the house." A roll of chiefs, living and dead, was called out, and tobacco was smoked in pipes. Their hosts ended the evening with a wonderful performance that was enacted with humour and drama as the dancers mimed a variety of characters.[76]

The next day, men from the village portaged the party's cargo, while the chief steered the canoe through the rapids. They continued on to Gitlaxdamks, which Chismore described as "one of the finest Indian towns I ever saw."[77] Chief Maas Gibu, Clah's brother-in-law, welcomed them. Chismore marvelled at the house's grooved planks and two large uprights, upon which rested large spars that supported the roof. A cover over the smoke hole in the centre of the roof could be turned as the winds shifted. The floor was made of planks.

According to Chismore, Clah "prevailed on me to engage [Maas Gibu] to accompany us to Kis-py-aux [Kispiox] on the Skeena."[78] Chismore might have considered this an example of Clah's schemes to fleece him, rather than as an attempt to protect Chismore from a possible hostile reception along the route of the grease trail, which was controlled by the Nisga'a from Gitlaxdamks.[79] Nevertheless, Chismore was aware that individuals could only carry goods over their own territory. Their neighbours would then take the produce on the next leg. He observed Nisga'a families loading boxes of grease on their backs and noted that each man and woman would carry 120 pounds. The load was secured with "a thong fastened to the boxes, and dividing into two parts, one of which passes across the chest and the points of the shoulders, and the other over the forehead."[80]

Each day, Chismore moved ahead of his party to hunt. When he failed to return to camp one day, Clah was concerned: "We think our Docder [doctor] Lost himself."[81] Along the trail, which Chismore thought resembled a highway, sat sweathouses in which tired travellers could have a steam bath from heated stones. The trail also included bark huts for shelter in bad weather and sheds strategically placed on boundaries where trade was negotiated. The track was peppered with the graves of those who had died en route.[82]

While Chismore praised the landscape as idyllic and noted the customs of the people, Clah recorded the arrangements he made to have his goods carried along the trail, how far the party walked each day, and where it camped. They passed the abandoned Western Union Telegraph line, where Chismore had served as medical officer to construction workers. People from Kispiox had cut down all the poles and removed the wire because, according to Chismore, they blamed the telegraph for the measles epidemic that broke out while the line was being built. At Hagwilget, Clah and Chismore parted company. Chismore arranged for transport down the Skeena River, and Clah traded with the Gitsxan and settled disputes that had arisen on previous trading trips.[83]

Chismore's description of his journey up the Nass and along the grease trail is revealing on a number of counts. It offers an outsider's assessment of Clah that confirms impressions gained from the diary, and it provides a naive yet detailed description of a trading trip through the Interior. Because Chismore's account is composed of observations of events and processes divorced from their larger cultural meaning, it obscures Clah's true role. Chismore relied on Clah to organize and guide his exploratory expedition, and he needed Clah to translate for him. Chismore appreciated Clah's quick intelligence, but he realized his guide could outsmart him in his own milieu. Chismore understood that local peoples' movements were constrained by territorial boundaries, but he did not realize that Clah had negotiated their passage across these boundaries. On the other hand, Chismore, the interested outsider, gives details Clah would never record in his diary. Clah was not an observer of society but rather a chronicler of his own activities. Scenery and people that Chismore found exotically strange and noteworthy, Clah took for granted. Tsimshian and Nisga'a tolerated without comment conditions that newcomers found physically challenging, whether it was mosquitoes or the fast flowing rivers that provided the only highways into the Interior. Stuart Sherman's observation that a diarist does not "grab hold of everything" but is selective is well illustrated through a comparison of Clah's and Chismore's records of the journey from Fort Simpson to Hagwilget.[84] The two accounts corroborate each other in terms of chronology, but their authors' expectations and concerns differ.

A few days after returning to Fort Simpson, Clah joined a convoy of four canoes that planned to trade furs up the Coast across the Alaskan border to Sitka. The men took a cargo of eulachon grease and forty boxes of goods with them. By this time, the border was policed by American customs officials who tried to charge duty and check their cargo for illicit liquor.[85] The party had to battle high winds, and because this was their first trip to Sitka, the men had to stop at a village to ask for directions. The slave they spoke to, however, did not speak Tsimshian. They received directions from occupants of a passing canoe and then crossed the open sea to Sitka.[86] They bathed and washed at a hot springs before continuing on to town.

Clah returned to Fort Simpson on 19 August with six black bear skins and seven beaver traps. The following day, he bought a canoe and uniforms from three American army deserters. He immediately dressed six young men in the blue uniforms and had them "playing Lik[e] American soldiers."[87] Clah took constant delight in these pseudo-military shows. The wealth he was able to generate through the fur trade enabled him to mount great displays. The most spectacular occurred in 1862, when Clah decked out four hundred men with uniforms and guns and had them fire at midnight as part of a New Year's celebration. The group then retired to Clah's house, where they played music and Clah taught them to act like soldiers. Unfortunately, Clah does not say where he acquired so many uniforms and guns, not to mention brass instruments. He presumably knew how soldiers behaved from observing them in Victoria.

Clah's involvement in the fur trade was a high point in his life. He accumulated much wealth, which he used to improve his status in the T'amks House and among the Gispaxlo'ots. He used his familial connections *kinship* among the Tsimshian and the Nisga'a to gain access to the lucrative trade *network* on the Nass River and in the Interior among the Gitxsan. As a reliable and effective operator, he cemented relationships with HBC officials and missionaries. Clah's single-minded endeavour to improve his own lot, however, also antagonized many people, particularly when he tried to claim his debts. And his relationship with missionaries was sometimes stormy, for they disapproved of his trading methods and lack of humility as he embraced his role as entrepreneur. In the 1870s, this entrepreneurial spirit would take Clah on a new journey, this time in search for gold.

4

Chasing Gold

The period of Clah's life dominated by the gold rushes – from 1871 to the late 1880s – was transitional in many ways. The gold rush era overlapped with the appearance of fish canneries, the industrialization of an activity that had been the basis of existence for Aboriginal peoples. In response to these economic changes and before he established himself near the Nass fisheries, Clah moved his family away from Fort Simpson, first to the house he built at the mouth of the Skeena River then upriver on the Nass. As Clah asserted his claims to land in these areas, the provincial and national governments began the process of formally dispossessing the Tsimshian and Nisga'a by surveying the land and establishing reserves (see Chapter 6). At the same time, the revival of Christianity at Fort Simpson, marked by the arrival of Methodist missionary Thomas Crosby, reinvigorated Clah's commitment to evangelical Christianity, which became a dominant part of his day-to-day existence. Clah's family life also expanded as he and Dorcas produced children who survived beyond infancy. By 1882, the couple had seven children, although most of them did not live into adulthood. The deaths of two of their sons during this period devastated the couple, and their distress is quite palpable in Clah's diary entries.

Clah increasingly became aware that he was an "Indian," without rights or status, in an evolving colonial society. There were times when he was unable to engage in activities that would give him an income to support his family. He successfully traded fish products, transported passengers to and from the goldfields, and freighted goods, but he found hard manual labour in the goldfields onerous and debilitating, partly because of the physical demands, but also because he was unable to distinguish himself.

He could not acquire special privileges or form relationships with those in power – he was but one labourer among many. It was also difficult for Clah to promote himself within his own society because the rewards for this work were relatively small. He tried to compensate for his sense of powerlessness by cultivating relationships with powerful government functionaries in the goldfields, people such as Matthew Baillie Begbie, the future chief justice of British Columbia; Peter O'Reilly, the future Indian reserve commissioner; and A.W. Vowell, the future superintendent of Indian affairs. In Alaska, he made friends with the governor, A.P. Swineford and maintained a correspondence with him over a number of years. In this context, Clah's increasing religiosity was a means of maintaining some control over his life, for he viewed his relationship with God as a personal one, not mediated through a church or a priestly hierarchy.

Gold and the people it attracted to northern British Columbia were the vanguard of colonial settler society, as many historians have pointed out.[1] Clah had interacted with newcomers from an early age, but these early interactions, in contrast to those he would experience during the gold rush era, had been by choice. *He* sought *them* out, whether they were traders, missionaries, or other people through whom he thought he could gain knowledge or advantage. Successive gold rushes – at Omineca, Cassiar, and Juneau and Douglas – brought a different form of contact, one that Clah did not find as comfortable or affirming. A fur trader had minimal contact with European or American buyers; most trading was done with Aboriginal hunters and trappers in environments that few newcomers had penetrated. In contrast, the discovery of gold brought miners rapidly into the Interior, along waterways and trails that Aboriginal people had used as a means of communication for centuries. The miners initially needed transport and guides to help them to the goldfields; once they were established, however, they treated Aboriginal people as mere labourers, more of an irritant than equal participants in the industry. The only work available to Aboriginal people was menial labour that required close association with miners, who often cheated them of their agreed upon rates of pay. Aboriginal people were discouraged from taking up mining themselves. The fur trade had rewarded individual initiative among Aboriginal traders; the mining industry discouraged it.

Although Clah's transition from the fur trade to the gold rush was rapid, it goes unexplained in his diary. It is not clear that he has left the fur trade until he states that he is setting out on a different journey with a different purpose. Clah continued to track down debts from his fur-trading activities for many years after he stopped working as a trader. He probably realized he could only continue to trade by offering credit, which he could not support. Whatever the reason for Clah's decision, he followed Robert Cunningham from trading to servicing gold miners.

Robert Cunningham had arrived on the Northwest Coast in 1863 as a lay assistant to William Duncan at Metlakatla. He offended Duncan's puritan morality, however, when he married his Tsimshian lover, Elizabeth Ryan, in September, rendering his relationship with Duncan untenable. After helping establish Quinwoch mission (the precursor of Kincolith mission) on the Nass River, Cunningham left mission work in 1866 to become a trader for the Hudson's Bay Company. A description written by a contemporary sums him up as a typical Englishman, with "his jolly round face, strikingly white skin and very light curly hair." When visitors happened on the Cunningham family sitting down to breakfast, Cunningham shooed his wife and children away, perhaps because he was sensitive to prevailing prejudices.[2] These prejudices did not stop him from running after other Tsimshian women, however, as is evident in a description of a domestic brawl Clah witnessed in 1869:

> Fort Simpson case about Jealouse Mrs Cunningham scratching her mans hand because Cunningham doing well in this place. He had sleeping to every womens outside the Fort[,] sometimes in the store ... Mrs Cunningham running runing about today. Cunningham[']s sweet[he]art was in the shop. But Mrs Cunningham was coming in the store an[d] founded Cunningham[']s sweet[he]art. Mrs Cunningham and one girl[,] they quar[re]ling about jealouse. Mr Cunningham used to be Minister[,] but now is [he's] falling.[3]

In 1871, Cunningham and Thomas Hankin, another HBC employee, won a government contract to upgrade trails leading from the Skeena River to the Omineca goldfields in the Interior.[4] They also established stores at the mouth of the river and near the Gitxsan village of Gitanmaax, which came to be known as the Forks or Hazelton.[5] The need to carry substantial cargoes upriver created opportunities for skilled boatmen.[6] A newspaper clipping attached to Clah's diary advertises Cunningham and Hankin's offer to freight goods from the mouth of the Skeena to the Forks for 21.5¢ per pound or to carry passengers with up to one hundred pounds of goods for $15 each.[7] The goods were carried by Tsimshian canoes.

Clah set out in May 1871 with a load of freight for Cunningham and Hankin, including ten traps, forty-seven cases of liquor, twelve ten-gallon casks of liquor, two hundred pounds of salt pork, and one hundred pounds of axes.[8] Clah took two white and five Aboriginal men with him, but even with their assistance the journey was hard going. As the men started up the Skeena River, they were passed by the steamship *Emma,* which soon grounded on a sandbar, one of many that dot the river. The next day, Clah's crew travelled twelve miles (19.3 kilometres) against strong currents on a rising river. Fortunately, the winds favoured them the next day, allowing them to rig sails. On Sunday, the men rested, and Clah nursed a sore throat, which would plague him for many years. Over the next two days, the party had to negotiate rapids and nearly lost its canoe and all the cargo. Worse was to come. The following morning, the men cut poles and portaged the cargo for two hours before reaching the Kitselas Canyon. The portaging in the canyon was so taxing that they had to hire extra labour. They worked all day carrying the cargo through the canyon and then went back for the canoe. Clah paid each of his assistants with ammunition and tobacco at a rate of twenty-five cents for a day's work.

After eleven days, the men had exhausted their initial stock of rations (thirteen pounds of bacon, one pound of tea, fourteen pounds of beans, five gallons of molasses, one hundred pounds of flour, and five pounds of sugar for seven men). Hungry or not, they had little choice but to push on, sailing another eight miles before encountering more rapids: "[O]ur canoe go roun[d] 3 [or] 4 times[,] two boys swimming across the river to save the Lienes [lines]."[9] Five men deployed lines to haul the canoe along the shore, while Clah and two others stayed aboard to steer. Despite their best efforts, the canoe was swept a mile downstream, and the back-breaking work had to be repeated. The men camped that night in rain that continued to fall the next day as they sailed to the next canyon. It was fortunate that they met an old man who gave them a large salmon. Two days later, the freighting canoe was ruined going through another rapid: "Our big canoe smash[ed] all pesise [to pieces], shallow an[d] strong cur-rent is the bad place for big canoe."[10] Although most of the cargo was saved, Clah had to send to the Forks for two smaller canoes. In the meantime, the men dried out their freight. Clah traded some dried fish and sent a man out to hunt grouse. He also had the good luck to encounter a Gitxsan man who owed him money from a debt incurred seven years previously. The party eventually managed to reach their destination, after twenty-two back-breaking days.

Clah immediately bought a double-barrelled gun for $30.00 and ammunition for $7.50. He paid off a thirty-dollar debt he owed to two Gitxsan men, and he bought five dollars worth of medicine for his throat from a doctor. The following day, he set off downriver with two canoes. He made the return journey to the mouth of the Skeena River in three days, despite tides and winds working against him. On the descent, he passed thirty-one canoes taking miners to the Omineca mines; five of them capsized, at the cost of their cargo and one man's life.[11] Cunningham paid Clah a dollar a day, but he deducted ten dollars for the broken canoe and damaged provisions, leaving Clah with fifteen dollars. There was a distinct possibility that Clah could do better on his own. A month later, as Clah travelled upriver to trade 120 pounds of flour on his own account, he passed a convoy of thirty canoes at Kitselas Canyon that was hauling freight for Cunningham and another trader, William Woodcock.[12]

Even before he visited the goldfields in 1873, Clah sought out Euro-Canadians passing through on their way inland. In 1871, Clah met Peter O'Reilly, the gold commissioner who was on a nine-month marathon trip to the Omineca goldfields.[13] O'Reilly hired Clah to navigate his canoe over several days. Clah verged on the obsequious, addressing O'Reilly as "Sir," helping him hunt deer, and arranging for him to witness Tsimshian dancing. Clah also acted as O'Reilly's interpreter and constable. He tracked down a man who had murdered three miners in 1862. Clah's involvement in this case was no doubt partly motivated by Duncan's false accusation, at the time of the miners' death, that Clah had killed the men. After serving as an interpreter for an informer, Clah helped arrest the culprit and imprison him at Metlakatla.[14] Having established a personal relationship with O'Reilly, Clah wanted his help to collect old trade debts from the Gitxsan. O'Reilly suggested that Clah write to Lieutenant-Governor Joseph Trutch. A few months later, while visiting the Coast, Trutch sought out Clah, who explained his case but failed to resolve his problems.[15] This pattern repeated itself many times over the years. Knowing influential men was never enough to resolve Clah's legal and economic problems.

JOURNEYING TO THE GOLDFIELDS

Clah timed his first journey to the Omineca goldfields in 1873 badly. The peak of the rush was over, and 1873 proved to be a lean year for gold discoveries in the region. Clah started out in late April in a convoy of six canoes headed by Paul Legaic II. He made some money transporting six passengers by canoe. They paid him fifteen dollars per person, but most of this money went to his assistants, who were paid twelve dollars each. Clah then set out to walk the trail to Lake Babine with Legaic and four other Tsimshian. Conditions were difficult because the winter snow, which had not yet melted, was too soft for snowshoes by the middle of the day. The men set off early each morning while the snow was hard.

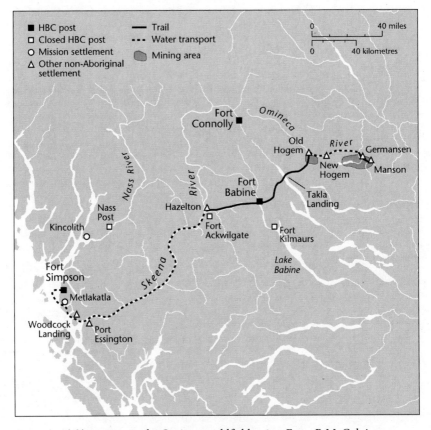

Clah's journey to the Omineca goldfields, 1873. From R.M. Galois, "Colonial Encounters," 124.

The mountains loomed on either side of them. They paid for transport across Babine and Takla lakes and reached the fast-flowing Omineca River after twenty days of travel. They carried on to Germansen Landing, a three-store settlement sixty miles downriver. By this time, the men were out of food. They mixed bacon remnants in their cups of tea. When that ran out, they desperately but unsuccessfully tried to hunt game.[16]

Once the party reached Omineca, Clah became ill. He treated himself with a mixture of Western and Tsimshian medicine then returned to work. He soon discovered that the men who employed him were also short of funds. They sometimes paid him in cash, more often in rations. Over the next few weeks, he picked up occasional work gardening or packing. After the thaw, he dug ditches for a miner. He then moved on to working the ground sluice for four dollars a day. After ten days on the sluice, however, Clah was exhausted and asked for his pay – ninety-three dollars for twenty-three days of work. Although the rate of pay was good compared to rates on the Coast, Clah had trouble getting money from his employers. Miners challenged the hours Clah claimed (Clah, of course, recorded the number of days worked in his diary) and told him they did not have the money to pay him. They offered him twenty dollars in gold dust and gave him a promissory note to cover outstanding wages.[17] Clah continued to ask Jenkins for the money owed him, and Jenkins gave him a gold watch worth forty dollars and another fifteen dollars worth of gold dust. Clah did not recoup the final $14.75 until the following year, when he met Jenkins on the Stikine River as he made his way to the Cassiar goldfields.[18]

Clah walked back to Omineca from Mansen Creek and obtained work shovelling tailings until he again collapsed from exhaustion. By August, he had had enough. It took him twelve days to walk to the Forks on the Skeena River. He descended the river by canoe and met his wife and children at Port Essington before pushing on to Fort Simpson. After four months away, Clah had earned only one hundred dollars in gold dust and concluded that the wages were not a good return for his hard work.

Clah therefore responded readily to a call by storekeeper, Lewis Hart, for fifty men to carry freight up the Stikine River, the main route to the Cassiar goldfields. At Tongass, across the Alaskan border, there were arguments over pay and rations. The Nisga'a refused to work for Hart unless he paid them in advance. The men eventually sailed along the Coast to Wrangell and then up the Stikine River.

The freighting trip up the Stikine River allowed Clah to become familiar with a waterway that had similar hazards to the Nass and Skeena rivers. Over the next eight years, he spent most summers at the Cassiar goldfields, usually taking his canoe to the highest point of navigation at Glenora and then walking up the trail to the mining region. When Stephen Redgrave, an ex-policeman from Toronto, arrived at Wrangell by steamship from Victoria a few months before Clah in May 1875, he described it as the most miserable place he had ever visited. The town was full of miners waiting for the ice to melt so they could go upriver and "poor wretched Indians," women who lived with white men who gave them food, clothing, whisky, and deadly diseases. Redgrave found the country fearful. The trail, which had been upgraded from an Aboriginal trade route to a track for miners and pack animals, ran among mountains covered permanently in snow. The lake was still frozen in May, making boat travel impossible.[19]

W.H. Pierce, Clah's nephew by adoption who became a Methodist minister, offers another account of the Cassiar goldfields and the people they attracted in *Thirteen Years of Travel and Exploration in Alaska*, which was written as if Pierce were a Euro-Canadian, not a Tsimshian familiar with the environment and people. He, like Redgrave, found Wrangell a depressing place populated by "miners, Indians and half breeds" as well as by "squaws," many of whom lived with white men on muddy, crowded streets as everyone waited for the ice to melt to take the trail to Cassiar. The miners took "their dusky mates" with them. These women, Pierce claimed, had developed expensive tastes. They sat at smoky fires in silk dresses, a practice Pierce found rather unbecoming for people who had been "raised on dried fish, fresh fish and all kinds of fish – and lived in bark houses with an open smoky fire-place in the centre."[20] The author pandered to the prejudices of settler readers, particularly when he expressed sympathy for the many miners who were so poor they lived on credit.[21] Pierce noted that the daily wage scale was three dollars for a labourer, four dollars for a miner, five dollars for a blacksmith, and two dollars a day for Aboriginal people. Aboriginal people's wages did not improve over the ensuing years, even when the mining process changed. In 1887, when Aboriginal workers at the Treadwell quartzite works at Douglas demanded three dollars a day, they were sacked, and Treadwell refused to employ Aboriginal labour.[22] While earnings were relatively low for Aboriginal people, food and other provisions in these remote locations were expensive.[23]

Clah arrived at the Cassiar goldfields at the start of the boom. His first year, although not as physically taxing as his season at Omineca and Germansen, did not bring his desired returns. The following summer, he decided that freighting goods and carrying passengers along the rivers and lakes of the Cassiar region would be more profitable than mining. He persuaded nine Tsimshian men, including John Ryan and Peter Quintal, to help him build a boat for freighting. Clah borrowed tools from a white friend – a whipsaw, two handsaws, and two planers – and sold fifty pounds of flour to buy food and materials. His partners also contributed small amounts of money to buy nails. It took the men eleven days to finish the boat.[24] Two days later, they carried two tons of cargo for storekeepers from Laketon on Dease Lake to McDames Creek. They sailed 103 miles along Dease River and through five lakes. They hired a local friend as pilot, charged four passengers five dollars per person, and charged four cents per pound for freight. Clah's partners were well satisfied. Two weeks later, they were paid $180.00 in greenbacks for the freight (possibly the first time Clah had been paid in American currency) plus $51.87 from passengers. Each of the nine partners received $25.50 and agreed to sell their interest in the boat to Clah. Clah thanked Jesus for his good luck, "I only Bad man when I younger. I always break Gods Law. Now I triet [try] to be good man[,] pray to Him and every day."[25] Clah's success did, however, cause resentment among some of his erstwhile partners back at Fort Simpson. When Peter Quintal complained to the new missionary, Thomas Crosby, Clah was forced to defend himself against accusations that he had cheated his men. The argument became a protracted dispute, and Crosby threatened Clah with imprisonment if he did not pay eleven dollars to resolve it. Clah instead appealed to Duncan at Metlakatla as a magistrate, who did not uphold Crosby's case against Clah.[26]

Although Clah was pleased to be an independent entrepreneur again, there were increasing signs of changing attitudes within the racially disparate population. Several times during the season, miners and officials made transport arrangements with Clah only to renege with no compensation or apology. Clah was offended when a restaurant owner he knew did not bother to clean the table after the previous customer, "a squaw," left or to bring him milk when he ordered it. When Clah used the term *squaw* for the first time at the Cassiar goldfields, his diary reflected increased racial stereotyping in the region.[27] He complained about two "coloured" men who did not pay him for their passage and a "black" employee who was lazy: "says he woulden take fourty dollars If anybody told me to swimming in the Creek."[28] In 1886, Clah observed Americans in Alaska rounding up Chinese and shipping them out of Juneau; at another time, he noted that "Boston men" did not like the Italians who were coming to work in the goldfields.[29] Clah met Frenchmen, Spaniards, and Mexicans, but it was high-status provincial officials and store owners who commanded his attention – people he referred to as gold commissioners, lawyers, and judges. When George Cook tried to cheat him, claiming Clah had made eleven trips for him rather than the twelve Clah recorded in his pocketbook, Clah called on three Euro-Canadians, whom he describes as lawyers and a judge, to support him. All they did, however, was warn Clah to look out for rascals.[30]

On his return to Fort Simpson, Clah paid his debts and the wages of seven men he hired to build his house. When the fishing season opened in March, he bought fish and paid men to salt it. It was at this time that he bought the land at Laghco.[31] A few days later, he left for the Stikine River. Once again he paddled to Glenora, where his crew packed the cargo on their backs to walk up the trail to Dease Lake and Dease Creek. Clah found his old boat undamaged and ready to start freighting and transporting passengers. He charged five dollars per passenger and three cents a pound for freight. From late June to late July, he freighted goods for storekeepers Whittacker Wright and James F. Calbreath, and throughout August he transported passengers.

In 1877, 1879, and 1881, Clah again worked from May to August at the Cassiar goldfields, even though he did not have his boat, which he discovered abandoned on a woodpile in 1881.[32] Finding work was much more difficult without the boat. In 1877, Clah worked for businessmen, taking goods and passengers along the river and lake system of the region. But in 1879 he had trouble finding work. At Dease Lake, he found that hundreds of Aboriginal people had preceded him. By early July, Clah complained that he had not had any work for two and a half months and had run up a debt of one hundred dollars. With so much labour available, Clah's potential customers became fickle; they promised to hire him and then engaged his competitors. Many of Clah's potential customers were people he regarded as friends, people whom he had known for many years such as David, a lawyer: "Now[,] about 5 oclock afternoon[,] lawyer Daved [David]

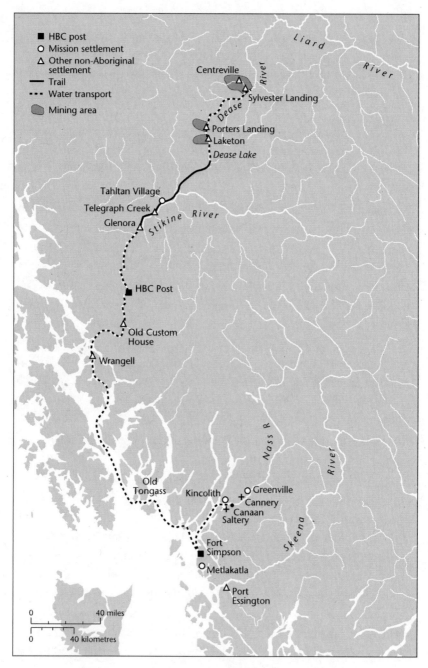

Clah's journey to Dease Lake, 1875. From R.M. Galois, "Colonial Encounters," 126.

Back out. he says ill [he'll] gone in Dease lake. Mr Bredy [Brady] says[,] ['][H]ow much mon[e]y you paid Arthur Wellington Clah for you stopping him [delaying him][?'] Daved says[,] [']Oh[,] Clah[,] his [he's] good friend to me[,] he not want mon[e]y.['] Now I found bad luck this time year all summer[.] some friends wants give me work, someone jumped[,] and some back out. What bad luck I have this time."[33]

The best deal Clah made in 1879 was buying a watch for ten dollars and selling it for twenty to pay off a debt.[34] He faired no better in 1881. Even before Clah left for the goldfields, his wife accused him of being a lazy "do nothing." For a man who had always tried to be ahead of the game, this was a telling comment on his narrowing options.[35] Gold Commissioner A.W. Vowell noted in his report to the provincial secretary and the minister for mines that there had been no gold discoveries at Cassiar in 1880-81.[36] The boom had peaked in the mid-1870s. Once he arrived at the goldfields, Clah hired himself out to carry freight for businesses, and he earned about two dollars a day or fifty dollars a month for his work.[37]

By this time, Chinese miners had arrived in large numbers. Two hundred arrived on two steamships at the beginning of the season. When Clah and his friends were offered accommodation in a house in the Chinese section of Dease Creek settlement, they refused to take it, claiming it stank. From late June, Clah worked for Rufus Sylvester, who, according to Vowell, was "noted for his enterprise and liberality," giving prospectors goods on credit.[38] Sylvester seems to have paid Clah well, with no arguments about hours or rates of pay. With gold mining in the doldrums, Sylvester turned to trading furs with the Kaska, an Athabaskan-speaking people of the region. Clah transported 1,400 pounds of furs, valued at between three and four thousand dollars, to McDames Creek.[39] Not long after this trip, Clah left the Cassiar region for the last time to return to the Nass River, where canneries were beginning to intrude on Tsimshian and Nisga'a life.

Meanwhile, up the Alaskan coast, two miners, Richard Harris and Joe Juneau, had been shown quartz with traces of gold by a local chief in October 1881. They immediately laid out a town site, Harrisburgh, which later came to be known as Juneau. The goldfields at Omineca and Cassiar were placer mines; they were worked by washing gravel and dirt through sluices and capturing the residue in tailings ponds. The quartzite deposits found at Juneau and Douglas Island had to be crushed in expensive stamp mills. Placer miners were soon replaced by industrialized mining. John Treadwell, a Californian carpenter, established a mill with five stamps in 1882, and it grew exponentially over the next few years. Clah made his first visit to Juneau in May 1882, just a few months after Harris and Juneau. He returned in 1886, 1887, and 1888.

The journey to Juneau and Douglas was a long trip by sea along the Inside Passage, but it was less arduous than the route to Cassiar because it did not require carrying provisions along inland trails. It was not, however, a journey Clah could make on his own; each year he recruited people to travel with him. In 1886, a Nisga'a father and son accompanied him, but it was not a happy partnership. The following year, Clah could find no one on the Nass willing to go with him and blamed his erstwhile partners for denigrating him. He eventually bought a sail, "one sail better [than] 20 men," and set out with a Nisga'a man, George Cook, his wife and two children, and an old acquaintance, Spanish Frank.[40] Although they experienced problems concerning the payment of duty on their cargoes of eulachon grease at the Port Tongass customs house across the Alaskan border, and although the two men had argued over the years about money owed to Clah, Cook and Clah enjoyed a successful partnership over the summer.

Clah took fish products, eulachon grease and smoked eulachon, to sell at Juneau. He wanted to ensure that if he did not find work, he would not go home empty-handed. He had taken fish products to trade in Wrangell the previous year on his way to Dease Lake, and he continued to trade them on his subsequent journeys up the Coast. He sold most of the eulachon grease to a store in Juneau at $1.25 per gallon, for a total of $100.00.

Clah tried mine labour on Douglas Island but decided after a day's work and an aching back that he was too old for mining. While his friends worked, Clah read the Bible and preached to those who would listen. His next venture was placer mining with a miner, William Meehan, of the Ready Bullion Company. Clah set up and worked the sluices and earned $2.50 an hour. The main activity on the island, however, was at the Treadwell quartz mill. Clah met the owner, John Treadwell, who gave him dinner and some flint he had brought from Idaho. He thought the flint could help Clah identify gold-bearing rocks when he went prospecting. For the six weeks Clah worked on Douglas Island, he lived in a tent. By early August, he was back on the Nass River, where he fished for salmon.

Before Clah returned to Juneau and Douglas Island, he stocked up on eulachon products to trade. By this time, the Alaskan townships were

[handwritten marginalia: late 1880's, ... immigration, ... move in the ... "Oregon Country".]

racially segregated. The Aboriginal town was located half a mile from Juneau and housed a thousand people.[41] The aging Clah was disturbed by the licentious and boisterous behaviour in the camps.[42] There were dance halls in Wrangell, Juneau, Douglas Island, and Yukon, where Clah travelled briefly in 1886.[43] He observed white men buying dances with Aboriginal women for ten cents worth of candy.[44] Aboriginal men also frequented the dance halls because they enjoyed the opportunity it gave for men and women to dance together.[45] In 1887, Auk Tlingit from the Juneau area provided alternative entertainment when they celebrated the peaceful resolution of a long-standing conflict with the Sitka Tlingit with dances and gifts that attracted a large crowd in Douglas. This was free entertainment in which men, women, and children could participate. Clah remarked that it was ironic that the government had banned this type of dancing, while dance halls run for profit were allowed.[46]

Clah occasionally visited the dance halls, but his Christian sensibilities were greatly offended by those who worked or played on Sundays. At the gold towns, Sunday was the busiest day of the week, because it was the only day miners could get away from their claims and come in to wash and mend clothes, collect supplies, and take in some entertainment.[47] The quartz mills, however, never closed down; they noisily crunched rock day and night. There was no church in Douglas, and a friend suggested to Clah in 1887 that he try street preaching in Douglas as was practised in Victoria by the Salvation Army.[48] A few weeks later, in August, two Quaker preachers, E.W. Weesner and J.H. Bangham, whom Clah had met in Juneau, came to town because they wanted Clah to interpret for them. Clah refused because he would have to use Chinook Jargon to reach the diverse people in town and, as Clah explained, the trade language's vocabulary was too limited to communicate the Christian message.[49]

Perhaps the most important event during Clah's sojourn in Douglas was a meeting with the governor of Alaska, A.P. Swineford, at Archer's Store on 23 September 1887. Clah was introduced as William Duncan's preacher. Later that day, Swineford visited Clah in his tent at the very moment he was recording their earlier encounter in his diary. Swineford chatted with Clah about Duncan's plan to set up a new mission community at Port Chester on Annette Island (later named New Metlakatla) in Alaska. He urged Clah to come to Alaska and become an American citizen.[50] Swineford also invited Clah to come to Sitka with him. Clah accepted. At

Sitka, the governor presented him with two letters, one addressed to Clah and the other to the people of Port Simpson, inviting them to come to Alaska.[51]

Clah's final sojourn in Alaska, in 1888, was short and disastrous. He did not take his own canoe but went as a passenger with two white men he knew well from the Nass River, Harvey Snow and William Robertson. Both had pre-empted land on the Nass, where they maintained small-scale fishing and trading businesses. As the men paddled away from Port Simpson on a foggy morning in August, Snow offered Clah "hell water." Clah refused and watched the men become drunker and drunker. On the third day, when Clah tried to take charge of the boat, Snow and Robertson swore at him and threatened to abandon him and his cargo on an island. Snow was not too drunk to trade eulachon grease for a gallon of whisky at the Tongass cannery, which he and Robertson consumed while they anchored in the fog. A few days later, Snow sold the rest of his cargo of grease. Encouraged by Robertson, Snow broke his agreement to continue to Juneau and decided to go back to the Nass River. After berating Clah for getting in the way of his and Robertson's plans, Snow paid Clah's steamer fare to Juneau.[52]

Back at Douglas, Clah visited his good friends Mark and Sarah Archer, who ran the store where Clah had met Swineford. He regaled them with details of his visit to Sitka, particularly how he had impressed the governor with his dedication as a preacher and a Christian who gave food to the poor, shelter to strangers, and medicine to the sick. But reliving past glories did not make Clah's situation more pleasant. After Clah sold his stock of trade goods, he had difficulty finding work. Despite frequent prayers, he was short of money and food. Even the weather was against him. One evening he bought himself three loaves of hot bread, but as he carried them home through the pouring rain, the wet bread disintegrated: "Just like flour so I don[']t threw out because I Boughted [it with] to my mon[e]y."[53] Never discouraged, he concocted new plans. He would make and sell curios. The previous year he had watched George Cook carve beaver bowls from green alder wood. It had given him the idea of taking "black marble" (probably argillite) with him to Alaska.[54] Although Clah set about carving totem poles and bowls, he was probably not a proficient carver. He could not sell his curios and eventually offered them at half price. He also gave away a bowl to E.W. Weesner, the Quaker missionary who had given him a Bible.[55] When it became clear that Clah had no future at the Alaskan goldfields, he returned to the Nass River and the canneries.

CLAH, THE INDEPENDENT PROSPECTOR

Over the years, particularly in those years that he did not travel to the established goldfields, Clah went on short prospecting trips. Although Clah and his companions were far from the main gold rush centres, they often encountered newcomers who tried to intimidate them and scare them away. In 1885, for instance, Clah travelled up the Nass and Tseax rivers to the Kitsumkalum Mountains.[56] As Tsimshian and Nisga'a prospectors pegged claims, they were threatened by newcomers. Those daunted by these attacks left, but Clah saw a religious analogy in the battle for gold. Bad miners abandoned their claims, just as bad Christians abandoned their faith. But both were gifts from God: "[W]ho back out from prospecting[,] he his [is] unbelieve Christian."[57] It certainly took strong faith in the existence of gold to continue prospecting. Clah was convinced he could find gold below the surface. Still more white miners arrived and challenged him. Clah heard that people were making fun of Aboriginal prospectors, calling them ignorant and incompetent. Most of the Tsimshian who continued to come to the mountains in the hope of quick returns were not willing to persevere in the face of these intimidatory tactics: "One time I have seen small pox come in town[,] and everybody leave the house fraiden [afraid] to catch pox. This sames [this is the same as] our indian miners. 2 men leave[,] they [all] wants go home[.] They all[,] 40 people[,] leave this same hour and this same day."[58] Clah, by contrast, persevered, but without much luck.

Clah often had to negotiate with local Aboriginal landowners for access to their territories. In 1877 and 1880, when he went up the Nass River as far as Lakwip, Clah was accompanied by a Gitanyow chief, Luuxhon, and some of his men. During the trip in 1880, the Gitanyow were uneasy about the nearby Eastern Tsetsaut, with whom they had fought in 1861. Clah believed they wanted to turn back because "I know them [in their] hearts[,] they not lik[e] anybody spoiling hunting grounds."[59] Before he went to the Kitsumkalum region in 1885, Clah was reminded that Gispaxlo'ots who did not pay five blankets to enter the hunting grounds at Kitsumkalum Lake were turned back.[60] Many of Clah's later prospecting trips were blocked by owners trying to prevent their hunting grounds from being disturbed.[61]

Clah's many prospecting journeys did not lead to wealth or even occasional discoveries of gold. Most of his trips lasted only a few days because he did not have the resources to make more extended ones, and they were speculative rather than based on evidence that gold might be found.

FAMILY MATTERS

Although the goldfields drew Clah away from his home territories most summers in the 1870s and 1880s, he was occupied with hunting, fishing, wood gathering, and communal activities for the remainder of the year. During his involvement in the fur trade, Clah was fortunate to have Port Simpson as his primary winter location. Not only was the HBC fort located there, the fort also provided him with easy access to the Nass and Skeena rivers and to coastal regions to the south. As fur trading was replaced by other economic activities, Clah experimented with living in other locations.[62] Although his temporary house at the mouth of the Skeena River gave him access to the freighting business that had been servicing Omineca goldfields for a few years, Clah turned his attention to the Nass River in 1877. After a short prospecting trip, he, with the assistance of four men, started building a house at Aiyansh, near Gitlaxdamks, on his wife's land. On 7 November, he collected his family from Port Simpson and took them to the new house, only to find that his workers had stopped work in his absence. So, during a cold and snow-bound November, the family completed the house on their own. The land Clah claimed was half a mile wide by a mile long.[63] On Christmas Day, to celebrate the completion of his new house, he gave a great feast for from three hundred to four hundred people. He called it a Christmas feast to ensure that Christian niceties were observed. Only a few months after the celebration, however, Stephen Redgrave, Clah's old associate, pre-empted the land.[64]

While Clah fought for his rights to the land, he built another house on land closer to the Nass fishery at Laxk'a'ata, a village that Clah renamed Canaan and called his "happy place." Clah claimed rights to this land through his father, but the Nisga'a at the Anglican mission at Kincolith made a successful counterclaim when the Indian reserve commissioner,

Peter O'Reilly, laid out reserves on the Nass River. This counterclaim led to a protracted fight between Clah and the Nisga'a.

At Canaan, Clah and his family planted potatoes and other vegetables, and they had ready access to the eulachon fisheries. Although Dorcas was closer to her Nisga'a family than she had been at Port Simpson, when Clah returned from the goldfields in November 1887, she complained that people were shunning her and the children because they were poor. Even Christian friends refused to help her, and she was forced to turn to white friends for food. Clah's diary entry about this incident offers a rare glimpse of how Clah's family fared during his many absences. We can only hypothesize about the family's predicament. Dorcas must have been concerned about how she would manage that summer, because she wanted to accompany Clah on his northern expedition. He reminded her of her responsibilities to the children and grandchildren and ordered her to stay on the Nass and plant potatoes at Canaan.[65]

Clah and his family were clearly in difficult straits by the late 1880s. He had trouble finding work, and his wife was apparently struggling to cope in his absence. The family had moved away from their home at Port Simpson, only to find that the land they owned on the Nass was no longer indisputably theirs. In the meantime, the house in Port Simpson, which Clah had rented out as a store for ten dollars a month, had been demolished when the renter, a white man named J.R. Linton, was caught with whisky by the Indian agent.[66] Clah and Dorcas were caught up in conflicts with pre-emptors, Nisga'a claimants, and the federal and provincial governments, which were in the process of containing Aboriginal people to inadequate reserve lands.

There were also personal tragedies. In 1882, Clah expressed pride in his seven children: Martha, Rebecca, David, Andrew, Fanny, Elizabeth, and Albert. But only a year after Albert, the youngest son, was born, Andrew died, and David followed a few months later. Two other daughters outside of Clah's primary family, Ida and Maggie, also died at about this time, as did two grandsons in 1887.[67]

In August, when Clah returned from his first trip to Juneau to find Andrew sick in bed, looking like death and thin as a bone, he quickly obtained medicine from the missionary A.E. Green. When the medicine had no effect, Clah turned to prayer. Over several days, Andrew seemed to get stronger, but his health deteriorated, and by 12 September Clah realized his son was close to death. The family decided to leave Nass Harbour, where they had resided since Andrew became ill, to travel to their house at Canaan. Andrew insisted on walking to the canoe, but he died as they paddled up river: "When I was half way[,] my dear Son Andrew Arthur Wellington Clah gone to[,] died 2 oclock this afternoon[,] aged 9 years and a half … poor Dear Son. Mother cried and sisters an[d] brothers cried. Some fishermen coming [a]longside my Boat[;] some were taking net in. also grandmother lucy Addosk met he[r] on the way. She was on top the tree taken indian apple. She call the Boat ashore … she come it down on tree and jump crying in my Boat[,] so I got up my place."[68]

The distraught family took the body inside the house as people from up and down the Nass River gathered. "We coulden sleep that night[,] as I felt weak[.] son[']s mother just like to be crezy [crazy] because our child die." The couple decided to bury Andrew at Canaan. Clah travelled to Port Simpson and Kincolith to announce that a Christian funeral would be conducted by Green.

While the family was still grieving, a measles epidemic broke out at Port Simpson. Over three weeks, fifty children became sick, and several died, some from starvation. David caught the disease. By 3 January, the family believed he was near death. The boy got up from his bed to confess his sins, while family and friends knelt to pray for him. David recovered, but the epidemic continued. Many children became sick, including Clah's youngest son, Albert. Clah bought medicines and boiled water for the children to drink. In the latter part of January, there were funerals nearly every day. In early February, David, who had seemed to be fully recovered, caught a cold while out hunting. His health deteriorated rapidly. Clah begged the local missionaries for medicines, called in a Chinese doctor, and went down to Metlakatla to try to persuade missionary Hall to visit David. The Chinese doctor was hesitant about treating the sick; he was worried that, if a patient died, the missionaries would blame him and he would be imprisoned. Yet the Tsimshian begged him for help. Clah started treating David himself with castor oil as a purgative. He then asked another Metlaktla missionary, William Collison, to come to Fort Simpson. Throughout David's illness, Clah resorted to prayer, but on 27 February David died after a month's illness. He was thirteen years old.

Fifty or sixty people came to the house to mourn. The Riflemen's Company collected six dollars and bought white flannel and black and white cotton for funeral decorations. Thomas Crosby and others came to pray. Two days later, David was buried with the Riflemen's Company in attendance. Ten days of mourning followed. Clah expressed his grief through continual prayer, despite his wife's pleas for him to stop.

Clah and Dorcas now had four daughters, a son, and a grandchild. A few years later, in 1888, William West, the husband of the couple's oldest daughter, Martha, died. Although everyone believed that he and his companions had drowned – some of their possessions and the boat had been found – their remains were not recovered. Rumours that the men had been murdered were confirmed when West's decapitated body was found buried on Dundas Island.[69] Clah did not express in his diary any suspicions he might have had about the murderers or their motives. The loss of a son-in-law made the whole family's existence more precarious, for West had contributed to the household economy.

When daughters Ida and Maggie died soon after, Clah went to the "witch man" Billscan (or Billscon), whom he blamed for the deaths of seven of his children. Although Clah had tried to appease Billscan by giving him tobacco, when Maggie died, Billscan stood outside the Clah house laughing. Clah was worried, if not unnerved, by the man's power. He dreamed about him and thought he was seeking retribution. Unfortunately, Clah does not disclose what he had done to offend the man.[70]

Unrealized Dreams of Gold

Clah's hopes for making a fortune at the goldfields were never realized. In the early years, he did profit from his ventures transporting goods and people to the mines. It was, however, arduous work, as the description of his trip up the Skeena in 1871 testifies. As he became older, Clah found it increasingly difficult to sustain the hard physical labour demanded of miners, and he was unable to utilize the skills he had as a boatman and navigator. Although Clah was at home when several of his children died, his years at the goldfields kept him away from his family for extended periods of time and at some personal cost to himself, his wife, and his children. Clah's life and that of his family were unsettled in other ways. The family moved from Fort Simpson to the Skeena and then to the Nass

River, where their rights to land were continually under challenge, before returning to Port Simpson.

As the fishing industry, canneries, and hop fields became the main means of making a living, Clah worked more closely with his wife, children, and sons-in-law. Although the goldfields had been difficult and frustrating places for a Tsimshian man to negotiate, Clah had forged relationships with storekeepers, lawyers, and officials that enabled him to establish working conditions in which he could survive, if not prosper. He nevertheless depended on these people to offer him work because he could not make his way successfully as a prospector. The canning industry, however, would put even more constraints on Clah's activities. Not only was piece-work poorly rewarded, the industry itself exploited fish and land that had sustained Tsimshian and Nisga'a since time immemorial and denied them access to their inherited rights.

5
Food Production and Wage Labour

Modernizing trends in food production had an enormous impact on the Tsimshian, including Clah and his family. The seasonal food-gathering activities of the Northwest Coast continued, but they were distorted by the industrialization of fishing, particularly the introduction of canneries in the late 1870s and early 1880s. Before the appearance of canneries, the Tsimshian and their coastal neighbours had caught and processed fish for trade, their own consumption, and as an integral part of feasting. Fishing sites were inherited, and rights to them were carefully protected. As canneries mushroomed at the mouths of rivers and along the Coast, the government intervened to regulate access to fish. Regulation affected Aboriginal fishermen in two ways: first, it impinged on their traditional rights to fish and shaped how they could use the catch; and second, it created seasonal wage labour for men, women, and children. Aboriginal people increasingly worked in the canneries, and for a short time they engaged in hop picking in Washington State. In the late 1880s and 1890s, when the hop fields flourished, there were large annual migrations of families from the north Coast. Clah visited the hop fields on two occasions.

As the fur trade declined and salmon fishing was constrained by the canneries, the Tsimshian turned increasingly to horticulture. They acquired a taste for potatoes and other introduced vegetables and supplemented their diet with them as their access to fish, berry patches, and other traditional foods became restricted. The Tsimshian had to learn new skills – clearing land, planting, weeding, fertilizing, and harvesting crops. They sold surpluses for much needed cash.

Clah and his family had to make radical adjustments to their lives to accommodate these changes. The women spent several months each year working long hours in canneries, fixing nets, cleaning and slicing fish, and putting fish in cans. Before the canning season, they prepared their gardens for planting; after the season, they harvested the crops. The men were employed for short periods as fishermen, they helped in the gardens, and they fished and hunted for their family. Some engaged in wage labour at the sawmills. A few Tsimshian ran small businesses, including their own stores.

TSIMSHIAN FOOD PRODUCTION

Tsimshian traditionally relied on marine resources and supplemented their diets by hunting and gathering a limited range of plant foods such as berries, crabapples, and roots.[1] Because these food sources were seasonal, Northwest Coast peoples developed a variety of food-preservation techniques that were, in turn, supplemented by the introduction of new European methods. The region was rich in fish, including the anadromous salmon and eulachon (smelt); trout and herring; and deep-sea fish such as halibut. Herring roe, seagull eggs, and seaweed were also important sources of food. The seasonal round of food collection began in spring, when eulachon swarmed in the millions up the Nass River. Throughout March, people kept a look out for signs that the fish were coming. In 1865, Clah "shew [saw] a grow [crow] catching small fish in his mouth[.] but I catch the fish from the grow [h]is mouth on the 13 March 1865 about mouth nass river."[2] Others found eulachon in the stomachs of seals or detected their appearance in the arrival of large sea animals such as seals and dolphins and birds such as eagles, ducks, and seagulls. As the eulachon swam up the river, the sky became thick with birds: "[S]ea call [gulls]. Just [looks] like snow where them fly of. they catch more fishs than man. eagle birds eat much fish everyday."[3]

Weather conditions were unpredictable in the spring. The river was often still frozen, and people fished with nets and poles through holes cut in the ice. In those years when the ice had begun to break up, fishing conditions were much more hazardous. In 1886, ice was moving on the river when the fish run started: "[M]ay be 5 hundred fishing poles brokin [breaking] every tide." People were forced to fish from canoes, using a combination of nets and spears. One person would pull on the oars, while the other handled the net. The fishers competed with the birds for eulachon.[4] Occasionally, it was so cold the fish froze before they could be harvested: "21 March 1866[,] small fishes But not one live at in the river of at nass. The[y] all frossing [frozen]. because too much cold[,] everybody can catching Deatt [dead] fishs on the sand that day."[5] In other years, the sheer weight of the eulachon dragged nets out of the fishermen's hands: "[S]mall fishs too t[h]ick[;] no time to hook it up[.] put net down on water[,] in about 3 minut[e]s the net was full. Some fishin[g] men very Smartt an Q[u]icker, some fisher men little too slow[:] the fish take the nets away."[6] Eulachon could be dense in some parts of the Nass River and scarce elsewhere. In the bumper year of 1892, there were few fish in Fishery Bay, which, as the name suggests, was usually abundant with fish, while the fish were plentiful at Canaan.

At about the same time that the eulachon appeared, the herring started spawning in coastal bays and island waters. Fishermen seeking herring roe would set out materials such as kelp or hemlock branches in known spawning areas for the herring to spawn on.[7] Spring fishing was particularly good in 1889, and Clah was in the area to take advantage of it. He collected seaweed and caught halibut off Dundas Island then travelled to the Nass River, where there were more eulachon than anyone could process. To top it all off, Clah collected a ton of eggs in a single day.[8]

The first of the eulachon were eaten fresh. After the stringencies of late winter, people could be close to starvation. But most of the catch was preserved. Eulachon was prized first and foremost for its oil, usually referred to as grease. The fish were left to rot in pits in the ground for ten to twenty days and then boiled in bentwood boxes, using hot stones to keep the water at a boil. As the oil rose to the top, it was ladled off. The rest of the fish was then pressed to release more oil.[9] Men collected the wood for the fire and women processed the fish. After Clah built his house at Canaan on the Nass River, the family kept its grease-making and other tools in the house. The tools were destroyed or stolen on several occasions by people from Kincolith who were trying to assert their rights over the land Clah claimed.

Eulachon were also dried, smoked and, after the introduction of salt by Europeans, salted. In the spring of 1892, which was particularly productive, Clah's family packed away ten coal cans and two Indian boxes (one nine-gallon and one fourteen-gallon) of grease; four tons of dried fish, which they stored in a thirty-gallon barrel; three barrels of salted fish;

Aboriginal people processing eulachon on the upper Nass River, ca. 1884.
BC Archives, C-07432.

and two hundred pounds of smoked fish.[10] Of course, Clah's family was not alone in producing so many eulachon products that year. Excess supply lowered prices.

Herring roe were dried on rocks and then stored.[11] In March 1892, when Clah heard that the government had passed a new law banning people from taking herring roe, he reported: "[M]ake everyone cried for that news. Because Indians like fish eggs." The law does not seem to have been enforced, though, for Clah reported collecting herring roe in subsequent years.[12] His entry does, however, reflect concerns over increasing government interference in Aboriginal people's activities.

Eulachon, particularly the oil, was a valuable trade item. It was sold to Aboriginal people who did not have access to eulachon runs and to those engaged in other activities, such as mining and logging. It was also sold to white traders, including those who worked for the HBC and small dealers on the Nass and Skeena rivers.[13] There were years when Clah did not harvest eulachon himself but bought the grease and dried fish. When Clah planned a trip to places where eulachon was not available, he made sure he took some, along with herring roe and seaweed, with him to trade. In 1887, when Clah was en route to Juneau with George Cook and his family, Clah and his companions were invited to a meal by a Stikine doctor who offered them seal oil instead of eulachon oil: "Break dried halibut in pieces puted [put it] in wash Basin mix[ed] with seal oil. one for me[,] one for George Cook an[d] his wife. steamed dried root in kettle. cutid [cut it] small, mixed [with] sealoil. wetted dry herrings eggs poilet [boiled it] little, mixed with seal oil." Mrs. Cook reciprocated by giving their hosts dried eulachon and eulachon grease.[14]

People in the Interior prized salty foodstuffs from coastal regions because they did not have access to salt. Seaweed was always in high demand. During the 1880s and 1890s, as salmon fishing became industrialized, eulachon, herring roe, and seaweed continued to be harvested by Tsimshian and other Aboriginal peoples.

At the end of the eulachon, kelp, and herring roe harvest, the salmon arrived. Spring salmon (also known as chinook), as the name suggests, were the first to come. These salmon are large but not as abundant as other species. They were followed by sockeye, which ran from mid-summer to late August; humpback (pink), which arrived in July; and coho and chum, which ran in the fall.[15] Although Clah had often been away for the summer fishing season during the fur trade and gold rush years, in 1892 he was nevertheless nostalgic about a time when life was more measured and less hurried:

[T]he way of old people. spend 3 months stay at Nass river. moving down lah-collums [Lax Kw'alaams], Metlekatlah or Skeenah [Skeena] river make everything slow an[d] right. some were hunting some places travel [to] trad[e] the fish grease cros[s]ing [to] Queen Charlott[e] island some places, gone down Bala Bala [Bella Bella] some gone up north trade grease [in] Alaska[,] Stickeen [Stikine], taco [Taku], chilcate[,] Sitka, cots-noo

Clycany [Kaigani]. Some old people were Rich[,] all gone up Skeenah river fishing salmon in first July. But New people[']s ways fishing [on the] Nass river [after] 3 weeks [they] go home. [Then they] start out hunting seal or bear in [for] a week or 2[,] they keep thinking about time for fishing [for the canneries].[16]

It is ironic that Clah regretted the loss of a slower pace of life, for he had always been an enthusiastic adopter of the latest innovations and new technologies, rushing from one new opportunity to the next. But, as a man in his sixties, he had become aware of the costs of these changes. He felt increasingly disempowered as the colonial juggernaut of canneries and land seizures rolled over his people. The Tsimshian and their neighbours became poorer as ever more restraints were imposed on their activities. They were forced to find new means of maintaining themselves as the old economy based on trade, exchange through the potlatch system, and subsistence was undermined.

Tsimshian also became dependent on imported provisions such as flour, rice, sugar, molasses, bacon, tea, coffee, tobacco, and alcohol. Although alcohol was not as socially destructive as it had been during the fur trade era, it was still readily available. People needed money, vouchers, or trade items to buy these goods at stores that sprang up along the Coast. Although most stores were run by newcomers, some Tsimshian did set up their own businesses. Paul Legaic II, for instance, established a store up the Skeena River during the Omineca gold rush, and Alfred Dudoward ran a store at Fort Simpson. Nevertheless, most stores were run by newcomers who had come to the region to establish fish-processing plants or sawmills, which operated on credit. Aboriginal labourers were either partly or fully paid with food rations such as flour and bacon. These dried and preserved foods were also convenient provisions to take on extended trips. Clah took store foods with him on his expeditions during the gold rushes. In preparation for his journey to the Cassiar goldfields in May 1876, Clah borrowed flour, coffee, yeast powder, sugar, black tea, butter, tobacco, and sugar from Joseph Pierce. On a shorter prospecting trip in 1881, he took flour, sugar, coffee, and butter, which he expected to supplement with meat from hunting.[17] Robert Cunningham gave Clah rations of tea, beans, molasses, bacon, flour, and sugar for his crew when he freighted goods up the Skeena River in 1871. Not only humans but also their animals had to adjust to a changing diet. One morning, as Clah prepared a meal, he saw that an "old hen an[d] a chi[c]ken was come longside me. the young chi[c]ken crying for something to eat. I pity them[.] gave the mother an[d] young chicken piece of bread. The[y] eat it. walk out happy. about 2 minut[e]s 2 young dog came in crying for something to eat. I cut loave bread give to them. thee smelled don[']t want live lik[e] whit people. thee not proud. But thee never seen Befor[e]. So I give them dry fish. now thee eat[,] thee happy walk way."[18]

As Clah became older and looked back on the changes that had occurred over his lifetime, he realized that reliance on introduced foodstuffs had made people poor and dependent on processed foods: "But new people very poor[,] using very much whit[e] peoples food[.] we don't know how to using sugar. Making small spoon[,] we call teaspoon one full of sugar. But new people take 3 full of sugar to make one cup. I have seen one place using s[o]upspoon of sugar one cup of tea. About old Indians[,] first whit[e] people came[,] don[']t taste molasses[,] no taste sugar[,] no rice[,] no bread[.] thee smelled and puted [put it] out."[19] Introduced foods were not only used for everyday sustenance but also in ritual feasting. Molasses and bread were common items at feasts, as were green apples, rice, and alcohol. In February 1871, when Clah gave a feast to celebrate his son David's birth, the food distributed included ten boxes of biscuits that had cost eighty-four dollars and twenty-eight gallons of molasses that had cost twenty-eight dollars. Clah recorded that he had spent $395 that month, presumably to acknowledge the birth of his son, whom he hoped would inherit the chiefly name Gwisk'aayn (Kuskin).[20]

In the late 1870s, when Clah was travelling to the goldfields in summer, he decided to invest in horticulture. Although his motivations for moving from Fort Simpson to the Nass River are not entirely clear, one of them was certainly his desire to gain land on which to grow vegetables and fruit. Clah eventually cleared the land and planted crops at Laghco, the land he had bought south of Port Simpson before his move to the Nass River. By the late 1880s, horticulture and wage labour at the canneries had become dominant activities in the lives of Clah and his family. In 1891 and 1898, the family also made two trips to work as day labourers at the hop fields in Washington State. Nonetheless, Clah continued to search for gold. On prospecting trips up the Nass and Skeena rivers in the 1890s, he found nothing worth reporting in his diary, and long-distance canoe trips had ended for Clah by the late 1880s. Clah continued to paddle to nearby destinations, but his trips to Victoria, Vancouver, and Washington State were by steamship, as was a trip to visit William Duncan at New Metlakatla in 1907.[21]

Canneries

As with so many of the new forces that transformed the lives of people on the Coast, canneries began on a small scale and then quickly dominated people's lives. Although the first canneries had been established on the Fraser River in 1871 and on the Skeena River by 1876, it was not until 1880 that Clah directly experienced the impact of cannery production on the Nass River. Newcomers had been involved in the fishing industry in the area for a number of years. James Grey, Harvey Snow, J.J. Robinson, and Stephen Redgrave had pre-empted small sites on the river for commercial fishing. These men lived in close proximity to the Nisga'a, trading with them, sometimes employing them, and setting up stores to service the mainly Aboriginal population. They were conscious that they were on Nisga'a land. When Grey and Robinson received Crown grants for their land, the Nisga'a residing there were forced to give up their gardens and move their houses. This caused so much resentment that, according to the missionary A.E. Green, Grey was only able to get his land surveyed after he agreed to build a sawmill on it.[22]

Snow, with whom Clah travelled to Alaska in 1888 (see Chapter 4), lived with his wife and children at Laxgalts'ap (Greenville).[23] Clah shared a closer relationship with James Grey, who had come to the region as a miner. The two men had met on the route to the Omineca mines in 1873 and 1874. After Grey pre-empted land on the Nass River in 1874, Clah often stayed with him and bought lumber from him as he was building his house at Aiyansh. Clah considered Grey a supportive friend at a time when the Nisga'a were ridiculing him and had refused to help him build his house. Grey, in return, might have found an ally in Clah, for Grey was also under pressure from the Nisga'a to leave because his Crown grant of thirty-five acres was adjacent to Laxgalts'ap.[24] According to Department of Fisheries records, Grey had four boats with eight fishermen and sixty shoremen working for him by 1883.[25] One year later, he was hiring Chinese labour, and Clah was working for him, collecting wood for his smokehouse. Grey established a cannery in 1891, but by that time he was also a heavy drinker.[26] He relied on a diversified economic base – potato crops, a sawmill, and a fish-processing plant – to support himself.

The appearance of H.E. Croasdaile on the Nass heralded the start of industrialized canning in the region. Clah first mentions Croasdaile as Robinson's partner in March 1879, and Croasdaile eventually purchased Robinson's Crown grant.[27] The fact that Clah freighted cargo for Croasdaile and Robinson in 1879 suggests the two men operated a store. The following summer, Croasdaile was involved in a commercial fishing operation. Local people were infuriated when his foreman erected a large salmon trap in the river. Rev. Green had to intervene to stop them from physically attacking Croasdaile.[28] Croasdaile employed men who fished in four boats and half a dozen women who worked onshore. When Clah asked Croasdaile to hire Dorcas, Croasdaile refused. He did, however, give Clah a few hours of work cutting staves. At this time, Clah and his family were in dire straits. He was sick, and his family was subsisting on salmon bones boiled in water. He found Croasdaile a hard man with no sympathy for poor, starving Indians. If they could not pay, Croasdaile would throw surplus salmon back into the river rather than give them to hungry families. Nor would he extend credit to Clah, unlike most of the store owners in the region.[29]

In 1881, Croasdaile applied successfully to the Dominion government for a one thousand dollar grant to remove snags from the river so that steamers could come upriver to his cannery, which was located about nineteen kilometres from the mouth of the river.[30] When Clah returned from the Cassiar goldfields in August, the cannery system had been put in place. Men, women, and young people awoke to a bell at dawn and worked sixteen-hour days. Men received a dollar, women seventy-five cents, and youths twenty-five cents a day. Clah worked for the blacksmith for $1.00 a day, while his young son David earned $1.25 for a week's work. In addition to long hours and low pay, the goods sold at the cannery store were overpriced. Naturally, people complained. Clah threatened to write a letter to the Indian commissioner in Victoria, I.W. Powell, but to no avail.[31] Clah found assisting the blacksmith physically taxing. He also undertook odd jobs such as carrying lumber or loading boxes of salmon tins onto steamers for transport south. Finally, in September, Clah was able to escape wage labour by going salmon fishing on his own account and salting his catch.

Croasdaile's cannery, Nass River. 1882. BC Archives, B-03546.

In early November, Clah received a letter from Port Simpson Council asking him to return to the village. He felt rather ambivalent about this invitation, for he only wanted to go back if work was available. In the meantime, he had offers of work from the storekeeper at Fishery Bay and from a cannery operator, William Ward. Clah decided to take the job at Fishery Bay – building a wharf for seventy-five cents a day.

At the time, Clah was negotiating the marriage of his daughter Martha to William West, the son of Chief Niisho'ot (Albert Nelson).[32] The family travelled to Port Simpson for Christmas and the wedding, which took place the following day. Altogether, it was an exuberant day. The soldiers' and firemen's bands played in the streets, while another band played in the wedding house. That night, Clah and Dorcas' youngest son, Albert, was born.[33] There was much feasting at Port Simpson that season.

On 2 January 1882, Clah, as a senior Gispaxlo'ot, was called to a meeting to discuss the inauguration of a new head chief. This is presumably the reason he had been called back to his community. At the same time, reports reached Port Simpson about conflict at Metlakatla between William Duncan and William Ridley, who had been appointed bishop of Caledonia in 1879 and based himself at Metlakatla. Several Metlakatla chiefs were contemplating moving back to Port Simpson to escape growing tensions between the two men.[34]

By March, Clah and his family were back on the Nass River for the eulachon season, making grease and salting fish. Clah lost twelve dollars worth of grease and his fifty-dollar canoe while trying to land his cargo in a heavy wind. Dorcas and Martha McNeill were devastated by the loss.[35] Luckily, this did not represent the family's entire eulachon harvest. A few days later, Clah set out for Juneau, hunting and trading along the way. At Wrangell, he sold grease and salted and smoked fish. Clah does not reveal what his family did in his absence. In December, Clah's wife and daughter were cleaning tin cans at one of the canneries, while Clah was looking for a canoe to take them down to Port Simpson for Christmas. Unable to buy or borrow one, the family spent Christmas at Canaan and feasted on food given to them by the store owner, McKay.[36]

The exploitative nature and uncertainty of cannery employment became even clearer in 1883. Clah and his family received another offer of employment from William Ward, who was establishing a cannery at Cape Fox. With help from local people, Clah built himself a temporary log cabin in anticipation of his family's employment over the summer.[37] But the promised work did not materialize. Clah's wife and children returned to the Nass River to make fishing nets at one of the canneries – Rebecca and Dorcas finished a 209-yard net by early May. They returned to Cape Fox, but Clah complained that only his daughter Rebecca had work. Clah had been without employment for sixty-five days and had exhausted his reserves of cash to feed his family.[38] When nothing else worked out for Clah, he turned to prospecting but returned empty-handed.

The following year, Clah returned to the canneries. In April, he worked for James Grey doing odd jobs, collecting wood to smoke fish and freighting barrels of salted fish. He spent some time at Canaan planting seeds in his garden and then set out rather late in the season to look for contract work at the canneries. The canneries paid fishermen either wages or by

Tsimshian fishing fleet, Skeena River. BC Archives, AA-00193.

contract. Those who earned wages were paid regardless of whether they were out catching fish. Under the contract system, fishermen were paid on a per-catch basis.[39] It would seem, from Clah's descriptions, that the canneries hired some fishermen in anticipation of the season because they could not know exactly when the salmon would arrive. By contrast, contract fishermen, who were not paid as they waited for the fish, ran up debts for food and other provisions at the cannery store. Fishing was undertaken in "double-enders," boats about twenty-six feet long that were crewed by two men (or, occasionally, women). The puller rowed, while the captain laid out and hauled in the net. The boats were usually towed out to the fishery. Once the net was let out, it drifted with the tides. After the crew hauled in the catch, the boats were towed back to the cannery or some other convenient location where the fish were unloaded.[40]

Clah needed a puller to work with him before he could get a contract. He hired a man at a dollar a day, or thirty dollars a month. Clah's contract with the cannery was six dollars for every hundred salmon. The first day, the two men caught 78 fish, the next day 189. When the fishermen brought in their catch to the cannery, the fish were counted. On the following Saturday, Clah caught even more salmon, but the cannery would not take them because newly introduced fishing regulations had banned fishing on the weekend. The following Saturday, Clah arrived at six in the morning to ensure that his catch would be bought, but he discovered that the cannery had an oversupply. By the middle of the week, Clah had to stop fishing so Dorcas could mend his old torn net.[41]

In August, Clah hired a new man, Henry Smith, to work with him, but the two men soon had a falling-out over pay. Smith had tuberculosis and, according to Clah, was too sick to work most days. Although Clah had offered him a dollar a day, Smith demanded $1.25. Clah retorted that if he paid him that, he would make no money himself. As a compromise, Clah offered Smith his gun, ammunition, and shot to enable him to go hunting, but this offer was not accepted by Smith, who threatened Clah with a stone axe. Clah decided to take some time out from cannery fishing, to fish on his own and salt his catch.[42] A few days later, he was back at the cannery, complaining to the boss that Aboriginal people were paid too little while the store charged too much.[43] Clah was not the only unhappy fisherman. Others demanded an extra two dollars per hundred salmon, but to no avail. Clah hired a new puller at a rate of two dollars per hundred salmon. Sadly, his net broke again. As he waited for repairs, he went down to meet the steamer *Otter*. His boat capsized as he drew alongside the steamer, and his gun, worth ten dollars, was lost in the river. After this run of bad luck, Clah decided to return to prospecting.[44]

Although the canneries paid women lower wages for mending nets and canning fish, their work was more consistent than men's. They too railed against low pay and poor conditions. Chinese contractors supervised and paid them. In 1891, the women refused to wash the day's catch of 3,700 fish until their pay of ten cents an hour was increased. Their nervous boss eventually agreed.[45]

No canneries operated on the Nass River between 1885 and 1887, and Clah continued to go north to Juneau in summer. He picked up casual jobs on his return, such as working for James Welch at the HBC store at Nass Harbour, or he went fishing on his own behalf. After 1888, new canneries expanded Clah's opportunities for work. By the early 1890s, two or three canneries operated on the Nass River each year.[46] Clah occasionally travelled to canneries farther afield such as the Claxton cannery on the Skeena River, and he once travelled by steamship to the Brunswick cannery at Rivers Inlet.

However welcome the work, pay and conditions remained poor. In 1888, many locals decided to go to Victoria because the new cannery run by A.J. McLellan was only offering contractors twenty-five cents apiece for spring salmon and five cents each for sockeye. Over the next two years, news arrived that the government was issuing licences to fishermen who wanted to sell fish to canneries. At a meeting held at Port Simpson, the community decided to send a letter to the provincial government to ask it to stop licensing cannery fishermen. Three hundred licences were issued for the Skeena River canneries in 1890, however.[47] The federal government had introduced new regulations for British Columbia in 1888. Fishers were to register their equipment and their fishing location. The government had also started to enforce a law that had been passed in 1879 that stated that Aboriginal people could fish for their own needs but needed a licence to sell fish. In this way, the federal government ensured that commercial fishing could be done only under licence. The regulations also specified the type, location, and size of nets, extended the weekend closure from 6 a.m. on Saturday to 6 a.m. on Monday, and controlled, through licences, the number of boats engaged in commercial fishing.[48]

In 1889, the Nass cannery paid forty-five dollars a month for captains and forty dollars a month for pullers. Contractors were paid thirty cents per salmon. The following year, the cannery cut the captains' and pullers' pay by five dollars, and it paid nine cents per sockeye salmon if the fishers used their own boats and six cents per fish if they used cannery-owned boats and nets. In Victoria, by comparison, wages were forty-five dollars per month.[49] Clah lamented that most families earned nothing beyond what they gleaned from the brief fishing and canning season.[50]

Unlike the male-dominated fur trade and gold rush industries, cannery-based fishing used the labour of the whole family. In Clah's case, the women and children had more regular and reliable employment. They worked at the canneries when Clah went prospecting, trading, and transporting. The women were employed to make and repair nets. They also worked on the cannery floor doing jobs – cleaning and processing the catch – that were gradually taken over by Chinese workers. They worked from early dawn until the late summer sunset, which made for a long working day.

Clah's diary reveals that there were many other tasks associated with the cannery business such as building wharves, making wooden buoys for the nets, carting building materials, and freighting packed salmon to steamers for shipment to Victoria. Historian Diane Newell suggests that chiefs or other high-ranking Tsimshian recruited labour for the canneries, but Clah was not recruited in this way.[51] He either approached the cannery manager or was asked by the manager to come work for him. This may explain why most of the work Clah undertook at the Nass River canneries was not fishing but other work directed by the boss.

Canning seasons in the 1880s and early 1890s were short because they focused mainly on spring salmon and sockeye. Spring salmon runs were unpredictable and unreliable, and the main catch, sockeye, ran from the beginning of July for four or five weeks. Thus, fishermen were employed for only a few weeks a year, while women were employed over a longer period, preparing nets in the spring and repairing them until the end of the season. Other cannery work was undertaken outside the actual fishing period. Although the canneries provided Aboriginal workers with some income, they left much of the year free for other activities. Clah and his family used this time for hunting, collecting berries, prospecting, trading, horticulture, and work in the hop fields.

THE HOP FIELDS

As the sockeye season drew to a close in 1891, Clah noted that three hundred people, including Clah and his family, were waiting at Nass Harbour for steamers to take them south. The *Princess Louise* arrived on 16 August and received 150 passengers and 2,500 cases of salmon. At Port Simpson, another 160 Tsimshian waited on the wharf. Some boarded the *Princess Louise,* paying $3.00 each ($1.50 for young children), while others took the *Boscowitz,* which only charged $2.00. At Victoria, the passengers changed to another steamer, which took them to Seattle. After a cup of tea, Clah and his family stood on the wharf and admired the big city as they waited for recruiters to come from the hop fields. They then boarded a train for Snoqualmie, which was fifty-five miles away. It was the largest hop farm in the region. Clah estimated that more than two thousand other people were working there by mid-September.[52]

The hop industry had been established in western Washington in the 1860s, and it flourished until 1910, when the fields were wiped out by aphids.

Princess Louise steamer at Port Simpson, 1888. Photographer: Richard Maynard. BC Archives, A-04178.

As in salmon canning, workers were needed only for the short, intensive harvesting season. Hops were planted with cuttings from old stock in spring and picked in August–September. The vines were trained along poles about fifteen feet high, which were then lowered to the ground by pole pullers during harvesting. The hops were then dried in kilns.[53] The pole pullers controlled production by deciding which poles to lower and which pickers to assign to a pole.

As soon as Clah and his family arrived at the hop fields, they were each allocated a number and started picking hops from five or six in the morning until seven o'clock at night. More Aboriginal people continued to arrive, including Clayoquot (Nootkans from Vancouver Island) and Klikitat (from eastern Washington). The pole pullers were Haida who, Clah complained to the head supervisor, favoured their own people by giving them the best hop vines and Clah the bad ones.[54] Clah and his family nevertheless picked four boxes a day at a dollar a box. After eighteen days' work, Clah had fifty dollars. The family continued working for a few more days, but by then the drying houses were full, the weather was unreliable, and work was sporadic. With more time on their hands, people gambled on the horse races, and the Haida put on a dance show, for which they charged twenty-five cents per person.[55]

Eight years later, after working at the Brunswick cannery at Rivers Inlet, Clah again took his family to the hop fields. The Wellingtons were recruited in Seattle by J.J. Metzler. He paid their train fares to Cedar River, but they discovered on their arrival that there was no work. Cedar River was a much smaller farm – 20 acres of hops compared to Snoqualmie's 350 acres. The farm did not grow or provide food, and the situation was made worse for Clah's group when pigs invaded their tent and destroyed their provisions of flour, potatoes, lard, bacon, and dried fish. After nine days of idleness, the hop picking began. Forty to fifty people worked in the fields for one dollar a day and no rations. Clah's party decided to move to a larger ranch located ten miles away at White River Valley. They discovered that the conditions were even worse.[56] By the end of the season, however, Clah was reasonably satisfied with the pay, if not the conditions of work. Steamship companies, however, took advantage of the hundreds of people going down to Washington State each year by charging exorbitant prices for the return passage from Victoria to Port Simpson and other northern villages.[57]

HORTICULTURE
Horticulture at home did not pay as well as the hop fields, but Clah and Dorcas could work to their own schedule and expand their gardens when they became too old for migrant labour. They put in long hours tending their garden. Clah criticized his neighbours for improvidence, for failing to plant crops in spring. He claimed that modern people relied too heavily on goods from the store instead of produce from the land. He implied that previous generations had cleared the land and grown their food. His claim, while not historically accurate, suggests that Clah was concerned that people were losing their capacity to produce their own food.[58] Foreign traders had introduced the potato to coastal communities in the late eighteenth century, and the Haida, having experienced the collapse of the sea otter trade, had seized the opportunity to produce a trade item that Europeans valued. By the mid-1830s, the Tsimshian were buying potatoes from Haida and trading them at the HBC's Fort Simpson post. Soon after, John

Work, the chief trader, cleared land for potato gardens within the fort.[59] In *A Pour of Rain,* Helen Meilleur describes the difficulties the HBC officers had establishing gardens in the area. Dense vegetation had to be cleared and massive tree roots removed before the waterlogged ground could be drained and fertilized with seaweed. Planting began in April or May, depending on the weather, and crops were harvested in October. Following success with potatoes, the HBC experimented with other crops: onions, radishes, turnips, and fruit trees. After the initial harvests, Aboriginal women did most of the planting, hoeing, and harvesting.[60] Horticulture soon spread to all coastal peoples.

Clah purchased land at Laghco in 1876 because there was none available at Fort Simpson. Dorcas brought in the first harvest in late September that year, and Clah accused Lugeneth and his wife of stealing potatoes and turnips from his garden.[61] Dorcas and other family members had presumably prepared the land and planted the crop at Canaan because Clah does not mention doing any gardening himself. It is likely that Dorcas had worked in gardens before, but there is no evidence in his diary that Clah had previously undertaken horticulture, although he had freighted potatoes for people such as James Grey on the Nass River.

By the late 1870s, potatoes had become a staple in the diet of Aboriginal peoples of the Northwest Coast. Clah describes many meals that included potatoes. In 1880, the family planted onions, carrots, turnips, cabbages, and potatoes. Clah was fully engaged with gardening; he complained of exhaustion and cuts on his hands. The garden fed the family and produced a surplus, which Clah sold.[62] But the climate made gardening difficult. Apart from the soggy ground, the weather was often too cold for either planting or harvesting: "Too wet weather everyday[.] our seeds in garden where flooded of [out of the] ground[.] was too wet raining everyday[,] every weeks[,] every months[.] we all thinks our seeds in ground die."[63] In a cold year, the potatoes would freeze in the ground. Even after they were harvested, crops spoiled from the cold. In response to these problems, Clah was open to horticultural advice from many different sources. The constable's wife told him to plant apple trees over old boots and seaweed mulch.[64] Missionaries and government officials gave him a variety of seeds to plant along with hints on how to do it.

The biggest problem, however, was the shortage of land. As soon as Clah claimed his father's land at Laxk'a'ata (Canaan) and began gardening, the Kincolith (Gingolx) people made counterclaims and planted gardens on the land. According to Clah, they stole his crops out of the ground and out of his house: "[G]one up canaan my place when use to be plainten [planting] potatose [potatoes] every year. Builten [building] 14 years ago when I got up I have seen when I got up is the great the[y] sdray [destroy] my garden[.] Nearly all stoaled [stolen] of by Kingaleg [Kincolith] Christian this same people use to be plaintian Closet [planting close to] my house ... carrits [carrots], cabbages, onions. Break the window[,] steal everything Belongs me."[65] Despite his anger over other Aboriginal people's resistance to his land claims, Clah was well aware of the underlying issues, for he noted that his ten acres comprised most of the good land in the area.[66]

Perhaps the relentless demands of the Kincolith Nisga'a wore Clah down, or perhaps he decided it would be more convenient to have his garden near Port Simpson. Whatever the reason, Clah and his family went to Laghco in February 1891 to start clearing the land for a home and garden.[67] They pitched two tents and set to work, despite snow and heavy winds that blew down their tents. Two days later, Clah injured himself cutting a log: "I walk lame[,] one of my leg like [a] hook."[68] The family continued clearing timber and burning it off for a month before they returned to Port Simpson. Over the next few years, the family gradually cleared the land, and Clah tried to have his claim recognized through a land survey (see Chapter 6). In the end, Indian Agent Charles Todd promised Clah ten acres, not the forty to fifty acres he had requested.[69] In the meantime, the family continued to cultivate its gardens. They had to contend not only with the inaction of the government and the competing claims of other Tsimshian but also with cattle that wandered about the unfenced gardens. With no survey, Clah could not build a house to store produce. In 1894, cows that belonged to Rev. Thomas Crosby and the mission doctor Albert Edward Bolton ate most of the potato crop: "[A]nimals taste my sweet potatose [potatoes,] sweet as sugar[.] the[y] camping in my garden[,] not go out." Instead of bringing in a harvest of a ton and quarter, as the family had done in the previous year, they brought in less than half a ton.[70] These were difficult setbacks for an aging couple. Dorcas complained that she worked hard clearing the land every year for no reward, while Clah struggled to build yet another house. Luckily, their widowed daughter, Martha, had married Henry Wesley. Wesley took on much of the responsibility for provisioning the family and the hard physical labour of building a new house. As Clah and Dorcas moved between Port Simpson and Laghco throughout the 1890s and 1900s, various family members joined them from time to time.

Although new kinds of food production came to dominate certain aspects of life on the Coast, Clah and his family continued to hunt and gather. In the winter months, Clah hunted deer, bear, porcupine, mountain goats, ducks, and other birds. He often had bad luck, as he put it, and came home empty-handed. Clah's diary is so centred on its author that it is difficult to determine how members of his extended family contributed to food production. Women and children certainly collected berries and other plants, which they cooked and preserved. In his later years, Clah and the women in his household combined hunting and berrying trips, suggesting that the hunting and berry grounds were in the same areas. Archaeologists Andrew Martindale and Irena Jurakic argue that berries were a staple food of the Tsimshian. They were eaten fresh or preserved as dried cakes or in eulachon oil. This is borne out by Clah's description of meals that frequently included dried berries.[71] Berries were also offered at feasts. On one occasion, a senior man insisted that a feast include berries, which had been bought from his wife.[72]

Several scholars contend that women's food-producing role was undermined by the introduction of European foods and the fur trade, which elevated men's hunting activities.[73] This argument ignores women's evolving role in cannery production and their primary role in horticulture, which became increasingly important in the mid- to late nineteenth century. While women's food-production did not generate as much wealth as the fur trade and the mining industry, they were a reliable source of food and some money.

Throughout the nineteenth century, the Tsimshian diet changed substantially, as did the means of food production. New foods such as potatoes were introduced early during the maritime fur trade, but the availability of such processed foods as flour, sugar, and molasses increased as Clah matured. Although Clah was introduced to wage labour as a young man, when he worked for the HBC, this source of income became much more common during the gold rushes and became entrenched with the appearance of the canneries in the 1870s and 1880s. Wage labour was a source of currency, either cash or vouchers, which had to be exchanged at company-run stores for food and other goods. Despite the industrialization of fish processing during Clah's life time, subsistence food production continued, although government regulation made it difficult. Martindale observes that although the market economy introduced by the fur trade affected Tsimshian wealth, the subsistence economy remained intact because the fur trade did not generate food.[74] Clah's diary demonstrates that maritime foods were produced and traded throughout the fur trade and gold rush eras, not only by Aboriginal but also by European traders. When it became too difficult to trade fish products, people turned to horticulture.

6

Land Matters

On 4 August 1888, Clah wrote in his diary: "All the chiefs on the nass river wanting to be Boston [American] citizen[.] wanting no english citizen Because [they] Rob the indians. take the indian[s'] land claimed themselves[.] english government give piece of land to every indian tribe[.] called indian reserve[;] nobody owned [owns it]."[1] By the late 1880s, Clah and other Tsimshian and Nisga'a understood very well that the provincial and federal governments were alienating their land without negotiation or compensation – they were converting Aboriginal peoples' pre-existing ownership rights into reserves that Aboriginal people did not own. Clah and others seriously considered leaving their homes to follow William Duncan and most of the Metlakatla Tsimshian to Alaska when the governor, Alfred P. Swineford, promised them their own land, American citizenship, and access to free education.[2] Duncan had moved to Port Chester on Annette Island, Alaska, aboard the steamer *Ancon* on 7 August 1887 and had been followed by eight hundred Tsimshian. But Swineford's promises were not fulfilled. He seems to have been surprisingly uninformed about US federal laws on Indian rights.[3] The legal status of the people of New Metlakatla differed little from that of Aboriginal people in Canada.

After Swineford met Clah at Douglas Island, Alaska, he entered into a correspondence with Clah to discuss the possibility of the Port Simpson Tsimshian migrating north:

> Referring to our conversation relative to the removal of your people from British Columbia to Alaska. I can only say that should they elect to make the contemplated change it will be my pleasure to contribute all in my

power to the success of any colonization scheme they may inaugurate. It is my opinion that should your people conclude to settle in Alaska they will receive every reasonable consideration at the hands of the U.S. government – they will, without doubt, be permitted to occupy and finally acquire title to at least 160 acres of land each, in severalty. They will likewise be accorded the benefit of our free schools, and in all aspects be accorded the rights and privileges of American citizens.

Yours very Truly,
A.P. Swineford
Governor of Alaska[4]

Clah was impressed by Swineford's promises and took his letters back to Port Simpson to discuss them with the community. Despite initial enthusiasm, however, the community never replied to Swineford. A number of chiefs from the Nass River also considered the possibility of moving across the border to a country they thought would recognize their rights and treat them as equal to other citizens. Clah mulled over the attractions of an Alaskan exodus for many years.

Although Clah canvassed the Tsimshian about the move to Alaska, he never contemplated moving there independently of the rest of his community. His competitive nature and single-minded pursuit of his own interests were constrained by his desire to remain a member of, and seek status among, his own people. These countervailing pressures are evident in his pursuit of various land matters after 1875. The dispossession of Aboriginal lands by settlers and the colonial state created tensions between Aboriginal peoples and governments and among Aboriginal peoples themselves as they vied with one another for access to vastly reduced territories, which were defined as reserves.

Clah's anger and frustration over his inability to overcome the colonial authorities' control over land policy is obvious through much of the diary. He naively thought that his friendships with influential colonists – including politicians, judges, lawyers, and bureaucrats – would enable him to negotiate his own land deals. He was disappointed over and over again, although he never gave up trying – so much time and energy for so little in return. Unlike his negotiations with Swineford on behalf of the Tsimshian, most of his battles were fought single-handedly for his own

McNeill land at McNeill (Shoal) Bay, ca. 1900. BC Archives, I-75533.

personal advantage. As Clah's entry for 4 August 1888 illustrates, however, the broader conflict over land formed a backdrop for all of Clah's personal odysseys. Clah documented community meetings and discussions in which he participated; however, he was often absent at the goldfields or fishing and hunting when Tsimshian chiefs and elders discussed strategies to maintain control over their lands.[5] Clah's diary gives a glimpse, but not a coherent picture, of the petitions, delegations, and meetings generated by the Tsimshian and the Nisga'a in their fight for control over and a fair distribution of their land. More importantly, the diary illustrates the bemusement Aboriginal people experienced when they contemplated the conundrum that the ownership of *their* land had, through some sleight of hand, passed to Queen Victoria and her government, who then allotted them small parcels in the form of reserves, which they no longer owned.[6]

Clah's land negotiations included various plots of land: on the Nass River, first at Aiyansh (Gitlaxdamks) and then at Laxk'a'ata (Canaan); at Laghco, south of Port Simpson; at Port Simpson (land claimed by the HBC); and in Victoria. These negotiations highlight different aspects of the complex politics of land on the Northwest Coast. Although Dorcas and her children might have had rights to the land at Aiyansh, Clah seems to have bought it from the government and then forfeited on his payment. He claimed the fishing station at Canaan through his paternal line. Clah apparently had no traditional rights to the land at Laghco, which he had bought from another Tsimshian and which later became incorporated into a reserve. The land under dispute at Port Simpson was Gispaxlo'ot territory to which Clah had rights as a member of the tribe. And the suburban blocks at Shoal Bay in Victoria were claimed because they were part of land bought by W.H. McNeill that was inherited by his wife, Nisakx (Martha) and, on her death, passed on to her nephew and then her nieces. Clah was trying to both assert his and his family's inherited rights and defend rights generated by the colonial state.

CHANGING LAND TENURES

Tsimshian land was claimed through lineages or houses. Members of a particular house, in Clah's case the T'amks lineage, owned rights to delineated territories for hunting, fishing, berry picking, wood collecting, and other resources. According to Viola Garfield, the head of a house could claim certain food- and resource-gathering areas and pass them on as private property. Although land could be inherited or pass to a new owner, it was indivisible and could not be broken up into smaller allotments.[7] Clah, who became head of T'amks in 1870, would not have been free to take land for his own benefit without the approval of his house. The territories owned by house groups were exploited under the direction of the head of the house. The fragmented nature of land ownership on the Northwest Coast, the fact that land was scattered over wide-ranging territories, and the aegis under which each area was claimed caused difficulties for individuals, kin, and tribal groups when the colonial state began to incorporate small areas into reserves, excluded other territories, and encouraged settlers to claim Aboriginal lands.

Before the Tsimshian began to move to Fort Simpson after 1834, they had lived in ten tribal groups in winter villages near the Metlakatla Pass.[8] At Fort Simpson, they formed one village with separate tribal sites. Clah's Gispaxlo'ots tribe was located adjacent to the HBC's fort. Ligeex, as head chief, built his house in a prime position, and other Gispaxlo'ots houses were arranged around it according to rank.

Land matters do not seem to have concerned Clah before the mid-1870s. He wintered at Fort Simpson, where he took advantage of changing circumstances to improve his wealth and status among the Tsimshian. In 1868, he held a feast to celebrate the building of his T'amks house on Gispaxlo'ots land, which was not under dispute.[9] Within a few years, however, every house he built mired him in conflicts over land ownership. These disputes resulted partly from Clah's desire to pursue every possible personal advantage in a rapidly changing economic and social environment. They also stemmed from the colonial state's restrictions on Aboriginal economic activities.

Clah first confronted the changing realities of land ownership in the late 1870s, when he decided to move his winter residence and plant gardens. Although he had already bought the land at Laghco, he moved from Fort Simpson to the Nass River via a brief sojourn on the Skeena River. He finished the house at Aiyansh by late November 1877.[10] By August the following year, he had moved lower down the Nass River to Laxk'a'ata and was bemoaning his poverty: "I am very poor since I commence start built place at Nass river lagh-ader. I have no friends with me. So I did say I called my relations an[d] brothers an[d] friends[,] some laughing [at] me because governmen[t] take all [money] from me[.] they said every year to pay my land."[11] This entry suggests that Clah had bought the land from the government without realizing that he would have to pay for the land in installments and would likely forfeit his payments. The land was almost immediately pre-empted by Stephen Redgrave. Clah complained to I.W. Powell, the Indian superintendent for British Columbia, who passed his letter on to the chief commissioner of lands and works. Clah explained he had built a house on the land: "I stayed there for winter, in the spring I built another house near the mouth of the River as a fishing house, the same as all the Indians do, and now one man Redgrave has come up and taken my land on the upper nass, or he says he has taken it."[12] There was also a petition from other Gitlaxdamks residents, who complained about Redgrave's pre-emption of land near their potato patches that they had earmarked for growing turnips. A cover letter from the Church Missionary Society (CMS) missionary Robert Tomlinson expressed concern that men such as Redgrave were coming to the Nass River to claim Aboriginal land ahead of the government, which was delineating reserves.[13]

The allocation and survey of reserves on the Mainland had started under a joint commission of the federal and provincial governments in 1876, but it proceeded slowly.[14] Commissioner G.M. Sproat was due to visit the Coast in 1881. He had been encouraged to visit by missionaries such as Robert Tomlinson and William Duncan who were concerned about the rapid influx of newcomers. After 1866, it had become almost impossible for Aboriginal people to obtain land by pre-emption. Under the pre-emption system, an individual could claim unoccupied and un-surveyed land and, after certain conditions had been fulfilled, obtain a certificate of improvement and a deed of conveyance. Joseph Trutch, as chief commissioner of lands and works (and later lieutenant-governor), not only made it difficult for Aboriginal people to access land through the colonial legal system, he did not recognize any pre-existing Aboriginal title.[15] The only land available to Aboriginal people was on reserves. Once reserves were allotted, Aboriginal people had to vie with one another over access to the land, which was designated by the government as communal land and which could not be individually owned.[16]

Reserve allocation was delayed when Sproat was replaced as Indian reserve commissioner by Peter O'Reilly, who did not arrive on the Coast until October 1881. He worked efficiently, sacrificing careful research and consultation with Aboriginal people for quick results. His hurried visit to Tsimshian and Nisga'a territory caused years of dispute and unrest on the Coast. Underlying O'Reilly's allocation system was the settler ideology enunciated by Trutch – the land was owned by the Crown, not Aboriginal people, who had no right to ask for more land than was deemed necessary for their basic needs. When the Tsimshian requested a reserve that would encompass the entire 350 square miles on which Port Simpson and Metlakatla were located, O'Reilly refused, "I explained it was not the intention of the Dominion government to lock up so large an extent of land of no practical use to them."[17] O'Reilly's observation reflected colonial attitudes towards indigenous land use; he implied that if land was not being used productively, it should be locked away for effective development.

In May 1879, Clah travelled to Gitlaxdamks to inspect his house and land. Despite their quarrel, Redgrave treated him to dinner. Both men then set out independently for Wrangell and the Cassiar goldfields. Their paths crossed a few days later, when Clah visited Redgrave's camp to preach to

an assorted group of miners and Tlingit from Cape Fox. At another encounter between the two men, Clah launched into a conversation about
their disputed land and claimed there was a law that prohibited Redgrave
from taking up land alongside an Indian village. Unfazed, Redgrave retorted
that he could easily clear out the village. The next day, Clah reported his
concerns to A.W. Vowell, gold commissioner at Cassiar, who sent him to
see the local justice of the peace.[18] A few weeks later, Clah met Chief Justice
Matthew Baillie Begbie, "quit[e] nicely looking old man," who took notes
on Clah's case against Redgrave after conferring with Vowell, who had
confirmed that Clah was a "good man to everybody."[19] Given that Redgrave
is not mentioned by O'Reilly when, as reserve commissioner, he visited
the Nass River in 1881, it is most likely he had left the region without ob-
taining a Crown grant. In the meantime, Nisga'a people had moved to the
land Clah had claimed and delighted in pointing that O'Reilly had listed
all the houses at Aiyansh except Clah's.[20]

ALLOCATION OF RESERVES

The saga of the land at Laxk'a'ata (Canaan) was much more protracted.
Clah and his family settled there in 1878: "Arrived Canaan[.] my new land
the great God gaven to me to live with only an[d] wife[,] 5 childrens. I
have no mon[e]y[,] no the bit[,] no cents. I only live [on] potatoes an[d]
fish[e]s."[21] Nevertheless, Clah's new home had a garden from which the
children could take food, and he started to build yet another house, where
his daughter Mary Elizabeth was born. This time, Clah did not fight a
pre-emptor for his land but Nisga'a who had settled at Kincolith at the
mouth of the Nass River. This Anglican mission village, which had been
established in 1867 by Arthur Doolan and Robert Tomlinson of the CMS,
gradually attracted Nisga'a from the upper Nass River. By the time Clah
decided to live a few kilometres upriver and on the opposite bank, the
inhabitants of the village had claimed the land on both sides of the river,
and the claims were recognized by O'Reilly in 1881. The Tsimshian and
many of the Nisga'a who remained in the upper villages agreed that some
of these fishing sites were Tsimshian, not Nisga'a, and that Tsimshian had
always built substantial houses on this land, which they had occupied for
two to three months each year during the eulachon fishing season.

The Methodist Missionary Society claimed the government favoured
the Anglican's representations on behalf of Aboriginal people over those

of the Methodists.[22] Clah supported this view in an affidavit appended to a formal complaint by the Methodist Missionary Society to the superintendent general of Indian affairs in the province.[23] Clah had first learned of Nisga'a claims to Canaan in October 1881, just before O'Reilly arrived on the Nass River, from Chief Mountain (Saga'waan) of Laxgalts'ap (Greenville), the Methodist village. Mountain warned Clah that the Nisga'a at Kincolith intended to claim the whole Nass River and shut the Tsimshian out.[24] Clah pinned his hopes on O'Reilly and followed him to Laxgalts'ap as soon as he heard of his arrival. He shook hands with O'Reilly and explained that he had left Port Simpson because there was nowhere for him to grow vegetables and that he now had two places on the Nass River. O'Reilly replied that he could not have two residences, so Clah asked him to confirm his right to Canaan. He believed that O'Reilly would support his case because the two men had been acquainted since the gold rush days at Omineca and Cassiar.[25] But when O'Reilly arrived at Canaan, he told Clah the land belonged to the people at Kincolith.[26]

The Tsimshian were disappointed by O'Reilly's high-handed proceedings. He had arrived without warning while most people were away from their villages hunting, fishing, and trading.[27] The reserve commissioner claimed that he discussed his land allocations with the Tsimshian and Nisga'a; they, however, described his visit as hurried and complained that he did not listen to them. O'Reilly based his decisions on his brief observations and conversations at Kincolith and the other Nass villages and ignored counterclaims and dissension among the villages. He allocated all the reserves between Gitlaxdamks and the mouth of the Nass River to the Nisga'a and left only a chain-wide commonage on the river frontage at the eulachon fisheries for other people to fish and process their eulachon catch during the spring season. Only Nisga'a were permitted to erect buildings and plant gardens. In many instances, O'Reilly specified which villages had rights over the reserves. Number 12 Reserve, "Lach-tesk"-Canaan, which contained 250 acres on the left bank of the river opposite Black Point Reserve, was allocated to the Kincolith people. O'Reilly noted that two "sub-chiefs," Clah and Moses McDonald from Port Simpson, had established themselves at Canaan and were present when he visited: "At the request of the Kincolith Indians I explained to them that they could use the frontage for fishing as they had been in the habit of doing, but that they must not interfere with the cultivable land."[28]

After O'Reilly left Canaan, Clah travelled up and down the Nass River to shore up his claim. He visited his wife's aunt, Martha McNeill, who was living at Kincolith. She assured him that the Kincolith people wanted to be friends with him and that some had even suggested he could build a house at Kincolith.[29] He then discussed his predicament with white men on the Nass such as James Grey, Johnny McMaster, and "Spanish Frank," who advised him to ignore the government and stay at Canaan. Then he went upriver to Laxgalts'ap, where the chief reassured him that his wife and children belonged to the Nass River.[30]

But Clah was not convinced by these statements of support and thought he should go down to Victoria to argue his case. In his usual fashion, Clah not only cited his Tsimshian rights to the land to support his claim, he also wrote to the commissioner of Crown lands to inform him that his family had occupied from ten to fifteen acres on the Nass River at Canaan since 1878. They had cleared and planted the land, but it had subsequently been included in the Kincolith reserve. He argued on the basis of settler rights that "[a]s this land was in my possession when it was provincial Crown land, you would confer a real favor by advising me what steps should be taken either to retain possession of my land or to secure compensation for the improvements made."[31]

Other Tsimshian shared Clah's anger over O'Reilly's decisions about reserves on the Nass River. Over the ensuing years, they held meetings and wrote letters to set out their ancient claims. Nevertheless, government surveyors arrived at Canaan on 22 October 1886 "to servey the land and giving away to stranger." By 1887, the Tsimshian were ready to work cooperatively with the Nisga'a to present a united front against the government, but the Kincolith council declined to join them, citing their exclusive claims.[32] Tsimshian and Nisga'a from Laxgalts'ap and some other villages journeyed to Victoria in mid-winter to demand larger reserves and a treaty. By way of reply, they were lectured to by the premier, William Smithe, and other officials (through a Kincolith interpreter) about how they would acquire the privileges of citizenship once they reached a requisite level of civilization.[33] In the meantime, the Nisga'a at Kincolith continued to vehemently oppose Tsimshian claims by damaging Tsimshian houses on the Nass River and stealing their fishing tools. They even fired on Clah and his family as they passed the village on their way to Canaan: "[W]hen I was passet [passing] Kingaleg [Kincolith] this evening[,] a dozen gun fired on top my canoe[.] children half crying."[34] In his affidavit appended to the Methodist Missionary Society's letter to the superintendent general of Indian affairs in 1888, Clah repeated his claims to Canaan, his father's land, "Our fathers for generations owned the mouth of the Naas as our fishing grounds, and had large houses there in late years. They had small houses for their fishing tackle. The Naas people often take our things and have burnt them."[35] The Nisga'a countered these accusations with complaints about Tsimshian vandalism.[36] Clah continued to plant crops at Canaan and to endure attacks on the house and garden throughout the 1890s. The Kincolith Nisga'a not only did their best to block others from farming on the Nass River, they attempted to regulate access to fishing as well. In 1884, they instituted a $1.50 tax on people who came from Alaska to fish. They also used armed patrols to intimidate visitors and challenge people coming up the river.[37]

O'Reilly's reserve allocations generated worries and tensions everywhere in the region. Chief Mountain believed that O'Reilly had allocated the Stoney Point Reserve (the main eulachon fishery) to his people from Laxgalts'ap. This seemed to be borne out by O'Reilly's report, which acknowledged that there were ten to twelve families from the village already resident on the land. Even so, the Kincolith people, accompanied by a band, marched to Stoney Point and hoisted their flag to lay claim to the land after O'Reilly left.[38] People once again hedged their bets by making simultaneous appeals to traditional rights and colonial authority. Employing flags and bands and invoking the Bible or the authority of the Queen showed just how well Northwest Coast peoples understood the symbols of British imperial power. They did not hesitate to wield these symbols against one another as well as against the colonial government. Only the Kincolith people remained adamant in their refusal to cooperate with the Tsimshian. Chiefs from Gitlaxdamks and Laxgalts'ap, in contrast, wanted a peaceful resolution of differences. At a meeting in 1887, one man raised a Bible and eagle feathers (a sign of peace) as he beseeched all present to make one heart and one law.[39] While this man said eagle feathers were stronger than the Bible as a statement of peace, Clah thought he had it the wrong way round. Clah was always ready to assert his Christian credentials and his rights, whether they were based in Tsimshian or British law.

When the newly appointed Indian agent, Joseph McKay, visited Port Simpson in 1883, Clah reminded him of their previous acquaintance in the fur trade. He hailed him as a true Christian before seeking clarification as to his official position as a justice of the peace, magistrate, or Indian agent. Clah asked who had sent McKay as an agent. Did he represent the Queen's law or God's law? He reminded McKay that a Christian should not take the land of another Christian and sell it. Nor should the Queen, who regarded all her people as her children, take their land from them without telling them.[40]

At the time that the Tsimshian were disputing Nisga'a claims on their fishing houses, they were also negotiating their own reserves at Port Simpson and on the coastal islands and the Skeena River. Although Clah was engaged generally with these broader struggles, he was, as usual, preoccupied with his own interests, including his property at Laghco and Port Simpson. In 1881, Clah received a letter from the council at Fort Simpson asking him to return, but he was reluctant to do so. He did, however, continue to visit Port Simpson for meetings, and he engaged in community matters as a senior member of the Gispaxlo'ots tribe.

CLAH RETURNS TO PORT SIMPSON

In 1885, Clah changed his mind and decided to move back to Port Simpson and build another house. Sudaał, William Kelly's wife, warned Clah not to build on land she had claimed, but Clah argued that all the Tsimshian wanted him to build there, on a lot eight feet wide and ten feet long.[41] Of greater concern was the intervention of the HBC. Its officer, R.H. Hall, wrote to Clah to notify him that the land was not on the Indian reserve but belonged to the HBC: "It is my duty to inform you that the land where you are building a house is not part of the Indian Reserve. It is nothing to me personally where you build but you might blame me at some future time if I had not told you that you are trespassing."[42] Hall wrote a similar letter to Paul Legaic II when he began building on Gispaxlo'ots land the following year.

Hall was in a difficult position. He worked and traded with Clah and Legaic and lived in close proximity to them, but he also served as the mouthpiece of his employer. Both Legaic and Clah replied by asserting their right to build on their tribal land. Legaic pointed out that he was building on the land where his uncle's house had once stood.[43] The

Gispaxlo'ots wrote several times to Superintendent Powell about the impasse with the HBC, arguing that he and Legaic already had houses standing on the land and wanted to build more. The HBC had not objected to them building on the land in the past, as long as they traded with the company. What is more, Clah argued, Powell had encouraged them to do so.[44] The HBC was willing to exchange some of the Gispaxlo'ots land for land east of the fort, but these negotiations dragged on for decades. In the meantime, Clah and other Gispaxlo'ots were left in limbo.

The Tsimshian claimed Lax Kw'alaams (Port Simpson) as Gispaxlo'ots land. When the first site of the HBC trading post at the mouth of the Nass River had been found unsatisfactory in 1834, the wife of the HBC surgeon (later chief trader Dr. John Kennedy), Ligeex's daughter, had asked her father to find a better location. He had offered his son-in-law land at Lax Kw'alaams.[45] In a submission to the McKenna-McBride Royal Commission in 1915, the Gispaxlo'ots stated that Ligeex had had a large house at Lax Kw'alaams in 1834, which he then moved so that the HBC could build its fort. Ligeex had successfully defended the site against northern peoples and would have killed Kennedy had he thought the HBC was claiming ownership of the land.[46] The HBC records, needless to say, do not mention Ligeex's role in the fort's relocation. They describe Loughlin Harbour (Lax Kw'alaams) as being thickly forested and having little evidence of habitation at the time the site for the fort was chosen by HBC employees.[47]

In 1862, unbeknownst to the Tsimshian, William Henry McNeill, then chief factor at Fort Simpson, had made a rough survey of one hundred acres delineated as HBC land on instructions from London. There had been, however, no formal conveyance of the land to the company. When the Methodists wanted to establish a mission at Fort Simpson in 1874, they had negotiated with the company for a site. Following these discussions, the HBC had again asked the government for a deed of conveyance for the one hundred acres it had claimed. On the eve of the reserve commissioner's arrival in 1881, the Fort Simpson Tsimshian and Thomas Crosby sought Powell's reassurance that the HBC lands would not include the village site. Powell agreed but asked them to wait for the commissioner's confirmation.[48] A plan for Fort Simpson included in a report by Powell in 1879 showed the HBC lands running behind the Tsimshian houses on the foreshore. But when O'Reilly allocated the reserve at Fort Simpson in 1888, some of the Gispaxlo'ots houses were set outside the reserve boundary on

HBC land immediately to the west of the fort.[49] O'Reilly's actions precipitated the drawn-out conflict between the HBC and the Tsimshian. In December 1885, when Clah was building his house in defiance of the HBC, he was clearly depressed. He observed that "Indian friends" who wanted to sell their land were intimidated by the government's claims, making Aboriginal people "poor our hearts like slave[.] we eat little dry fish every year."[50] A few days later, however, Clah celebrated the completion of his house with a dedication potlatch.[51]

In 1898, when Clah decided to build a new house for his son Albert on land he claimed had belonged to his father's brother, he first had to gain the agreement of the Port Simpson Council. Clah had antagonized some influential members of the council, including Alfred Dudoward and Lewis Gosnell, by signing papers that approved a survey of the Port Simpson township and a petition in support of the Salvation Army, and they were reluctant to oblige him.[52] But the HBC provided a more significant obstacle to his plans, as the proposed house was on HBC land. Clah and Albert eventually proceeded with construction of the house in 1907. They were warned by both Anglican and Methodist ministers that the HBC might sell the land to the railroad company. The HBC officer in charge of the post confirmed the ministers' claim and threatened the two men with legal action.[53] The following year, Clah went to Victoria to seek help from A.W. Vowell, the superintendent of Indian affairs for British Columbia, and Senator William J. MacDonald. In January 1909, he wrote to W.T. Kergin, a member of the Legislative Assembly who had offered to contact the general manager of the HBC on Clah's behalf. By December 1909, when Clah's diary ends, the situation had still not been resolved.[54] Conflict between the HBC and the Tsimshian continued until 1911, when the HBC closed its trading post, which did not reopen until 1934. In the meantime, the Tsimshian continued to occupy the land at Lax Kw'alaams.[55]

Having lost so many skirmishes over land, Clah was cautious about building a house at Laghco without an official survey to support his claim. In 1889, during a visit to Victoria, he had been told by O'Reilly, Charles Todd, and various other officials that it had not been included in reserve lands.[56] Three years later, he told Agent Todd he was waiting on a letter about the land at Laghco: "Charles Todd said to me that no man take the land from you. I said to him. I know But I understand the government Auction all Fort Simpson land. Charles Todd laughing at me. He said to government is not fooll[,] they not back out."[57] These were hardly reassuring words for a man who had lost several claims to land because of government interference in Aboriginal land matters. Although Todd promised many times to visit Laghco, he did not do so until 1893, when he advised Clah to look for more productive land. Clah ignored this suggestion, although he hesitated to build on the land before Todd completed his survey. He was again put off with promises and inaction. In 1892, 1893, 1895, and 1896, Todd promised Clah that the survey would be carried out. Clah eventually built his house without a survey.[58]

SHOAL BAY, VICTORIA

Another dispute, which centred on land Dorcas had inherited in Shoal Bay in Victoria, began in 1891 and was not resolved until 1907. Its origins went back to 1855, when William H. McNeill bought 246 acres for a dollar an acre on the outskirts of the town. He built a house in the southwest corner of his estate five years later.[59] McNeill retired from the HBC in 1863, and he married Nisakx (Martha McNeill), a woman he had lived with for many years, in 1866.[60] Prior to his relationship with Nisakx, McNeill had been married to a Kaigani Haida woman known as Mathilda, who died in 1850 after giving birth to twins, the last of their twelve children. When McNeill died in 1875, his estate was divided between Nisakx and his children.

Nisakx died in 1883 and was buried, at her request, next to her husband at Ross Cemetery in Victoria. A tombstone and an iron fence encompassed both their graves. Her property at Kincolith mission was bequeathed to her nephew George Niy'skinwaatk, and her estate at Shoal Bay was divided among Mary McNeill, the wife of William Henry McNeill's oldest son; Mary's son, Donald; Lucy Moffatt, William's daughter who married Hamilton Moffatt, a government official; Nisakx's nephew George Naskinwat (Niy'skinwaatk); and Catherine Armour, Nisakx's niece. Dorcas and her two sisters, Emily Barton and Lucy Yatze, were not mentioned in the will, but when their brother George Niy'skinwaatk died, they inherited his share of Nisakx's estate.

Clah first became aware that his wife would inherit from George Niy'skinwaatk in March 1891. He immediately sought advice from missionary William Collison at Kincolith. The problem was that George had died intestate, and it would take many years to sort out the legal mess. Clah initially believed that Dorcas would inherit twenty acres of land worth the substantial sum of seven thousand dollars. The couple decided to travel to Victoria to investigate. Because Clah realized his English was not up to the legal complexities, Mary McNeill, a woman of mixed descent, acted as Clah and Dorcas' interpreter as they went from lawyer to lawyer. Dorcas and Clah spent two months in Victoria, in and out of lawyers' offices, trying to prove Dorcas' right to the land. They heard that Kitty (Catherine) Armour had sold her twenty-seven acres for five thousand dollars; in the meantime, they were still trying to prove that they had family ties to Nisakx and George Niy'skinwaatk without documentation to support their claims.[61] It all became too much for Dorcas. On one occasion, she was too drunk to attend a meeting at the lawyer's office: "[L]awyer Ebert ask w[h]ere his [is] my wife[.] we says she is sick[.] we tell lie to the lawyer[.] she was drunk."[62] They had to track down missionaries and other respectable non-Aboriginal people to confirm Dorcas' family relationships. Clah and Dorcas returned to the north with little to show for their many weeks in Victoria.

Once they were back in Port Simpson, Clah heard rumours that others were making claims on the land. They returned to Victoria in September on their way home from the Washington hop fields and were told that a decision on the division of the land would soon be made. A third trip to Victoria in early 1892 revealed no further progress, so yet another journey south was made in October of that year. Dorcas was again drinking. Clah made the rounds to lawyers, Indian Commissioner Vowell, and the HBC officer, R.H. Hall, but there were still outstanding questions regarding Niy'skinwaatk's kin. In the meantime, Clah learned that Martha McNeill's property would be auctioned at two thousand dollars an acre. Clah claimed that twenty-seven and a half acres belonged to his wife.[63] The auction appears to have been delayed for several months, for probate records give a date of 13 June 1893.[64] Frustrated after days spent walking around Victoria viewing the new buildings springing up in the town and faced with the possibility that the land might revert to the Crown, Clah observed, "[B]etter whit[e] people don[']t take no land up north because they had no will from them [their] fathers."[65] The inequities of the colonial land system were blatantly obvious to him. As he fought for rights inherited from his father that were being ignored by the reserve system, his wife's rights under colonial law remained in legal limbo. Much to the amusement of Hall, Clah suggested one solution might be to take his lawyer north as his slave.

Later that year, a letter came from Mary McNeill asking for power of attorney to act on behalf of Dorcas and her two sisters. Because the three sisters were scattered about the north, it took several months for Clah to collect their signatures to be vouched for by Dr. Bolton, the local justice of the peace at Port Simpson.[66] Given that Mary McNeill and her son, Donald, had an interest in the Shoal Bay land, allowing them to act on behalf of the three sisters was not a sensible move.[67]

Throughout 1894 and 1895, the Clah family received contradictory accounts of the status of the Shoal Bay land. Clah continued to make trips to Victoria without resolving the impasse. In July 1895, he had the good fortune to run into Justice David on the street in Victoria. David had been a lawyer at the Cassiar goldfields with whom Clah had had extensive contact. He invited Clah to visit him. A few days later, Clah arrived at David's home, where he was invited to stay for supper. He chatted with his hosts for three hours, and David advised Clah to cancel the power of attorney. Two days later, the judge accompanied Clah to his lawyer's.[68]

Clah hounded every possible influential contact: the commissioner of Indian affairs, the Indian agent, and Dennis Harris, whom Clah described as a lawyer but who was actually a real estate and financial agent who became a trustee of Martha McNeill's estate.[69] The three men claimed that the land the three sisters had inherited was twenty-three acres, while Donald McNeill, who held their power of attorney, claimed it was fourteen. This discrepancy troubled Clah, who realized that he should act urgently on David's advice to rescind the power of attorney.[70] As Clah walked around Victoria collecting conflicting advice, he became increasingly anxious. When McKay suggested he should take an offer of four hundred dollars for fourteen acres, Clah refused: "You[r] skin whit[e] an[d] my skin red. But our Blood this [is] same colar [colour] as you[r] Blood. I hope our Queen will help all my trouble."[71] He was referred to a real estate agent, who invited Clah to have his likeness taken with his grandson William Beynon and who apparently agreed to take papers to England for him.[72]

Lawyers acting on behalf of the heirs of George Niy'skinwaatk wrote to the attorney general in June 1898 to ask that $1,888.19 (the proceeds from the sale of Niy'skinwaatk's) land be distributed by the trustee of the estate, J.C. Prevost, to the Indian heirs: "The Indian Agent at Metlakahtla naturally finds it somewhat difficult to make the Indian understand how it is that they cannot obtain the money which they know to be in the hands of the Registrar of the Supreme Court and the Official Administrator."[73] In late 1899, Clah visited Vowell and McKay in their Victoria offices, and they told him the money would become available in three months' time. In mid-1900, however, a letter arrived that informed Clah and Dorcas that the matter was going to the High Court.[74] A few months later, the couple received notification that Dorcas would receive eight hundred dollars from sale of the land, but the years passed by without any money being paid. Clah continued to seek help from the Indian agent and from lawyers when he visited Victoria. Finally, on 22 August 1907 Dorcas received $825.50. The lawyers' fees (presumably already deducted) were $107.50.[75]

Clah complained in 1905 that he had lost $1,800 over the business, mainly travelling to and from Victoria. One can only hope that this was a gross exaggeration, for he did not recoup the money. It is difficult to tell whether Clah's attempts to intervene in the legal process by calling on the colonial officials and lawyers of his acquaintance sped up the slow-turning cogs of the system. One suspects that all the meetings, long walks from office to office, and letters and documents had little influence on a colonial government that treated Aboriginal people as non-citizens and their financial interests as irrelevant. At the same time, it is noteworthy that many top officials welcomed Clah into their homes and offices over the years. Although they often kept him waiting or asked him to return at a more convenient time, this might have been a response to Clah's ignorance of office hours and system of business appointments rather than rudeness on their part. These men clearly found Clah engaging, but their friendship did not extend to helping him resolve his problems.

It suited settler governments to consider Aboriginal people as ignorant about matters of land ownership.[76] But colonized peoples not only had to operate within their own understandings of ownership, they also had to decode the ownership rules of the settler state. When the HBC established its trading post on Gispaxlo'ots land at Lax Kw'alaams, the Tsimshian welcomed the company because the fort facilitated their trade in furs and gave them ready access to a range of products at the store. The HBC was tolerated as a guest. The transformation of the guests into the owners of the land and the Tsimshian into guests on a reserve was difficult to grasp because the Tsimshian and other Aboriginal groups had never been informed about, let alone involved in, the transfer of land. In the late 1880s, many Tsimshian and Nisga'a clamoured for a treaty because they believed it would recognize their rights and help them deal with land on an equitable basis. They refused to enter into discussions that would merely change the size and number of reserves because these discussions did not address their concept of land ownership.

LAND LESSONS

Clah's land dealings illustrate the depth of Aboriginal people's understandings of land ownership as well as the frustrations they felt when the colonial state refused to deal with them. His move to claim land in several locations in the late 1870s attests to his realization that land would be the next source of wealth after the fur trade and the gold rushes. He observed that newcomers could pre-empt land by establishing themselves on it, and it appears he thought he could do the same. Unlike newcomers, however, he could only claim the land through means recognized by the Tsimshian and Nisga'a. So he bought land at Laghco. Procuring land as an individual had not been a traditional means of transferring land ownership, but transfer of land by gift had been recognized. Perhaps acquisition of land through payment of money and goods could be seen as an extension of this practice. The two sites on the Nass River where Clah built houses were claimed through inherited rights, even though Clah appears to have paid the government for land at Aiyansh. Dorcas and the children had established rights to the land at Aiyansh, and Clah claimed Laxk'a'ata (Canaan) through his father. Once his ownership of the Nass River sites was challenged, he was willing to negotiate a change of tenure as long as he was recompensed for the improvements (a European concept) he had made to the land by clearing it. Although he was dogged in pursuit of his own interests, he was flexible enough to realize that if he could not have his claims recognized, he could at least use settler law to his own benefit. When Clah grasped that the rights under colonial law did not apply to Aboriginal people, he railed against the state that had reduced him to the status of a slave with no land.

Ironically, the only land Clah was able to use unchallenged was the land he had bought at Laghco. Yet he could not own it because it was part of the communal reserve. His house at Port Simpson was not on the reserve and therefore was subject to the ongoing dispute with the HBC. The Gispaxlo'ots, who had benefitted from their close relationship with the HBC during the fur trade era, found themselves dispossessed because of their physical proximity to the trading company. Clah's many journeys to Victoria and his voluminous correspondence (most of which has not survived) concerning his land claims demonstrate his ability to engage with the introduced system of law and administration and to argue his case using both Tsimshian and colonial concepts of land ownership.

Dorcas' inheritance of land in Victoria took the family much deeper into the colonial legal system than they had been before, making it even more difficult for Clah to promote his own interests. The family was not interested in the land itself, but in the wealth it represented. Under the terms of Martha McNeill's will, the land should have been sold after her death and the proceeds distributed to her heirs. Had this happened, her brother, George Niy'skinwaatk, or her nephew would have benefitted from the estate. As it was, the land was not sold until after the death of the nephew, to the benefit, ultimately, of his sisters. Clah was at the mercy of lawyers, the McNeill family and, towards the end of this long saga, Indian agents who acted as his wife's representatives. His knowledge of the legal system evolved with each new complication: the necessity for a will and the repercussions of an intestate property; the apparent need for power of attorney, and the realization that this involved an element of trust in the disinterest of the person with that power; the difficulty of releasing the money from the courts after the legal process eventually ground to a halt; and the need, throughout the process, to prove who the inheritors of the estate were and their relationship to one another. This last requirement must have seemed foreign to Clah and his family, who came from communities in which everyone knew everyone else and their status and relationship was known to others. One has to admire Clah's perseverance in pursing what he believed was owed to him, much as he had pursued trade debts over many years, and his willingness to draw acquaintances and friends into his affairs to help him surmount countless obstacles. Tellingly, the land in Victoria, over which he had no traditional rights but which he could access through a Canadian legal system in which his wife was treated as a person with legal rights, was the only land dispute resolved in the couple's favour. In all other matters, Clah was treated as an Indian who was neither a citizen nor a recognized legal entity, as someone who only had a communal identity and no individual rights.

7

Becoming a Christian

Although the colonial state disrupted and in many instances destroyed Tsimshian usage and inheritance rights to land, the influence of the Christian missions and the process of becoming Christian was much more equivocal. Of all the voyages Clah made during his lifetime, his spiritual journey to a full understanding of and identification with Christianity was the most important. Mission literature generally refers to conversion and converts in a manner that suggests that religious change was a clear-cut process with an unambiguous outcome: it entailed replacing an existing set of beliefs with a new one, as if a person's spiritual and moral universe disappeared down a black hole to be replaced by another superior universe. Many scholars realize that the process of religious change is much more complex than this, but they also understand that it is difficult to analyze because, in the case of new Christians, there are few first-hand accounts of the conversion experience. Clah's diary is a rare example of this genre.

The diary, however, is much more than one man's spiritual and moral journey, for it also gives insight into the relationship and tensions between missionaries and the communities that adopt them. This chapter and the two that follow trace Clah's gradual adoption of Christianity and his urge to teach others about his new understandings. They also explore the politics of religion, both among the Protestant denominations on the Coast and among the Tsimshian themselves. Clah was grateful to William Duncan and, later, Thomas Crosby for opening his eyes to different aspects of Christianity. These missionaries were also seen by Clah and many other Tsimshian as conduits for changes that we associate with modernity. They offered access to the colonial system, including trade networks, industrial developments such as sawmills and canneries, and modern infrastructure, for example, housing, stores, wharves, churches, and roadways. Although many Tsimshian were willing to tolerate the foibles of these men of God to gain these perceived advantages, Clah was his own man. He wanted to associate with missionaries and take advantage of their teachings and links to colonial society, but he could not tolerate being subservient to them. They, in turn, found Clah a difficult man to deal with – a devout Christian and admirer of much they stood for who would not accept their authority over his life.

ACCEPTING CHRISTIANITY

Clah was born a Tsimshian, an identity that he wore like a skin. But he became a Christian as an adult, and this identity developed into his primary persona, the one that distinguished him from other Tsimshian and, he believed, gave him a unique place in Tsimshian history. Clah's evolution into an active and evangelizing Christian does not conform to any of the popular missionary narratives of conversion. He did not experience an epiphany or have a sudden revelation. It is not even clear from his diary when Clah accepted Christianity or when the religion came to define him. In 1887, he claimed that "Gods power given to me [in] Victoria [in] may 1 1853[,] when I 23 year of age."[1] But this entry, thirty-five years later, is his first mention of the purported event. In his first diary, which he began keeping in 1859, Clah recorded that he worked at the HBC fort at Fort Simpson in 1853 and went to Victoria in 1855.[2] He first mentions William Duncan as a language teacher, not a Christian missionary: "And after that time [1858] and when Clah 27 years old and he have been learning School. Clah is head school an[d] of Tsimshen an[d] of North[,] and it was Wm Duncan teaching to Clah an[d] english language."[3]

Clah's early diary entries do not articulate a strong Christian commitment. In later diaries, however, as he assesses his life retrospectively, he often refers to himself as the first Tsimshian Christian. It is William Duncan's diary, not Clah's, that offers a description of Clah's early (if not first) response to Christian knowledge:

> Today we came to the great fact of the Gospel – Salvation by the death of Jesus. I had a great deal of trouble (rather pleasurable labour) in getting

my Indian to comprehend the Mighty truth. I am glad to say however I succeeded. And this is the first instance of my doing so ... As every step to the truth brought him additional light, so it made him more earnest & more enquiring. Now and then he gave a long sigh & stared at me with such eagerness that I felt sure he was grasping truth which he felt precious. When he understood the main fact his countenance which is usually lowering – lit up beautifully & was followed by a delightful softness of manner – quite a contrast to his usual sullen and haughty demeanour. I felt encouraged. I had prayed [for] the Lord to be especially present with us & I believe He was.[4]

The first sign that Duncan's teaching had stayed with Clah came three years later, when Clah recounted an encounter with some Nisga'a as a group of Tsimshian were rowing across a lake with them in Nisga'a territory. His companions warned the Tsimshian to speak only in Nisga'a. If they spoke in any other language, they would disturb the beings who lived at the bottom of the lake, who would capsize their canoe. Clah dismissed their fears, retorting that the "Great Father in heaven is God," who made all things.[5] In February 1862, in mid-winter, Clah and several companions paddled south to Victoria. It was so cold that at times they had to cut through the ice to continue their journey. On reaching northern Vancouver Island, they were caught in a storm at night. For five hours, the men were buffeted by winds. They could not tell from which direction the winds were coming and became convinced they were going to drown. Clah, however, reassured the faint-hearted that he had prayed to God and Jesus Christ, who would take care of them and save them.[6] Two years later, returning from another trip to Victoria, he again called on God to save him and his companions from drowning during a storm.[7]

Four years after Duncan had expressed the belief that he had convinced Clah of the truth of salvation through Christ, Clah was calling on God and Jesus to come to his aid in times of stress. This was the year of the devastating smallpox epidemic, and many Tsimshian were looking for explanations for and escape from the catastrophe. On 21 June 1862, they turned to the Christian God for help and burned all their ritual paraphernalia in the hope that relinquishing their past practices might appease Him:

[A]ll the Indians in tsimshens thee will Burned as all lots the things with fire. about an half Day an[d] the[y] wants [make] Sacrifices to God and want thee will God tak[e] away sickness from them. [T]his the way burned all bad things[,] an[d] all the Chiefs in Tsimshen burn all [h]is Music with Fire called Nohhnohh [Naxnox], an[d] other kinds we called Ahamelk [amiilk, masks]. burnt them all poor all tsimshen. thee afraid to gone [going] to Die. thee make God Angry an[d] in every year. thee always Teelling lies an[d] stealing, Murder kiling [one] another. Drunkness an[d] fighting. An[d] we never do Right In God Shight [sight]. But we often doing wrong an[d] In our Lifs [lives].[8]

Clah used the opportunity to charge his people with a range of Christian sins – lying, stealing, murder, and drunkenness – before he returned to his house to pray to God to save them and clean them of their sins.

Close brushes with death in 1862, in particular the smallpox epidemic, seem to have solidified Clah's belief in Christianity. He believed the Tsimshian had brought God's wrath upon themselves through their behaviour and decided that he would abide by the Ten Commandments. He was therefore deeply hurt when, a few weeks later, Duncan, now residing at Metlakatla, accused Clah of murdering three white men. Clah protested, "['Y]ou maken me ashame[d] yesterday[,'] Clah said. Clah asking to Duncan[,] [']Mr Duncan[,] What you say to me first time you teach me in Gods word. You saying to me kill another[,] lie[,] stealing murder[.'] no. 2 Duncan you say to me Clah[,] [']will you not to any more bad ways[,] pray to God and every day three times a Day. Then I will Believe what you saying to me.['] An[d] I pray to God an[d] every day. and now you blame me Clah murder 3 whit[e] men."[9]

The God Clah prayed to in the early 1860s was vengeful but could be placated by prayer and good behaviour. Throughout his adult life, Clah distinguished between good and bad behaviour or doing right and wrong. God could see and hear all that he did, and Clah, as God's amanuensis (see Chapter 2), kept a record of people's actions, a moral accounting of the Tsimshian and their neighbours. In these early years, Clah perceived God as a saviour. He prayed to him in times of danger and under threat of death. Later, God would become much more companionable, someone Clah could communicate with at any time.

Clah embarked on his role as evangelist in the latter half of 1863. As he travelled the Coast, from the upper reaches of the Nass River to Victoria in the south, he sought out "poor blind" people to whom he could preach.[10] He frequently criticized what he referred to as the "old-fashioned ways" – the dances and rituals that formed such an important part of the winter activities of all Northwest Coast peoples – although there is some evidence that he remained ambivalent about the power of these rituals. In 1864, after refusing to participate, he was told that if he did not take care he might die. That same evening, Clah recorded that his wife almost died.[11] The incident must have challenged his certainties over what was right and wrong.

Looking back many years later, Clah claimed that his criticism of Tsimshian ceremonies and his attempts to stop them put his life in danger. On Christmas Day, 1892, he recalled how he had spoken out against the elite secret society ceremonies, which involved the ritual consumption of dog and human flesh. His criticism so enraged the Tsimshian and Nisga'a that they tried to kill him: "Smash all my fresh [flesh]. Smash my bone with axes an[d] hammer to cut my head [off] thr[o]w in deep water. Because I break the law." Others wanted to enslave him and sell him to the people to the north.[12] Generally, Clah preferred preaching to people who had not yet encountered Christianity rather than recalcitrants who, knowing of Jesus, refused to acknowledge his superior powers.

Between 1863 and 1873, Clah's Christian observance became a more regular and normal part of his daily routine.[13] He knew he still had much to learn about the Bible, and he participated in classes with Duncan at Metlakatla on his frequent visits to the mission. He continued to believe that if he did not humour God through good behaviour, he would be sent to a bad place of darkness when he died.[14] When the murderer of Clah's uncle died violently, Clah believed God had punished him.[15] If people behaved properly, God would save them and they would live forever. God would also take care of them when they were sick, for, Clah believed, he pitied and saved the poor.[16] Clah expressed an increasing intimacy with God as he came to regard him not only as a distant observer of human doings on earth but also as someone with whom he could communicate.

Clah acknowledged his lapses, for instance, when liquor made him "like the devil, I feell very bad that day[.] perhaps If I die[,] God the great

Father in heaven angry with me Because I am only bad man Against Him."[17] Clah transgressed in other ways, too. When he hosted the feasts that elevated him to lineage head of T'amks, he angered Duncan, who raised the black flag at Metlakatla, presumably to symbolize the death of a Christian.[18] Seven months later, Clah had another argument with Duncan, who referred to him as a hardened deviant, rescinded his appointment as a constable, and demanded the return of the constable's coat and belt.[19] Duncan did not elaborate on Clah's deviance. Had Clah once again fallen from Christian grace or, as is more likely, had he taken liberties in his role as constable, using his authority for his own purposes?

Another important lesson Clah had learned from Duncan was that it was a sin to travel on Sundays. This Protestant injunction was almost impossible to keep on the Coast, where survival and prosperity depended on long journeys, particularly during the fur trade and gold rush eras. Over the years, missionaries themselves found it impossible to keep Sunday as a day of rest.[20] Clah, in his usual pragmatic way, railed against those who travelled or worked on Sundays (including missionaries) even as he did it himself when it suited his purposes.[21]

A BRIDGE TOO FAR

When Duncan abandoned the HBC fort and set up his independent village at Metlakatla in 1862, he hoped to attract all the Christians from Fort Simpson. His timing was fortuitous, for the move coincided with the smallpox epidemic and many, including Paul Legaic, decided that Metlakatla was a safe haven from the disease. Duncan rarely visited Fort Simpson after the move but instead sent Tsimshian evangelists to preach in the village.[22] Ever ready to promote Christianity, Clah made his house available to the preachers. In late 1873, Duncan decided to encourage conversions at Fort Simpson by inviting people to celebrate Christmas at his Christian village. The Metlakatlans prepared large banners that stated "Welcome to our brethren of Fort Simpson" and "To you is born this day a saviour Christ the Lord" to greet visitors.[23] The Fort Simpson Tsimshian were welcomed with a prayer on arrival, and then Duncan and his assistant missionaries, Mr. and Mrs. William Collison, shook hands with them all. A hymn, newly translated into Tsimshian, was sung, and flags flew on Christmas Day. The following day, the guests were entertained with a magic lantern show, and the festivities continued over the week according to the usual pattern of Christmas and New Year's festivities celebrated at Metlakatla.[24]

Clah, perhaps as an assertion of independence, declined Duncan's invitation, as did many older people who had resisted evangelization. He records that the atmosphere at Fort Simpson was despondent. Seeking to lift community spirits, he invited men in the gambling house to an impromptu Christian service. On Christmas Eve, forty to fifty people responded to the invitation. Clah began by asking if they wanted to continue the old, bad ways or follow the new path of God and Jesus Christ.[25] He rewarded those who agreed to turn to God with clay pipes and tobacco. The next day, the group spent four hours in Clah's house, where he introduced them to the Christmas story: "Because I teaching them about our Saviour Jesus Christ. He was borne into the world to save sinners."[26] The assembled Tsimshian also hatched a plan to prove that Fort Simpson was the equal to Metlakatla in piety, energy, and industry.

For three days, the Tsimshian laboured to build a bridge between the two parts of the Fort Simpson village that were separated by sea at high tide. Half the tribes were located on Rose Island, while the other half resided near the HBC fort on the mainland. This bridge would unify the Tsimshian symbolically and practically. On the morning of 26 December, men in eight canoes set out to cut wood. The next day, a bell was rung to call the people out to start building, and a cannon was fired at the end of the day when the bridge was half finished. The following day was Sunday, a day of rest. Clah and "an old indian doctor named Whaigty" spent the day preaching to the nine tribal groups, "preaching all dark hearts. Now who got heavy hearts when I telling about what is right in Gods word[?] they all moved[,] old men and womens. All says[,] right[,] we turn our hearts to God and we believe our lord Jesus Christ."[27] On Monday, the bridge was completed, and the completion was marked by the firing of two cannon and a Christmas feast.

On New Year's Eve, Clah invited everyone to his house for prayers, which commenced at midnight. Guns were fired, and music was played to welcome in the new year. Clah continued to take advantage of this revival in interest in Christianity by walking around the village and preaching each day. On 3 January, those who had gone to Metlakatla returned. They were welcomed back with handshakes, but they were both jealous of and shamed by the new bridge built by the old people who had stayed home.

The next day presaged the beginning of a new era. It was Sunday, Duncan, as usual, had sent one of his preachers, Samuel Pelham, to take a service at Fort Simpson. Pelham, however, discovered he had to compete with Alfred Dudoward, who rang a bell for a Methodist service, and Clah, who walked round the village preaching from Matthew 5:16-17.[28] These were verses well chosen for the circumstances:

16 Let your light so shine before men, that they may see your good works and glorify your Father in heaven.

17 Do not think that I came to destroy the Law or the prophets. I did not come to destroy but fulfil.

Through his bridge-building enterprise, Clah moved from being a minor preacher to a competitor to Duncan and an advocate of the soon-to-be-established Methodist mission. Duncan sent constables to Fort Simpson to confirm what had happened, while Samuel Pelham and Alfred Dudoward started a whispering campaign against Clah. In retaliation, Clah called them to a meeting at his house, where they were confronted by Clah's supporters. The next day, a Metlakatlan man destroyed the bridge, the symbol of the resurgence of (non-denominational) Christianity at Fort Simpson.

Duncan's attempt to split the Fort Simpson Tsimshian had encouraged Clah to formulate his own Christian philosophy, which formed the basis of his evangelizing for the rest of his life: "God the father told me to teach all the people. Now I do what my father said to me to tell all the people about Him."[29] Clah asserted his direct, unmediated link with God and his independence from any Christian church. This assertion did not, however, represent a claim to independent priestly office. Throughout his life, Clah learned willingly from those who he acknowledged possessed superior spiritual knowledge. The day after setting out on his own ministry, Clah and Alfred Dudoward attended a Bible class taught by Samuel Pelham. The following Sunday, all three were again preaching.

THE METHODIST MISSION

Alfred Dudoward and his wife, Kate, had converted to Methodism on a trip to Victoria in 1873. On his return to Fort Simpson, he had participated in a memorial feast for a Gitando, Kommahen (possibly G̲amayaam), at which he promised members of his tribe that he would not stop feasts or the giving away of property. This promise might have been a way to reassure his people that his adoption of Methodism would not interfere with his Tsimshian obligations. Clah's grandson William Beynon advances the plausible argument that Dudoward, who had been expelled by Duncan from the Anglican Church after expressing a wish to be initiated into the Xgyedmhalaayt (Cannibal secret society), turned to Methodism to shore up his prestige.[30] Nevertheless, Dudoward had been a member of the Christmas expedition to Metlakatla. It is not clear whether Clah's bridge-building project provoked Dudoward to invite the Methodists to establish a mission at Fort Simpson, but the exclusion of Clah and his house from the meeting that agreed to the invitation strongly suggests that this was the case.[31]

In response to Dudoward's letter of invitation, the Methodist Missionary Society sent William Pollard to investigate the situation at Fort Simpson. Upon his return from a trip to Port Essington, Clah found Pollard in residence and signalled approval of the Methodist presence by allowing his four children to be baptized with the Christian names Martha, Rebecca, David, and Andrew.[32] Pollard's favourable reports resulted in the installation of Thomas Crosby as resident Methodist missionary to the Tsimshian.

Religion on the Coast was now highly politicized. Although Pollard paid Duncan a courtesy call before he left Fort Simpson, the two men had quarrelled.[33] Duncan and the Anglicans were outraged by the Methodists' move into what they regarded as their territory.[34] Once the Methodists arrived, Duncan started visiting Fort Simpson more frequently and sending more evangelists, but the community had made its choice. When Thomas Crosby took up permanent residence, Duncan realized he had lost Fort Simpson. But he made sure the Methodists did not benefit from his earlier work when he transported remaining timber at his old station to Metlakatla.[35]

The Crosbys, Thomas and Emma, arrived at Fort Simpson at the end of June, when Clah was at the Cassiar goldfields.[36] In her correspondence, Emma Crosby describes a lively scene, "[W]e were greeted by cheers from the Indians who were out in hundreds. Flags were flying and guns fired as we approached. The landing was crowded with men, women and children."[37] It was clear that these missionaries were welcome. Emma Crosby, however, did not reveal to her mother that their main sponsors at Fort Simpson were the Dudowards. Inverting true power relations, she refers to Alfred Dudoward as Thomas' interpreter and mentions two "half breeds" (Alfred and Kate) in whose house the school was being conducted. She wrote that she thought the couple might be able to assist the missionary.[38]

When Clah arrived back at Fort Simpson in early October, the Crosbys immediately visited him at his house.[39] Clah contributed enthusiastically to the church fund established by Crosby on his first day in the village. Now that there were weekly church services at Fort Simpson, Clah stopped preaching while he was at home, but he continued when he was away on his travels. In December, Clah was summoned to Metlakatla to give evidence in a case before Duncan. He took the opportunity to talk to Duncan about the Methodists. When Duncan explained that they had no right to be at Fort Simpson, Clah advised Duncan to heed his own teaching to love one another, otherwise he and Crosby would set a bad example for the Tsimshian. Clah appears to have treated the Methodists as a welcome addition to the community, one that provided an alternative to Christian authority and a vibrant new form of worship.

In 1875, class meetings were held in the evenings at Fort Simpson. Clah does not describe what occurred in these meetings, but over the ensuing weeks his attitude and language changed.[40] He no longer regarded God merely as a stern overseer of human behaviour who must be humoured through good behaviour to ensure eternity in the afterlife. God could now bring joy to this life. His diary began to include entries such as "Great Light came down from heaven," "the Spirit of God upon our hearts," "preaching and pray[ing] to Our God Holy Spirits came upon us. light came down upon our hearts," and "preaching first class to[,] we feell happy. We know now where we go when we die and we know who is the great King. Is Jesus Christ our lord ... If we give our hearts to God[,] He will sent His power and Spirit[.] then we have no more trouble."[41] Clah had clearly picked up the revivalist language that Crosby employed in his services. Crosby's early reputation as a preacher was based on his emotional and stirring delivery.[42] One woman recalled that "[d]uring a sermon he [Crosby] dashed back and forth with such speed on the platform, his coat-tail flew, he pounded the desk, waved his arms, squatted and stared at his flock."[43] Crosby's style was very different from the restrained and austere practice favoured by Duncan.

CLAH THE CHRISTIAN

Clah did not disregard the dour side of Christianity, but his happiness increasingly depended on successful communion with God. He had a literal understanding of the influence of Christianity. The site of religious feeling was the heart, not the soul, which he rarely mentions other than in hymns and the sermons of others. The heart could be a heavy burden that could drag one down; if one loved God, however, it could be light. Clah first used this imagery when he accompanied Crosby on an evangelical expedition up the Nass River. In one village where the inhabitants did not respond to Crosby's preaching (Clah had presumably translated), Clah declared that "they [are] all wicked people. Dark heavy hearts. They hided they [their] light. They wants darkness."[44] Although this attitude might have reflected Crosby's view of non-believers, as historian Susan Neylan notes, Clah developed, by 1886, his own interpretation of the heart as the receptacle of religious feeling.[45] In that year, when Clah searched Port Simpson for those interested in baptism without success, he reflected that the people had heavy hearts that weighed from fifty to a hundred pounds. He likened the people of Port Simpson to people of the Old Testament who could not escape God's wrath, people who drowned in the flood with their heavy hearts while Noah and his family, with their light hearts, escaped. According to Clah, Lot and his family likewise ran from the devastation of Sodom and Gomorrah while the heavy-hearted died.[46]

Clah's preaching drew on both the Old and New Testaments yet, like many others in the Christianized colonial world, his attention was seized by a few characters from the Old Testament.[47] Clah, a Christian man from a hierarchical Tsimshian society, made numerous references to the "bad" kings Nebuchadnezzar and Saul. When the Tsimshian threatened to return to the old chiefly feasting system, Clah reminded them of how King Nebuchadnezzar of Babylon had tried and failed to pit his power against that of God by worshipping golden images. He reminded them that Saul had been given power by God but had had that power taken away when he disobeyed.[48] Clah's concern with people looking back to the old ways also brought Lot and his wife frequently to his mind. When Lot's wife's faith wavered and she disobeyed God's commandment by looking back to the old city, she was punished by being turned into a column of salt.[49] In 1866, perhaps before he had a proper understanding of the Biblical passage, Clah interpreted this story as a parable about the disobedient wife: "My wife just like lot[']s wife[,] looking back[,] she wants runaway this day. But I have said right[.] I sent her [to the] country where she was before ... my wife[,] she always had bad words against my face."[50]

Susan Neylan and some anthropologists, including Jay Miller, suggest that the Tsimshian were able to assimilate Christianity because they could easily translate Christian ideas, particularly of heaven and light, into existing Tsimshian concepts. There are two problems with this idea of translatability. First, the anthropological knowledge on which it is based was gathered after Christianity was well established on the Coast; therefore, it is difficult, probably impossible, to know to what extent Tsimshian beliefs had already been influenced by Christian notions. Were Tsimshian accounts of heaven and light in the twentieth century the same as Tsimshian beliefs in the mid-nineteenth century, or had they been influenced by the widely disseminated Christian concepts of heaven and light? Second, if there was translatability between Christian and Tsimshian beliefs, it could have undermined Tsimshian understandings of Christian concepts just as easily as it could facilitate them.[51] Certainly, there is no evidence that Clah tried to equate pre-existing Tsimshian beliefs to Christian concepts. He relied heavily on the Bible when he preached; if he did not have his Bible with him, Clah could not proselytize.[52] Clah rarely referred to pre-existing Tsimshian beliefs in his attempts to convert others, except to disparage them (the flood that existed in Tsimshian adawx is perhaps the exception).[53] When Clah refers to light coming down from heaven, the light illuminates the heart, not the Tsimshian world. It is a personal illumination, not a means of enlightening the group or society as a whole. In Tsimshian accounts of Raven who stole the light that brightened the world, this sudden illumination blinds some creatures. According to Clah, in contrast, Christianity would make poor, blind hearts see.[54] Clah's view that the heart rather than the soul was the repository of religious feeling is not a translation of Christian beliefs but rather his attempt to articulate his spiritual state.

Clah saw his Christianity as a challenge rather than a counterpart to previously held beliefs. His claims to a direct link with God (in heaven) defied Tsimshian belief that only chiefs had access to heaven. Marjorie Halpin points out that during Tsimshian halait rituals, "chiefs [had] special and direct access to power of heaven, whereas the powers acquired by others were as mediators between heaven and man, and thus weaker in potency."[55] Clah's motivations for conversion and his use of Christianity were strongly influenced by his life as a Tsimshian, for Christianity enabled him to assert his status among his fellows by claiming Christian powers. His refusal to affiliate with a Protestant denomination and work under a missionary enabled him to claim a direct communication with God. As a young man, he refused to be initiated into the *nulim* (Dog Eaters) secret society, which was open to people with resources who were not chiefs. On Christmas Day in 1893, he recalled that people said of him, "[I]s not right to break our law. we want him to dance this sames what we do, eat dogs fresh [flesh], this same we do. But he never believe what we commantment [commanded] to him[,] to dance as we to [do]. so our lord Jesus Christ told In my heart to love our God and obey His Comman[d]ment walk on His law."[56] The direct relationship between God and believer was not an exclusive right, and Clah urged others to establish their own connection with God rather than relying on missionaries to bring them to him.

Clah also accepted the Christian admonition to help the poor. Although he rejected many aspects of the feasting and potlatch system as anti-Christian, he recognized the system was a means of redistributing wealth within Tsimshian society, and he was most upset with Crosby when he tried not only to ban potlatches but also to make people retrieve goods and debts that had been distributed through feasting.[57]

To understand Clah's acceptance of Christianity, it is necessary to recognize that although Clah was aware that Christianity was a recent innovation on the Northwest Coast, he did not think it was a foreign import but rather a genuine Tsimshian religion.[58] As many scholars have noted, Tsimshian society was open to outside influences. The secret societies are thought to have been introduced by the Heiltsuk at Bella Bella, south of Tsimshian territory, not long before Europeans appeared on the Coast.[59] The prophesies of the Wet'suwet'en prophet known as Bini, who anticipated the arrival of European trade and technological innovations and the introduction of new religious ideas, were pertinent to the introduction of Christianity.[60] William Beynon suggested to the anthropologist Marius

Barbeau that Clah, as a very young child, might have witnessed a Bini revival in 1834, for he found a reference to the revival in Clah's notes.[61] Although Clah recognized that previous generations had not known about the Christian God, he nevertheless believed that God had looked after them. God had been there, even if they were not aware of Him: "13 wise old men were meeting[,] telling about old generations ... telling about before the flood and after the flood[,] after the flood when great Father lord of Heaven made people crew many they made every thing [illegible] to them people. For them use God[,] teach them how to make canoes. They made hard stone for axes[,] sharping in 5 months some 6 months some all one year. Made knives large moseal [mussel] shells spears for bone. Kill everything[.] some old wise men don't understand much about old generations."[62] Clah was genuinely shocked to hear from a white prospector that he, along with many people in Europe, did not believe in God: "[M]akes me so fraiden [afraid] because God knows me[,] an[d] him speaking against Him. Say very near half the people in the world not believe the Bible no hell and no God no Jesus." When he asked his prospecting partner if he believed that Jonah had been eaten by a whale, the reply was no – the whale's mouth is too small to swallow a man.[63]

Despite Clah's enthusiastic embrace of Christianity, Thomas Crosby was reluctant to welcome him formally into the Methodist Church. Crosby delayed the baptism of Clah and Dorcas, even though Pollard baptized Clah's children in 1874; Clah acquired a Christian name, Arthur Wellington, by 1875; and Crosby officiated at Clah and Dorcas' Christian wedding ceremony on 1 April 1875.[64] When Pollard returned to Fort Simpson in 1875 to baptize Crosby's daughter, Clah requested baptism, but Crosby intervened, suggesting Clah wait until the new Methodist church was built. Five years later, in 1880, Clah and Dorcas were belatedly told by Crosby that they had to take baptism classes. A.E. Green, the Methodist missionary at Laxgalts'ap (Greenville), agreed to prepare them. The Wellingtons were finally baptized ten months later in January 1881.[65] Crosby then asked the newly baptized Clah to seek out residents of Fort Simpson who wanted to be baptized without formal classes.[66] Why did Crosby, who was always eager to recruit new congregants through revivals and other spontaneous means, delay the baptism of the Wellingtons? Clah and his family had moved away from the mission in 1877, but that does not explain why they were not offered baptism before their departure. Perhaps Clah's inability to be an acquiescent church member explains Crosby's reluctance to formally bring him into the church.

Clah's encounter with Methodism not only broadened his understanding of Christianity, it also introduced him to new rituals. Duncan refused to introduce the sacrament of communion to the Tsimshian because he believed it could be confused with heathen ceremonies such as those of the Cannibal secret society. Crosby, an ordained minister, had no such reservations and admitted Clah to communion services following his baptism.[67] The Methodists also favoured Clah's kind of lay preaching. Crosby ordered Clah and several other Tsimshian to preach to every tribe long before Clah was baptized.[68] Clah accompanied Crosby on several evangelical expeditions. He took Crosby on his first trip to the Nass River, and he later accompanied him on the *Glad Tidings* up and down the Coast. Clah, however, generally followed his own proclivities, preaching whenever he could to whomever he encountered on his travels.

METHODIST REVIVALS

The Methodists also encouraged revival meetings. Under Crosby's leadership, revivals took the form of "[e]motionally charged group meetings" that resulted in personal transformations and heightened religious experiences.[69] The first Methodist revival at Fort Simpson occurred under the guidance of the temporary missionary Charles Tate and continued for some time after the Crosbys arrived.[70] Clah was away from the village for much of this time. There was another revival in 1877 that enveloped both Fort Simpson and Metlakatla. This movement peaked while William Duncan was away. A young, inexperienced minister, J.A. Hall, had replaced the missionary, and Duncan blamed him for encouraging an outpouring of religious sentiment, including reports of angels, exorcisms, dreams, and ecstasies.[71] Clarence Bolt notes that Crosby took advantage of Duncan's absence by visiting Metlakatla during the revival to encourage religious enthusiasm.[72] Duncan feared this behaviour harked back to the halait and other forms of Tsimshian religious expression. He believed he needed to closely supervise and control Christian observance among the Tsimshian because they were still children in the Gospel.[73]

Neither Duncan nor the historians who have subsequently analyzed these events have looked for connections between the simultaneous revivals at Fort Simpson and Metlakatla. Clah's diary provides important clues to the process at work. At the end of 1876, he notes that the Tsimshian were despondently turning away from Christianity because of petty squabbles and turf wars among the Anglican and Methodist missionaries[74] By 30 October 1877, when he returned from prospecting near the headwaters of the Nass River, the atmosphere had changed: "[A]ll people at home, re[ading] Bible[.] Spirit of God came. Some see Jesus[;] others pray the devel [devil.] Metlekatlah people this same, some will pray to hell."[75] Two days later, Clah went to Metlakatla, where he met Duncan and Hall. This suggests that a revivalist atmosphere was developing while Duncan was still at Metlakatla. The Metlakatlans wanted the Fort Simpson Christians to reconcile with Duncan, but Clah argued that the Tsimshian should combine to get rid of the Anglican and Methodist missionaries and form one church. Having proposed a solution to ease tensions between the Tsimshian churches, Clah left the Coast for the upper Nass River with his family.[76] It is apparent that the religious fervour at Fort Simpson and Metlakatla developed independently of both Duncan and Crosby, although the Metlakatlans did take advantage of Duncan's subsequent absence to fully express their emotions. Missionaries of established churches looked on from the sidelines as expressions of religious enthusiasm – which they had not inspired, did not approve of, and could not direct – broke out.

Clah's diary captures the essence of the revivalist spirit in his account of communal religious enthusiasm late in December 1886. Spontaneous prayer meetings were held each night. On the Sunday before Christmas, during a fierce storm, seven hundred people spilled out of the Methodist church and broke into public prayer, preaching, and song. Clah was highly susceptible to such an occasion. These were the times when the light and spirit of God were upon him, the times when people were converted or, as he often expressed it, converted themselves. He urged the crowds on: "I speak too[,] must go [a]head not look Back to the Devel."[77]

8

Parading and Preaching

On the surface, the 1870s were dominated by denominational tensions between Anglican and Methodist congregations. In reality, the introduction of Methodism at Fort Simpson was not the result of church initiatives but rather political gamesmanship among the Tsimshian. Denominational jealousies followed as the missionaries vied with one another for influence among the local people. Although relations between William Duncan and Thomas Crosby were strained in the beginning, they came to an accommodation and worked amicably as neighbours. Duncan probably had more in common with Crosby, despite his different views on revivalism, than he did with the leaders of Canada's Church of England. In 1879, the new bishop of Caledonia, William Ridley, arrived at Metlakatla. His arrival opened the rift between Duncan and church authorities that culminated in Duncan's 1887 move to Alaska, where he established New Metlakatla with the majority of Tsimshian from his mission.[1] Even as Duncan prepared to lead his people to the promised land, new religious movements were sweeping through the Northwest Coast. This chapter draws on Clah's observations of these dramatic events to show how he and his community strove for independence in religious organizations, spiritual autonomy, and control over evangelical outreach.

THE SALVATION ARMY AND THE INDIGENIZATION
OF METHODISM

Just as Methodism had been introduced to Fort Simpson by the Tsimshian couple, Alfred and Kate Dudoward, so the Salvation Army was introduced in the late 1880s by Tsimshian returning from Victoria.[2] Its personnel was entirely indigenous. Clah first mentions seeing the Salvation Army at Port Simpson in November 1888. Its arrival instigated another revivalist movement. While members of the Salvation Army prayed in the street, people were converted at the Methodist service in an agony of feeling that made the blood boil: "I have seen our great God[']s power sented down upon all Christian who was [at] morning Service[.] some were cried at the Spirit of God. Boil them hearts. our hearts warm as lik[e] hot water."[3] Clah held prayer meetings in his house and invited the Salvation Army; the Salvation Army instead continued its highly charged evangelical sessions in the street. This is not to say that everyone at Fort Simpson was caught up in the euphoria: "[P]rayer meeting every night in schoole house. Salvation arme [Army] keep singing an[d] cried to the lord. the night last[,] I was from schoole house meeting when was out in the street. I have seen Salvation arme praying in street. But some younger men stand alongside them were laughing[,] using rough words."[4]

The Methodist and Anglican missionaries were angered by the advent of a rival religious movement, even though the movement had no institutional structure behind it. The Salvation Army headquarters were not at first aware of the spontaneous eruption of followers on the north Pacific Coast.[5] By the time an official from the organization came north in 1896, the movement was well established.[6] Methodists and Anglicans found it difficult to ban the Salvation Army because it specifically disclaimed any intention of setting up a rival church. Moreover, the Salvation Army was composed of Tsimshian from the Methodist and Anglican mission communities who had not formally left the church and continued to depend on ministers and priests to administer the sacraments. Crosby, however, in a fit of pique, refused to administer them after the Salvation Army opened its own hall in Port Simpson in December 1894.[7]

The arrival of the Salvation Army signalled that a wider section of local people had become disillusioned with newcomer missionaries and their institutionalized churches. At Port Simpson, the Tsimshian had become increasingly frustrated with Crosby, and as early as 1880 the Nisga'a at Kincolith were talking about getting rid of the Anglican missionaries.[8] Their main object was not to expel missionaries but to gain control over their religious lives through the Salvation Army and other offshoots of the established churches: the Methodist Band of Christian Workers (and, later, the Epworth League) and the Anglican Church Army. Each of these groups formed its own marching band with uniforms and instruments. Their competitive parades through the villages of the Northwest Coast created a colourful pandemonium.[9]

The brass instruments used in the bands were imported, even though Aboriginal people had previously employed drums in ceremonies and shaman rituals.[10] William Duncan was given a complete set of brass instruments by a supporter in 1870. Not knowing how to use them, he hung them on the walls of his study until his assistant, William H. Collison, suggested hiring a musician to teach the Tsimshian to play. An ex-bandmaster from a Prussian cavalry regiment arrived in the winter of 1879, and a band was soon playing proficiently under the direction of a Tsimshian bandmaster.[11] According to Collison, other villages quickly imitated the Metlakatlans, procuring instruments at great expense and employing bandmasters.[12]

Even though the Anglicans claimed they introduced brass instruments and bands to the region, Clah had been experimenting with a marching band for several years. He must have witnessed military bands on his travels to Victoria. Whatever the genesis of the idea, he set up his own marching soldiers corps in 1862. The young men marched with guns and band instruments to herald the new year of 1863. Clah refers to the instruments as trumps (possibly bugles or cornets): "[A]nd we having nicily music an[d] good trump[et] an[d] when we going in Clah [h]is house an[d] we will learning how the soldiers an[d] play."[13] These celebrations continued the next day, when Clah's "troops" donned red and blue jackets and Clah played a flute to the accompaniment of two men on trumpets. The jackets were probably procured from army and navy surplus, as there were plenty of American military uniforms on the market by 1870.[14] In 1871, Clah added a music box to his collection of musical paraphernalia to accompany his marching men. It must have been a novelty at Port Simpson, for Ligeex sought to borrow it from Clah.[15]

By the 1880s, occasional militaristic displays were institutionalized in the Riflemen's (Clah continued to refer to them as "Soldiers") and Firemen's Societies. Although secular, these organizations performed important social and cultural functions at occasions such as funerals. As with so much of Tsimshian life, they were organized along crest lines. When Clah's

Salvation Army at Port Essington, 1897. BC Archives, A-06191
(photographer: Harlan I. Smith).

son David died in 1883, the Riflemen's Society took responsibility for the
funeral preparations.[16] Viola Garfield claims that chiefs led these two
organizations and were the bandmasters. Members of the two societies,
dressed in magnificent gold-braided uniforms, competing to produce the
best music.[17]

Historian Clarence Bolt, using mission-generated sources, argues that
Crosby introduced the Riflemen's and Firemen's organizations to Fort
Simpson to distract the Tsimshian from their winter feasts.[18] Clah's diary
suggests there was a pre-existing Tsimshian fascination with military
paraphernalia and band music. Without question, Tsimshian took the lead
in supporting the societies, training members in appropriate behaviour,
and purchasing equipment. As historian Susan Neylan observes, the brass
bands were a form of cultural collaboration through which the Tsimshian

Port Simpson volunteers, 1879. BC Archives, B-03552.

and their neighbours "adapted and adopted colonial forms to create new kinds of performative expressions."[19]

Before the advent of these new opportunities for display and role playing, the Tsimshian had used secular and religious performances to entertain one another through the long winter months. George Chismore, recounting his journey up the Nass River and along the grease trail to the Skeena in 1870, gives a detailed description of a performance he witnessed. After preliminary dances and pipe smoking, a song, accompanied by drumming and the clapping of wooden sticks, began outdoors. Eventually, as the music reached a crescendo, the performers came into the house. They were led by "two Indians *en Character* as savage 'Toodles.' By long practice in reality, they were enabled to be intoxicated with great fidelity ... the next couple, who were clad in mountain goat skins, and wore masks," had the audience in uproar. They were followed by other characters, one after another: "Thus they continued to enter and give place, each bearing some common article – the men with guns, pistols, knives, and paddles; the women with wands – until all the dancers, some

Nelson's Cornet band, Port Simpson, ca. 1900. BC Archives, PN-9331.

twenty or thirty in number were in the house."[20] The performers, some humorous some serious, kept the company entertained as they tried to outdo one another until the end of the performance was announced and everyone went home.

Just as the Tsimshian incorporated new religious and economic practices, so too did they adapt and enrich their amusements. On New Year's Day in 1900, Clah reported the great fun that ensued as members of the Soldier's Society played "chinamen. Negros. All kinds [of] play. Band boys work hard for new day 1900."[21] Neylan rightly contends that this absorption of social changes and new ideas was neither assimilation nor acculturation, although I disagree with her view that it was a form of resistance.[22] The performances, whether dances or bands, incorporated new elements into enduring patterns of social interaction that continued in spite of, rather than in reaction to, the missionaries' and governments' attempts to stamp out potlatch practices. Clah shows that these borrowings began to occur before there were concerted efforts to ban the potlatch or massage the Fort Simpson Tsimshian into the shape of European Christians.

The Salvation Army, with its band and public worship, did not supplant the Riflemen's and Firemen's societies. These groups continued to fulfill secular and semi-religious functions. The advent of the Salvation Army coincided with the establishment of the Band of Christian Workers by the Methodists and the Church Army by the Anglicans.[23] Crosby referred to the "intrusion of the Salvation Army" after he had established the evangelical Band of Christian Workers, which had been inspired by a similar organization in Ontario.[24] The Band of Workers was "composed of the most earnest Christian Workers ... They generally carried on street preaching or open-air services in their own villages, and also took trips with their Missionary, or sometimes alone to distant heathen villages. They were organised with a president and Secretary. They also carried a banner or flag with the name of the organisation, or Scripture texts, on it, such as 'God is Love': or 'Seek ye the Lord while He may be found.'"[25] Members of the organization carried drums, tambourines, and other musical instruments, which they played outside but not in church. The Church Army fulfilled a similar role among the Tsimshian and Nisga'a who lived on Anglican missions. J.B. McCullagh, the missionary at Aiyansh on the upper Nass River observed, "The Army marches through the town with its Band playing and banner flying, singing hymns and delivering short exhortations at the street corners."[26]

Crosby hoped that the Band of Christian Workers would provide an outlet for religious enthusiasm without compromising the parent church.[27] Although his strategy might have succeeded initially, he did not retain control of the group over the long term. Bolt chronicles the process by which the Tsimshian demonstrated their rejection of Crosby's oversight by playing instruments in church, building their own hall against Crosby's wishes, and organizing independent evangelizing expeditions. By 1894, Crosby had to admit that he exercised little control over the members' activities.[28] He tried to re-establish control by introducing yet another association, the Epworth League, in the latter part of the 1890s. This move was strongly opposed by the Band of Christian Workers.[29]

There was a strong rivalry between the Methodists and the Salvation Army from the time of the latter's arrival in 1888. It was not a benign competition but closely associated with other tensions in the community. In the first few months, many people laughed at the Salvation Army and ridiculed its adherents. Political factions soon became aligned with the organization, however, and it became an established part of the religious scene. In November 1892, the Methodists treated the Salvation Army as a serious threat and rightly so, for half the population of Port Simpson was attending Salvation Army services. There were prayers and meetings every night. Crosby's men were driven to imitate the methods of their rivals, singing on the streets before services.[30] There were also attempts to reach an accommodation with the Salvation Army, either by combining the two congregations or, when no agreement was reached, by sharing facilities.[31] Despite these efforts, the religious divisions reflected political tensions in the community that could not be resolved.

Alfred Dudoward was prominent in the politics of religion. Although he had been suspended from the Methodist church on more than one occasion, he returned after admitting his wrongdoing. He was, by 1892, chief of the Gitando and, with the support of his brother-in-law Albert, chief 'Wiiseeks of the Ginaxangiik, and members of the Git'siis tribe, who were aggrieved by the Salvation Army's interference in the commemoration feast of their dead chief, he attempted to force the Salvation Army out of Port Simpson.[32]

Despite the rivalry, or maybe because of it, there was a revivalist movement at Port Simpson at the end of 1892. People were attending meetings and services every day: "[A]ll our little children were stand[ing] singing out and cri[e]d[.] [A]ll says Jesus[,] His [He's] the Lord. That makes our hearts warm."[33] Although people might have felt closer to God, faith did not bring them closer to one another, and the friction between the two church groups continued, fanned by Crosby's fears of losing control of his congregation.[34]

The situation was complicated further when Chief Mountain of the Nisga'a invited all the chiefs and elders at Port Simpson to a feast at Kincolith to mark the raising of his gravestone. A meeting was held to discuss an appropriate response. Both the Methodists and members of the Salvation Army recommended not attending Mountain's feast. In a speech, Clah warned that they would break God's law if they participated. A couple of chiefs ignored the advice, however.[35] A few days later, Crosby called on fifty young men to accompany him on an evangelical trip to the Nass River. He hoped to reinvigorate his congregation and counter Mountain's celebrations.[36] At Port Simpson, the churches, led by the Salvation Army, voted to expel the errant chiefs. Emotions cooled over the ensuing year, and the chiefs were reinstated in late December 1893.[37]

As people dispersed to the fisheries and then to the canneries, inter-denominational rivalries continued. In December 1893, the manager of the Claxton cannery, with the support of both Methodist and Anglican missionaries, threatened to send away anyone who preached outdoors. In effect, he was banning the Salvation Army from holding services at the cannery.[38] By the time everyone had returned to Port Simpson for the winter, the stage was set for a major confrontation. Because no agreement had been reached the previous winter about sharing the Methodist church facilities, the Salvation Army decided to build its own hall. Although the Salvation Army had increasing support among the Port Simpson Tsim-shian, most of the chiefs and the village council opposed the organization. Neither Ligeex nor Niisho'ot (who had recently changed allegiance from the Methodists to the Salvation Army) would publicly support the Salva-tion Army. And, when invited, Crosby refused to lay the foundation stone of its building. Nevertheless, the new hall opened on 23 December 1893 with great fanfare from the Firemen's Society.[39] Paul Brentzen and his wife, who became captain of the corps, were strong supporters of the Salvation Army. They belonged to a dissident Eagle Clan (Laxsgiik) group, which had formed its own Gispaxlo'ots house in the hopes of usurping Ligeex's position as chief.[40] It would seem the family was using the Salvation Army to further its political ambitions – ambitions with which Clah was in sympathy. Clah's attempts to persuade Ligeex and Niisho'ot to support the Salvation Army were obviously a strategy to influence the wider political scene. Religious and Tsimshian politics were always closely aligned at Port Simpson.

Clah was allied with the Salvation Army throughout 1893. In Decem-ber 1892, he described himself as the captain and, maintaining the military analogy, suggested that the women should make war coats and caps for the soldiers of Jesus.[41] No doubt, Clah supported the Salvation Army for both political and religious reasons, although he does not make his pol-itical position clear. It would appear that he supported the Brentzens' putsch among the Gispaxlo'ots, but it could also be that, rather than act-ively promoting the Brentzens, he was motivated by resentment at Dudoward's use of the Methodists to support his own political agenda.

Clah was also disenchanted with Crosby. In January 1893, Crosby asked Clah why he did not support the Methodist Church. Clah cited Crosby's continuing demands for money. Clah had been taught by Duncan that his reward would come from God, not man.[42] Dorcas and Rebecca not only abandoned the Methodists but became committed members of the Salvation Army, while Clah continued to be eclectic in his religious adherence.[43] Prior to the 1880s, Dorcas had only been nominally Christian: "I heard my wife learning how to pray[,] as 20 years she never open her mouth to calling upon our Jesus Christ."[44] The Salvation Army arrived at a time when Dorcas was ready to dedicate herself to Christianity. She remained a devoted Salvationist for many years.

Over the next few years, the Anglicans, Methodists, and Salvationists competed vigorously at Port Simpson. In 1895, Clah recorded that the Anglican Church Army had been at the canneries (Collison had introduced the organization to Kincolith in 1892) and that the Band of Christian Workers was competing with the other Christian groups at Port Simpson. Although most people at Port Simpson were Christians by this time, on the Nass River there were many who were not, and they found the Church Army's use of drums infuriating and possibly sacrilegious.[45]

The rivalry between the church groups did not dissipate as Crosby tried to retain control over his congregation. In 1896, he asked the young Ligeex, Martha, to become head of the Band of Christian Workers. The elders advised her not to align herself with a faction but to remain chief of all the tribes.[46] When the Salvation Army headquarters finally sent an official to the north, Crosby tried to persuade him to focus his attention on villages where there was no established church. His request was ignored.[47] It was not only Crosby who tried to undermine the Salvationists, Tsimshian Methodists were also concerned about their subversive influence. They threatened the Brentzens, the leading members of the Salvation Army, while Alfred Dudoward and Lewis Gosnell circulated a petition in the village to have the Salvationists banned from Port Simpson. A few weeks later, it was reported that Dudoward was using witchcraft against Salvation Army adherents, including Clah's son Henry Tate.[48] The introduction of the Epworth League in 1899 increased rather than dissipated tensions between its members and the Band of Christian Workers.[49] In 1906, Clah received invitations from six companies to join them as they competed on the streets, and the Epworth League, the Band of Christian Workers, and the Salvation Army had formal drives to recruit members.[50] Clah avoid-ed formal membership in any group, happily attended their services, and preached to them when invited.

PREACHING TO THE UNCONVERTED

As the politics of religion unfolded in the winter villages over the decades, Clah continued to be more concerned with reaching out to those who had not accepted Christianity. He had happily served as a translator for both Duncan and Crosby when they arrived on the Coast but, as we have seen, he did not align himself with their evangelical agendas. Missionaries all over the world found it difficult to hand control of the church over to local people, even when the formal policies of their mission societies demanded it. Duncan and Crosby were no exception. Each man had handpicked acolytes who travelled to villages to preach, but neither man could tolerate an independent evangelist. Both men tried to rein Clah in as he took it upon himself to proselytize to those who followed their traditional religion. When Clah took a stand against Duncan's attempt to attract Fort Simpson Tsimshian to Metlakatla, Duncan ridiculed him. Crosby, likewise, was discomfitted by Clah's criticisms of the Methodist Church and Crosby's money-raising activities.

Clah began to evangelize during the fur trade, when he visited villages on the Skeena and Nass rivers. His preaching was quite an ad hoc activity. If he was in a village on a Sunday and could gather a few people together, he would take the opportunity to preach to them. To Clah, these poor blind hearts were not hot or cold but lost and unseeing. Because the uncon-verted could still be found at Fort Simpson, evangelism could continue at home as well.

It was the challenge posed by Duncan in December 1873 and the ap-pearance of Crosby and his revivalist form of preaching that galvanized Clah into serious evangelical activity. Although Duncan had ridiculed him, Clah began preaching on the Nass River in February 1874. He was not, however, confident about his knowledge of the Bible.[51] He asked Robert Cunningham to teach him as the two men travelled together. One Sunday, he arrived at a village where the people were waiting for a missionary to teach them. Robert Tomlinson was stationed at Kincolith, and the villagers wanted their own teacher. Having so recently convinced the Fort Simpson

Tsimshian that they could be a Christian community without a missionary, Clah showed no sympathy for the Nisga'a's plea: "[N]ow I get up and tell them[,] I say[,] [']all my friends[,] I have no News to telling yous dont to not trouble yourselfs to what you like to do. you not slave.['] Now one thing I have said to yours, [']pray to God[,] love him then He will give good min[i]ster in here and you fell happy.'"[52] Twenty years later, Clah remembered walking the grease trail between the headwaters of the Nass and Skeena rivers, trading furs while preaching from Matthew 28:19-20, to "make disciples of all the nations" and teach them. He travelled to the goldfields at Cassiar and north to Alaska, telling "friends about our saviour Jesus."[53]

Clah's prayers and preaching generally became more ardent when he was away from home. Perhaps he felt more vulnerable or maybe he had more time, particularly at night, to concentrate on his prayers. Those travelling with him had to join him in his prayers and listen to him preaching. In 1875, on his way to the Cassiar goldfields, he preached four times on Sunday at Fort Wrangell and was pleased that some of the local chiefs had come to hear him.[54] Walking up the trail to Dease Lake, he prayed all day Sunday and sometimes every other day as well. Once he arrived at the goldfields, the preaching became more spasmodic as he and his companions built their boat. A few weeks later, Clah was thrilled to meet some "Cassiar Indians" who had never before seen a Tsimshian. They exchanged gifts, and Clah took the opportunity to preach to them in Chinook Jargon, at which "they Bow down."[55] This was a rare opportunity to preach to neophytes. More often, Clah was disappointed by the Christians from Fort Simpson and Metlakatla because they tended to forget their Christian commitment when away from the missions. They worked or played on Sundays, breaking God's law.[56]

Back at Fort Simpson, Clah attended church and Crosby's sermons. When he and his family left Fort Simpson a few months later to live at Laxk'a'ata (Canaan) on the Nass, Clah behaved as he had on his earlier travels – he prayed with and preached to the family everyday. This pattern of preaching and praying continued for the remainder of his life, sometimes with more intensity, sometimes with less. During the family's time on the Nass River, Clah's preaching occasionally became so relentless he drove his children to tears: "[M]y wife says I will destroy them[.] she told me to not preach any more."[57]

Although Clah often forced his preaching on an unwilling audience, there were occasions when he was invited to preach to informal gatherings, in church, or to the various religious factions that were appearing along the Coast. In the mid- to late-1890s, Clah was more likely to preach to the Salvationists, Anglicans, or members of the Christian Band of Workers than to the Methodists, although he was happy to preach to anyone who would listen. When he became older and less mobile and no longer had the opportunity to proselytize among strangers, Clah focused his religious enthusiasm on his family. There were, however, many times when he would have felt quite alone were it not for the company of the Christian Trinity.

THE HEALING POWERS OF CHRIST

Clah's faith in God was reflected in his attitude towards ill health. He became accomplished at treating himself and others with both Tsimshian and Western remedies. He never overtly compared his ability to heal to shamanic powers, but it is difficult not to conclude that Clah took pride in his healing powers and skill, even though he believed that, ultimately, it was only Jesus who could heal the sick.

Clah and his community were surrounded by sickness. Measles and influenza epidemics carried off children and adults quickly. People suffered slow deaths from tuberculosis and venereal diseases and from wounds from accidents and fights. Clah's desperation over serious illness was most palpable when his own children fell sick, but he too was often unwell with throat infections, influenza, and many other unspecified illnesses. When Clah was alone on the goldfields and too sick to move, he prayed to God for assistance. He often administered purgatives, a Tsimshian remedy for a range of conditions, to himself. During the smallpox epidemic of 1862, he collected wild plants in the hope that Tsimshian treatments would keep the disease at bay. Yet even in these early days of Christian adherence, he believed only God had the power to heal.

When Clah's son Andrew became sick with complications from measles, he resorted to prayer – perhaps because he had no access to medicines. When Crosby brought medicine, it was too late, and Andrew died a few days later. Within months, there was another measles epidemic. Forty to fifty children, including Clah's, were sick each day during January. While the missionaries tried to treat people, Clah prayed for their recovery:

"Preach the children at nine oclock that night. My children's they have little stronger. We use midicin [medicine][.] not much good. But when we use prayer[,] we felt stronger."[58] Two weeks later, when David became seriously ill, Clah had no medicine. He continued to pray and went to Crosby for help. Clah was so desperate at this point that he also went to the Chinese doctor and back to Crosby, who gave him more medicine and suggested Clah pray. Clah called in the Chinese doctor yet again, and he continued to pray each day. Clah then asked Collison for help and a Tsimshian woman who had knowledge of traditional medicines. He tried castor oil as a purgative to clean out his son's bowels, but neither prayer nor medicines helped. In the end, he called on Christians to pray by David's bed as he lay dying.[59]

David's and Andrew's deaths, and the deaths of so many other people close to him, did not dent Clah's faith. (His faith wavered only during the sickness and death of two of his daughters, Ida and Maggie, when he became convinced that they had been bewitched and that prayer would be no use.) Clah's Christian faith was deeply felt and unshakable. He worked hard to win to God those who had not previously encountered Christianity, and he tried to ensure that Christians did not revert to their old beliefs or break strictures against work or travel on Sundays or the Ten Commandments. While private prayer was important to Clah, he relished public displays of faith and having an audience for his sermons. On the other hand, his faith was a deeply personal bond between himself and God, it could not be mediated through a missionary or an institutional church. Church buildings and services facilitated worship, but they did not control it. We know that there were many Tsimshian Christians who aligned themselves closely with church hierarchies, including Clah's nephew William Henry Pierce, who became an ordained minister and missionary, and Philip McKay (also known as Clah), who died in Alaska preaching to the Tlingit. Then there were the preachers Duncan sent to Fort Simpson from Metlakatla and those who accompanied Crosby on evangelical journeys. It is difficult to determine whether Clah, the individualist, was unusual or whether there were many others who functioned independently as evangelical Christians. The popularity of the Christian Band of Workers and the Church Army, as well as the early history of the Salvation Army on the Coast, suggests that there were many others like

Clah, individuals who wanted to control their own religious life and not be dictated to by an outsider missionary. Yet, as Clah's ambivalent relationship with Anglican and Methodist missionaries shows, we cannot discount the influence of missionaries on the Tsimshian.

9
Clah and the Missionaries

Clah's relationship with missionaries epitomized his attitude to modernity. He was interested in its benefits, but on his own terms. He craved the knowledge missionaries could give him, but not at the expense of his independence and autonomy. He wanted missionaries as friends and equals, not as authorities who dictated how he should run his life. He wanted their acceptance, not their judgment. He gradually learned that missionaries occupied a liminal space between the colonial state and the Tsimshian and that there was as much rivalry and politicking among missionaries as could be found in Tsimshian society. Clah regarded missionaries as religious teachers rather than as morally superior beings. He believed their role was to support and promote the interests of the Tsimshian in spiritual and practical matters, not to intervene in their lives.

Clah sought William Duncan out soon after Duncan arrived at Fort Simpson in 1857. Clah wanted to join the class Duncan was holding for mixed-descent children at the fort; he was hungry for the skills Duncan could teach him. Clah and Duncan soon formed a symbiotic relationship: they taught each other before Clah left for Victoria.

The Church Missionary Society (CMS) missionaries who followed Duncan to the Northwest Coast spread up the Nass River and then the Skeena to Haida Gwaii (Queen Charlotte Islands) to establish mission villages based on Duncan's Metlakatla model.[1] Robert Cunningham arrived in 1863 to assist Duncan, but the two men had a falling out after Cunningham married his Tsimshian sweetheart, Elizabeth Ryan. Cunningham joined the Hudson's Bay Company and then established his own business on the Coast as a fur trader and storekeeper. Arthur Doolan came to

Metlakatla in the same year as Cunningham and was sent to the Nass River north of Fort Simpson, where he established himself in the village of Quinwoch and then, with Robert Tomlinson, built a new Christian village at Kincolith.[2] Although Doolan returned to England in 1867, Tomlinson stayed on at Kincolith until 1878, pioneered another mission at Kispiox, and finally left the CMS around 1881 to run an independent Anglican mission on the Skeena River at present-day Cedarvale. Two other long-term CMS missionaries on the northern Coast were William Collison and James McCullagh. Collison spent periods of time at Metlakatla, Massett in Haida Gwaii (1876-79), and Kincolith (1884-1922).[3] McCullagh ran the mission at Aiyansh on the upper Nass River, which had been established by Tomlinson in 1878. In 1879, the Anglican Diocese of British Columbia was divided into three new dioceses. The northernmost was named Caledonia, and its first Bishop, William Ridley, was deliberately located at Metlakatla. Arguments between Ridley and Duncan about fundamental issues of doctrine and ritual ultimately convinced Duncan to establish his independent mission, New Metlakatla, across the border in Alaska in 1887.

Clah also had interactions with a number of other Anglican CMS missionaries. Henry Schutt, a schoolteacher, arrived in 1876 with his wife and two children to replace Tomlinson at Kincolith.[4] James Alfred Hall, an ordained minister, arrived in Metlakatla in 1877 and was immediately left in charge of the mission while Duncan went to Victoria. And Fred L. Stephenson arrived in the 1890s.

Thomas Crosby, the first Methodist missionary to make his permanent residence at Fort Simpson, arrived in 1874 and stayed until 1897. Alfred Green, who helped establish the Methodist mission at Laxgalts'ap (Greenville), remained there until 1890. Dennis Jennings spent some time in the region in the 1880s, as did the medical missionary Dr. Albert Edward Bolton in the 1890s.[5] Crosby, while based at Fort Simpson, engaged in itinerant preaching up and down the Coast, travelling first by canoe and later in the schooner *Glad Tidings*. Green and others acted as his deputies in his absence. After Crosby's departure, the Reverend S.S. Osterhout served Port Simpson for a number of years.

The Methodists relied heavily on Tsimshian missionaries to facilitate their evangelical work. The most prominent was William Henry Pierce, who became an ordained minister in 1887. As Clah's adopted nephew, he might have been brought up in Clah's household.[6] Pierce did the ground-work, establishing a number of Methodist missions on the Nass and Skeena rivers – including at Port Essington, Greenville, Gitsegukla, and Kispiox – ahead of the arrival of newcomer missionaries. He also helped establish missions outside Tsimshian territory at Bella Bella and Bella Coola and proselytized on the *Glad Tidings.*[7]

Clah's interactions with missionaries are instructive, particularly because he was, on the whole, well disposed towards them and interested in their Christian message. He was also well aware of their shortcomings. He knew missionaries had more Christian knowledge than he did but that they held no monopoly on that knowledge. He viewed missionaries as people to be cultivated for his own interests, as servants rather than masters of his community, as useful intermediaries in his dealings with secular authorities.

WILLIAM DUNCAN

Clah's relationship with William Duncan was the most complex. It began with Clah teaching Duncan Sm'algyax, and Clah learning English from Duncan. Clah's initial introduction to Christianity was a by-product of his language sessions. The process of translating Christian concepts into Tsimshian for Duncan evolved into a process of instruction. Duncan's attitude towards Clah in these early days was ambivalent. Clah acted as his eyes and ears in the village, and he encouraged Duncan to move out of the fort to work directly with the people. Clah accompanied Duncan on his first visit to preach to the nine Tsimshian tribes. Duncan had initially hired Clah to teach him Sm'algyax because there were no other candidates for the job. But he failed to recognized Clah's quick mind and capacity to absorb information and consequently hired a middle-aged Tsimshian woman who lived with one of the men in the fort: "She readily seized my meaning with relatively little trouble[,] which I find a great relief[,] for the young Indian I have had[,] I am sorry to say[,] is not so bright as I could wish and has severely taxed me sometimes [before] I got a word or an expression."[8] Yet Duncan soon called on Clah again for assistance. In June 1859, Duncan reported that a large group of Tsimshian was going to Victoria, "One of them is my most forward adult scholar[,] a young man named Clah[,] but a very bad man. He has made amazing progress and would have made more if others of the class could have kept pace with

William Duncan, missionary at Metlakatla, ca. 1870. BC Archives, A-08354.

him."[9] This observation epitomizes Duncan's view of Clah. He recognized Clah's abilities, including his quick intellect, but he did not believe he could control Clah and make a good Christian of him. Thus, Duncan could accuse Clah of killing white men, then hire him as a constable to control the liquor trade, only to strip him of his appointment when he went beyond the authority Duncan had vested in him. On other occasions, Duncan intervened to help Clah recover fur trade debts and relied on Clah to give evidence against Collins, the liquor trader. Duncan's friendship with Clah reached its lowest point during the events of 1873-74, when Clah stayed at Fort Simpson while others visited Metlakatla for Christmas and took a stand against the missionary by building the bridge to Rose Island (see Chapter 7). Duncan saw this as a direct challenge to his authority and influence at Fort Simpson.

Clah admired Duncan and generally regarded him as a friend, yet he could be deeply hurt by him, especially when Duncan accused him of murder and when he raised a black flag in 1868 to disown Clah because he had held a potlatch. Although Clah did not join Duncan at Metlakatla, he visited him frequently and made his house available to Duncan's Tsimshian evangelists when they came to Fort Simpson during the 1860s and early 1870s. He sympathized with Duncan's war with Ridley: "[O]ld brother Duncan out. they have 6 churchs out Gods house for 2 priest Qualing [quarrelling] themselfs. I feelt very sorry when I had [heard] Duncan his [he's] out. I pray to great God very much. because his old and first claimed Simshens [Tsimshians] an[d] every place of indians in Britsh Collumbia."[10] Some months later, Clah, using a mining analogy, accused Ridley of "trying jumping Duncan[']s claim" at Metlakatla. Duncan had written to the Fort Simpson Tsimshian to ask for their support against Ridley.[11] By 1886, the Tsimshian regarded Ridley not only as Duncan's foe but also as their enemy in the campaign to halt the surveying of reserves. He was seen as a government man bent on undermining Tsimshian interests.[12]

Ridley's disdain for others became evident in February 1888, when a canoe carrying Cunningham's wife, Elizabeth, the Reverend H.A. Sheldon, and three other people capsized in heavy seas at the mouth of the Skeena River. All of the occupants drowned. When search parties went out to look for their remains, Ridley was asked to supply them with food. According to Clah, the bishop laughed and said Sheldon had not belonged to the CMS and was not, therefore, his responsibility.[13]

On a visit to Victoria in 1889, Clah expressed his distaste for Ridley to his old friend Senator William J. Macdonald, who was a strong supporter of Duncan. He claimed Ridley was a bad man whom nobody at Metlakatla wanted.[14] By then, Duncan had moved to Alaska, and Clah saw him infrequently. The last time they met was in 1907, when Clah travelled to New Metlakatla at Duncan's invitation.

The arrival of the Methodists had also revealed another side of Duncan's personality to Clah – resentfulness and vindictiveness. In 1874, Clah reported that Duncan was jealous of the Methodists. There were rumours that Duncan and Tomlinson had threatened to punish Tsimshian who allied themselves with the Methodists by either sending sickness upon them or poisoning them. It was said that Duncan was going to blacklist those who had been baptized by the Methodists. In response, the Tsimshian, including Clah, turned against Duncan. Clah hosted a meeting for members of his house at which it was decided that they would no longer support Duncan.[15]

Yet, by December of that year, Duncan and Clah appeared once again to be friends when Duncan asked Clah for a witness statement in relation to a matter Duncan was presiding over as magistrate. Clah paddled to Metlakatla and remarked in his diary that "[o]ur brother Duncan was very kind to us."[16] The next day, Clah tried to act as a mediator to resolve the issue of the Methodists presence at Fort Simpson: "I give advice Old Duncan and all his people. because I had something about between them and Crosby an[d] Duncan jealous. he tells me everything about methodists ... Mr Duncan[,] ['][Y]ou teach us before[,] So what Gods says in Bible and to keep His Commandment. To Love one another[.] Jesus Christs tells this same love one another. Crosby teach us[,] and your teach all your people this same. Now you and crosby teach us Bad[;] then we all Bad.['] I said to him. [']I think myself everything will breaked up If we all Bad this yours.['] he says that so."[17] Instances such as this, in which the tables are turned as the new Christian lectures his teacher on Christian behaviour, are seldom, if ever, found in missionary annals, in which the missionaries always hold the high moral ground. Clah never acknowledged Duncan or any of his missionary acquaintances as morally superior; he freely criticized them for travelling on Sundays or breaking rules they had imposed on the Tsimshian.

As Clah and Duncan aged, their names became linked in the history of Christianity on the Coast. Duncan mentions Clah as his Sm'algyax teacher in the book he wrote after his first ten years as a missionary, and other histories expanded on this connection. For instance, in *Dayspring in the Far West*, M.E. Johnson claims Clah saved Duncan's life when Chief Ligeex threatened him in 1858.[18] The two men's friendship survived turbulent times, and each man symbolized for the other a turning point in his own life. For Duncan, Clah was associated with his early, uncertain years on the Coast, when he was filled with doubt and loneliness, overwhelmed by the task before him, but determined to proceed.[19] To Clah, Duncan represented new opportunities. He taught him to read and write and introduced him to Christianity. Armed with these skills and knowledge and the protection of the Christian God, Clah believed he represented the future of the Tsimshian. By 1887, when Duncan moved to Alaska, both men had toned down their youthful ambitions but were determined to continue along their chosen paths – Duncan to set up yet another mission community, and Clah to fight the colonial forces that were claiming his land.

THOMAS CROSBY

Clah's association with other missionaries was never as close as the one he shared with Duncan. Although Thomas Crosby remained at Fort Simpson much longer than Duncan, he maintained a rather distant and often strained relationship with Clah. Clah was not involved in the decision to invite Crosby to Fort Simpson, yet he welcomed the new missionary's presence in the village, was pleased to see his children baptized, and gave generously to Crosby's church-building fund.[20] However, Clah clashed with Crosby before he moved his family to the Nass River in 1877.[21] Their first altercation, in January 1876, was sparked by Crosby's heavy-handed intervention in the potlatching system, when he tried to persuade the Tsimshian to return goods distributed at feasts and suggested they should pay back their "debts": "About last night[.] Mr Crosby calling some people to settle old debts. But in our laws[,] when we gave away all our property[,] we not say to friends to take propertys back."[22] Clah was annoyed by Crosby's meddling in a complex system the missionary did not understand.

A more serious conflict was sparked when Crosby intervened in a dispute between Clah and his partners in the boat-building enterprise at the Omineca goldfields. Crosby acted on their complaint that Clah owed them money and insisted that Clah make a payment of eleven dollars. Clah refused and referred the matter to Duncan in his capacity as a magistrate.[23] This dispute heightened Clah's growing dissatisfaction with Crosby's interference in Tsimshian matters and constant demands for money from the Tsimshian to support his church-building projects. Clah accused Crosby of stealing from the poor and not paying his workers their full wages. In

Thomas and Emma Crosby with their children, ca. 1885. BC Archives, B-06308.

March 1876, Crosby accused Clah of lying and refused to shake his hand as he left church.[24] Yet only a few weeks earlier, Crosby had held class meetings in Clah's house. It is therefore difficult to determine just how serious these disputes were.

Although the disagreement between Clah and Crosby in 1876 might not have signified a permanent falling out, Clah (after his return to Port Simpson) expressed continuing frustration throughout the late 1880s with Crosby's demands for money from his congregation and his apparent inability to help the Tsimshian halt the government's inexorable alienation of their lands. In Clah's mind, however, the priest always remained separate from the man. However annoyed he might be over Crosby's activities, Clah still recognized him as a great preacher who could heighten his religious experience. In 1887, Clah walked around Port Simpson, recruiting people to be baptized by Crosby. Several initially refused because of Crosby's insistence that they first go through a Christian marriage ceremony. When Clah persuaded Crosby that this prerequisite was unnecessary, twenty people arrived at the church for baptism.[25] Two weeks later, Crosby led a revivalist meeting at which "the great God open our heart. His moving. He was with us in our meeting[,] the Spirit of God was in our meeting."[26]

Crosby, the flawed man rather than the inspiring preacher, antagonized the Tsimshian. They suspected that the money he raised was kept for his personal use rather than for the church or providing education for their children. They accused him of aiding the surveyors who were laying out the boundaries of their reserves. They resented his frequent absences from the mission on evangelical trips. They wanted an advocate and adviser as well as a preacher who would not only bring people to Christianity but also educate and develop their Biblical and religious understanding.[27]

A minor episode proved to be the final straw for Clah. In 1892, Crosby disregarded protocols and built a cow shed on Tsimshian land without their permission. Clah was particularly incensed because he had written a letter on behalf of the Tsimshian requesting that Crosby desist from building the shed. Despite his annoyance, Clah recorded this ironic riposte on 27 August 1892:

[W]hen I ask him. ["][F]riend I want to know If you read that letter which I give to you wednesday last[?"] he said yes. But I want to know what letter said.

[S]o he said to me. ["][B]ecause I found no Names on that letter[."] says[,] ["]If I found 2 [or] 3 names on[,] I [would] not built the house.["] I say[,] ["]well letter dont write himself[,] may be somebodys hand writed [wrote it]. But why not believe what letter said to you[?"]

I said him friend[,] ["][Y]ou the priest. But you spoil the people here.
you Built the houses every where. you know yourself indians want that
land which you built the place on. also one thing I want you stoped about
asking mon[e]y in church every Sunday[.] that makes everybodys heart
very low. If you [do] that in big city[,] the whit[e] pe[o]ple give you hell.
tie you [up]. you the man spoil this place[.] you never teach the people
right["] when I speak to him[,] he speaks very rough to me.[28]

A few days later, Crosby, close to tears, left Port Simpson for a visit to
Victoria without saying goodbye to anyone in the village.[29] In 1895, the
Tsimshian wrote to Alexander Sutherland, general secretary of the Methodist Missionary Society, requesting that Crosby be replaced. Their request
was fulfilled in 1897.[30]

Throughout the 1890s, Crosby had been distracted not only by a peren-
nial shortage of funds but also by the appearance of the Salvation Army at
Port Simpson. The enthusiasm with which the Salvation Army was embraced by many Tsimshian reflected the dissatisfaction they felt with
Crosby's leadership. This dissatisfaction had also been expressed through
the growing independence of the Band of Christian Workers and the high
number of congregation members placed "on trial," including the
Dudowards, stalwarts of the Methodist church.[31] Clarence Bolt suggests
that Crosby relied on revivals to maintain religious enthusiasm at Port
Simpson but did not follow them up with lessons to foster a deeper knowledge and understanding of Christianity.[32] The absence of any revivals
between 1882 and 1892 suggests that religious adherence was waning. The
1892 revival was, I have suggested (see Chapter 8), instigated by the presence of the Salvation Army. Unlike the interdenominational rivalry of the
1870s, Clah did not become embroiled in the religious politics of the 1890s.
He maintained a neutral position, but he was critical of Crosby's attempts
to undermine the Salvation Army and not sorry to see him leave in 1897.[33]

OTHER MISSIONARIES

Clah's relationship with the Methodist minister Alfred Green, who was
stationed at Laxgalts'ap from 1877 to 1890, was more amicable. It is possible
that their relationship was less troubled because they lived in different
communities. Clah only saw Green when he travelled up the river to fish

Clah with the Reverend A.E. Green, ca. 1970. BC Archives, A-02176.

or trade. When Green relieved Crosby at Port Simpson in 1890, however, their relationship deteriorated. According to Clarence Bolt, soon after he arrived in the village, Green criticized the Tsimshian for not leading godly lives, being too concerned with community council matters, neglecting the Sabbath, and indulging in potlatches and drinking.[34] Leading Tsimshian men met and decided that they wanted to have Green removed for denigrating their status in the community. Clah concurred and claimed that Green was working against Tsimshian interests by undermining their confidence in their own autonomy.[35]

At other times, Green proved himself to be a supportive friend to Clah. He provided him with medicines when he or his family was sick, and presided over the funeral of one of Clah's sons. Mrs. Green offered Clah seeds to plant in his vegetable garden, and it was Green, not Crosby, who prepared Clah and Dorcas for baptism in 1880. Clah maintained friendly contact with Green after the missionary moved to Vancouver Island and called on his assistance in his legal battles with the HBC.

Clah also maintained a significant relationship with Albert Edward Bolton. A qualified medical practitioner from Ontario, Bolton arrived at Port Simpson in 1889.[36] Because the Methodist Church was not prepared to support a medical missionary, Bolton looked to the Tsimshian for financial support. When he became a justice of the peace, he fulfilled three roles at Port Simpson: doctor, occasional preacher, and law enforcement officer. Judging from Clah's diary, his medical role was the most contested; however, in Bolton's own diary, there is no mention that the Tsimshian blamed him for deaths in the community.[37] Both diaries record that Bolton treated Clah's daughter Mary Elizabeth for dropsy or ascites.[38] She died in 1891 at age thirteen after suffering from the illness for four years. Although Clah had been grateful to Bolton a couple of weeks earlier for curing his son Albert of the influenza, he blamed the doctor for his daughter's death. According to historian Susan Neylan, Bolton claimed "bad medicines" were responsible for the tragedy.[39] A few days before the death, Bolton had warned the Tsimshian not to buy medicine from the HBC's store.[40] This explanation did not console Clah, however, and he claimed that everyone blamed Bolton for the bad medicine. The village council called a meeting two days later at which both Crosby and Bolton were accused of killing Tsimshian children during the influenza epidemic. His request for funds

Dr. and Mrs. A.E. Bolton with their daughter Isabella and Misses Spencer
and Lawrence, Port Simpson. BC Archives, B-07114.

from the Tsimshian were resented that year, as they counted their dead
since his arrival in the community two years previously.[41]

When the next crisis, a measles epidemic, threatened the community
in February 1894, people again called on Bolton's medical expertise. Although Bolton put in long hours ministering to the sick, Clah pinned his
faith on God because the doctor appeared powerless to halt the deaths of
vulnerable children.[42] Two years later, however, Bolton saved Clah's
daughter Martha's life when she and her baby almost died in childbirth.[43]

After the turn of the century, Bolton's role as justice of the peace looms
larger than his medical practice in Clah's diary. It was in these years that
Clah sought Bolton's assistance with Dorcas' claim on Nisakx's (Martha

McNeill's) land in Victoria. Bolton helped Clah obtain the signatures required to grant power of attorney and then helped him secure the cancellation of that power. Both applications required much paperwork and correspondence. Clah continued to call on Bolton for help with his land matters, even after the doctor retired to Victoria. Although dependent on Bolton for legal assistance, Clah resented his presence at Port Simpson in many ways. Bolton's role as JP cast him as both magistrate and policeman, inevitably creating tensions. When Bolton left Port Simpson in 1902, Clah refused to contribute to his final request for money for his medical services to the community over the years.[44]

When S.S. Osterhout came to the Northwest Coast in the late 1890s, he too became enmeshed in the internal politics of the Tsimshian. In 1900, the Methodists and the Salvation Army factions at Port Simpson were still at loggerheads. The chiefs and elders of the Methodist Church wanted to remove the names of the adherents of the Salvation Army from the church register and abused Osterhout when he tried to prevent them; some threatened to leave the church if he persisted.[45] Clah, who was not directly involved in this power play, maintained an amicable relationship with Osterhout, who agreed to his request to write a foreword for his 1901 diary:

Memoir of The life of one of Christianity's first converts
on the North-west Coast
Kept with a view to the production of a history of the same region
See Psalm XC-10
"So teach us to number our days that we may apply our hearts
unto wisdom"
S.S. Osterhout[46]

Clah approached other missionaries to make similar entries. In 1903, he complained that William Collison had kept his "Big Book" for five years without writing in it. Yet, with Duncan no longer available to offer advice and support, Clah came to rely on Collison, along with Green, particularly for assistance with land matters.

In 1891, Clah had collared Collison and Green to assist his bid for the McNeill land in Victoria. Green, who had by then moved to Nanaimo, travelled to Victoria to see Clah's lawyer and the Indian agent to confirm

Dorcas' relationship with Nisakx and Niy'skinwaatk, while Clah asked Collison, who was then at Kincolith, to help him with legal matters relating to the elder George Niy'skinwaatk's will. Green was a strong supporter of Nisga'a and Tsimshian land rights and was viewed by the government as a dangerous radical who fomented Aboriginal people's dissatisfaction. In December 1889, when Green was at Port Simpson, he had helped Clah in his discussions with the reserve commissioner, Peter O'Reilly, about land allocation in the village.[47] A few weeks later, however, Clah complained that Green was assisting the government and that the Tsimshian wanted him removed from Port Simpson because he had suggested that the Tsimshian had no power, which was no doubt the case. This incident yet again illustrated the missionaries' untenable position in dealings between Aboriginal peoples and the government. Although they possessed no power and little influence, missionaries were persistently blamed for their failure to successfully represent Aboriginal interests.

William Duncan's strong personality and idiosyncratic view of his role as a missionary – particularly his refusal to be ordained or to give communion – had divided the CMS and the Anglican Church on the northern Coast. Robert Tomlinson (who also refused ordination) remained a strong supporter of Duncan, while Collison got caught in the crossfire between Duncan and Bishop William Ridley.[48] Tomlinson had arrived in Metlakatla in 1867 and had helped to set up Kincolith mission the same year. He had moved to the Skeena River to establish a new mission in 1879 but had left soon after for England to lodge a complaint against Ridley.[49] He resigned from the CMS in 1881 and maintained an independent Anglican mission on the Skeena River.

Clah encountered Tomlinson over many years on the Nass River and along the Coast, but he did not form a close relationship with the missionary. The two men did, however, have a couple of personal altercations. In Clah's view, Tomlinson could be petulant and discourteous. In 1874, Tomlinson supported Duncan in his initial threats against the Methodists at Fort Simpson. He visited the fort in March to make plain to its citizens the consequences of rejecting the Anglicans and embracing the Methodists: "[H]e says will be no more Maryestrat [magistrate] at FS [Fort Simpson]. If anybody fight[,] no more law[,] no judge[.] and if anyone laying sick[,] give no metisin [medicine] ... Tomlinson and Duncan very jealous. People says all right. God[,] his [he's] the great judge[.] Jesus Christ[,] he his the great man of war and he his the great Docteur. If anyone believe Him[,] he helping us in His Blood. If anybody laying sick take Jesus[,] [h]is Blood may help pline [blind] people."[50] Thus, the missionaries' teachings were thrown back at them. The Tsimshian did not need the missionaries because God supported them. He was not jealous or acrimonious but helped those poor blind people in need. The Tsimshian ignored Duncan's and Tomlinson's threats and warnings. By January 1875, the majority of Fort Simpson people had moved to the Methodist Church and the Anglicans' personal animosities quickly dissipated.[51] Although Tomlinson refused to shake hands with the Fort Simpson people in January 1875, by April the following year he was visiting Clah's house, shaking the hands of his erstwhile friends, and visiting the sick and providing them with medicine.[52]

Until Tomlinson left Kincolith in the late 1870s, Clah generally referred to the village as "Tomlinson's place." He was a frequent visitor at the village where Nisakx often resided and where other Nisga'a relatives lived. The village was on the way to the Nass fisheries and Clah's house at Laxk'a'ata (Canaan). Clah sometimes travelled to the village from Laxk'a'ata for Sunday services. In January 1879, Tomlinson arrested Clah for supplying three women with tobacco (it is not clear from the diary why this was regarded as illegal). Tomlinson kept Clah imprisoned at Kincolith for several days, during which time his large canoe broke up. Tomlinson released Clah with a five-pound fine to be paid within four days. Clah was unable to return in the specified time, so Tomlinson doubled the fine, forcing Clah to borrow the money under threat of imprisonment.[53] It must have been difficult for the Tsimshian and Nisga'a to distinguish the missionaries' secular and religious roles when they indulged in such highhanded behaviour.

The schoolteacher Henry Schutt, who assisted Tomlinson at Kincolith, was put temporarily in charge after Tomlinson left. If Clah's observations are correct, the two missionaries had an unhappy partnership. The diary may, however, reflect Clah's disdain for Schutt. On 23 December 1879, he complained that Schutt "preach very rough" when he claimed God would cut down the villagers of Gitlaxdamks and Gitwinksihlkxw (Kitwenselco, Canyon City) for continuing their heathen ways.[54] A few weeks later, Clah regaled people with an account of his nephew Charlie Abbott's near-death experience. According to Clah, Abbott had seen heaven and the Lord, who showed him the mountains and all the streams of the other world. On hearing Clah's report, Schutt called him into his house. He laughed at Clah and assured him that dreams could not reveal heaven or God. Clah disagreed, pointing to biblical accounts of Jacob, John, and Joseph. "But that was then," said Schutt, "when God sent down his words to earth." Clah, who believed he had a direct link with God, disputed Schutt's reading of the Bible. The next day, Schutt took up the issue of dreams in his sermon, debunking Clah's views. But it was not only Schutt's religious views that raised his ire, Clah also judged Schutt immoral for his addiction to tobacco: "I seen last Christmas and New year[,] he cried about tobacco when he short. He sent some girls to ask somebody who may have tobacco to smok[e]."[55] Many of the missionaries were flawed characters in Clah's eyes. If he respected their biblical knowledge, he also admired their preaching. Schutt did not even have this redeeming feature.

Unlike Schutt, Robert Cunningham was a fallen minister. In many ways, Clah's relationship with Cunningham was the most intriguing, for Cunningham barely ranked as a missionary. Following his arrival at Fort Simpson in 1863, and his dismissal by the CMS two years later (see Chapter 4), Cunningham worked for the HBC and remained on the Northwest Coast throughout his working life. Clah knew him first as a missionary, but for most of their acquaintance Cunningham was a trader, storekeeper and, later, cannery operator. The two men went hunting and trading together, and Cunningham employed Clah and many other Tsimshian to transport goods for him during the gold rush era. Cunningham did not have to maintain dual religious and secular roles after he left the CMS. Missionaries tended to hold themselves aloof from the local people to maintain their authority, whereas Cunningham worked closely with the Tsimshian. Clah had an ambivalent attitude towards Cunningham. He admired his business acumen and worked for him willingly, yet he often referred to him as a fallen minister and was offended by his womanizing and other self-interested behaviour.[56]

The last of the Anglican missionaries with whom Clah established a relationship was Fred L. Stephenson, a young priest who resided on the Coast in the mid-1890s. Stephenson baptized one of Clah's grandchildren in November 1894, and over the next few months came regularly to Clah's house to give him Bible lessons as Anglicans, Methodists, and Salvationists battled for followers on the streets and in the churches of Port Simpson. Stephenson must have learned Sm'algyax quickly, for he could preach in the language by December 1894. He did not participate in the denominational wars, as is illustrated by his willingness to administer the sacraments to Salvationists when Crosby refused to do so.[57]

Although Henry William Pierce was Clah's nephew, they were not close. One might expect that Clah would take pride in Pierce's accomplishments in the colonial world – an ordained minister, married to a white woman, and sent out by Crosby to establish missions along the coast and rivers. But none of these accomplishments are mentioned in his diary. Clah noted encounters with Pierce, but there is little mention of Pierce's elevated position in the mission system. Clah neither expresses pride in his relative nor indicates that he might have anything to gain from a close association with him. Although Clah went to the newcomer missionaries for help or advice, he did not believe that Pierce possessed either the status or connections to help him. Perhaps Clah disapproved of or distrusted Pierce's close association with Crosby, or perhaps he recognized that Pierce occupied a lowly position within the pecking order of the mission system and had little influence outside it.

Other Tsimshian preachers who are mentioned in mission records such as Samuel Pelham, George Edgar, David Leask, and Philip McKay (Wilum Clah) are not identified as such in Clah's diary.[58] He sometimes reports that they have taken a service, as he himself often did, but his reports on their activities are just as likely to concern land matters or social visits to his home. Tsimshian and Nisga'a preachers might have spread the Christian message, but they were not agents of change or modernization in Clah's mind. Thus, their actions appeared to him no more noteworthy than those of any other member of Tsimshian or Nisga'a society.

CLAH'S DREAMS
Many of the dreams Clah recounts in his diary focused on his relationship with missionaries and priests. In one dream, two unnamed ministers preach God's word on top of a mountain.[59] In another, Christ gives Clah passages to read from the Gospel of Mark 1:1-8, in which John the Baptist predicts the coming of Jesus Christ. His reading is interrupted by Cunningham, however, who calls him outside because his canoe has capsized.[60] On

another occasion, Clah dreamed of William Duncan, Robert Tomlinson, William Collison, Fred Stephenson, and Thomas Crosby.[61]

But the most fascinating dream is one in which Clah encounters Robert Cunningham, the fallen minister, with three upright Anglican ministers, Arthur Doolan, William Duncan, and Robert Tomlinson. Doolan takes money out of a small box that belongs to Clah, while Duncan winds up his broken clock to make it work again. Most intriguingly, Tomlinson gives Cunningham a putrid piece of meat and Clah a fresh one, but Cunningham swaps them, taking the best for himself.[62] In this complex dream, Doolan represents the grasping missionary who robs the poor Tsimshian, while Duncan assists them. Tomlinson rewards Clah for being a good Christian but punishes Cunningham for his sinful behaviour. However, Cunningham, ever opportunistic, cheats Clah of his due reward. The dream symbolizes Clah's ambivalent feelings towards missionaries in general. Missionaries could be helpful and supportive, but they also stole from the poor Tsimshian. Some were noble, while others were under-handed and only interested in their own advancement.

In another dream, Duncan works in Cunningham's store selling whisky, while Cunningham teaches Clah how to pray.[63] The dream suggests some sort of Freudian transference of characteristics from the bad missionary to the good one. But this dream and the others do not support Frantz Fanon's claim that the world of the colonized is a Manichean one in which "the dreams of the natives are always of muscular prowess; his dreams are of action and of aggression."[64] Clah's world, as reflected in his dreams, was not a world of stark alternatives. As in his lived existence, Clah always appeared to be hedging his bets.

CLAH'S VOYAGES OF DISCOVERY AND DISAPPOINTMENT WITH MISSIONARIES

Clah gained practical and religious knowledge from missionaries and learned other important skills, particularly reading and writing. He relied on them for help and advice on a wide range of issues that emerged as he dealt with the colonial state and society. He rarely criticized the mission-aries' preaching or services. He enjoyed preaching himself, but if he could attend Sunday services, whatever the denomination, he would do so. He appreciated the revivalist services offered by the Methodists, but he also

valued Duncan's more sober style and the noise and drama of the Salvation Army. Tensions arose between Clah and missionaries when they
stepped out of their religious role to become administrators or mediators
between the Tsimshian and colonial authorities. He expected missionaries
to be religious leaders, not to demand money to maintain the church.
When Crosby first came to Fort Simpson, Clah and the other Tsimshian
gladly donated money to build a church. This paralleled their practice of
helping chiefs or heads of households build a new house that would have
significance for the whole tribal group. But ongoing demands for money,
as in weekly collections at church, were not part of Tsimshian protocols
and came to be resented deeply. Clah and the Tsimshian thought the missionaries were lining their own pockets with this money and not using it
for the good of the whole community.

Both Anglican and Methodist missionaries established town councils
that they used to impose their will. These councils had the potential to
create tension and conflict, and this potential was realized at Port Simpson,
where the Tsimshian became increasingly disillusioned with Crosby. Their
move to the Salvation Army and offshoots of the Methodist church – the
Band of Christian Workers and the Epworth League – was a strategy to
exert more control over their secular and spiritual lives.

Missionaries also ran into trouble when they attempted to mediate
disputes between Aboriginal peoples and the government, particularly
disputes over land alienation. Their inability to influence colonial authorities was interpreted by the Tsimshian (and neighbouring peoples) as
connivance with the state. On the other hand, Clah continued to consult
with missionaries and call on them for help with his personal land dealings.
He asked both Collison and Green (but not Crosby) to intervene on his
behalf with public servants and lawyers in Victoria as late as 1909, long
after Green had moved away from the Coast.

Clah wanted the missionaries as friends and sought their acceptance
and regard, but he did not want them gratuitously interfering in his affairs
or telling him what to do or how to behave. As a member of Tsimshian
society, he wanted the missionaries to create opportunities for the Tsimshian in the emerging colonial economy and to defend their interests; he
did not want them controlling the way the community ran its affairs. In
reality, it was impossible for missionaries to live up to these various expectations and demands and remain responsive to their mission societies

without becoming totally isolated within the settler society. William Duncan managed these conflicting pressures better than most missionaries, at least until he became old and too set in his ways at New Metlakatla. He was able to retain the respect of the Tsimshian among whom he lived and died while at the same time maintaining a loyal and influential following in Canada, the United States, and Great Britain.

Clah's diary reveals missionaries as all too human. They could be generous and loyal friends. They tended the sick. They helped the Tsimshian communicate with colonial authorities. At other times, they were petty, jealous, and vindictive. They sometimes fought amongst themselves and broke the Christian codes they preached. Most missionaries took on secular roles such as magistrate, justice of the peace, and head of community councils. They swore in Aboriginal constables and organized building and maintenance projects in the villages. These myriad roles put them in sensitive situations that had the potential to create conflict with the people they evangelized. Nevertheless, Clah, and presumably other people on the Coast, expected missionaries to fulfill more than a purely religious role. He saw them as agents of change, a role Aboriginal evangelists could not fulfill. The changes they brought, however, while having short-term benefits, did not live up to expectations and were overtaken by the imposition of colonial rule.

10

The Changing World of Feasting

Clah fraternized with missionaries but was never part of the missionary world; he observed their schisms, arguments, and work but did not participate in them. He did business with fur traders, gold miners, storekeepers, cannery operators, and other newcomers on the Coast, but he was not part of their social world. He sought assistance from judges, lawyers, and Indian agents in Victoria but was not part of colonial society. He visited Victoria frequently, but he never contemplated living there himself. He had a Welsh son-in-law but seems to have had little empathy for him, although he did stay in his house on trips to Victoria. William Beynon Sr., however, is rarely mentioned in Clah's diary. Clah travelled the Coast from Seattle in the south to Juneau in the north, from Haida Gwaii in the west to the goldfields in the Interior, but his social existence was firmly anchored at Lax Kw'alaams (Fort Simpson) and on the Nass and the Skeena rivers.

Clah's social and political world revolved around the Tsimshian and Nisga'a, but his participation in this world changed as he evolved from an ambitious and curious young man to a mature adult with influence and authority to an old man with waning status. The world of which he was part also changed radically, and these changes had a huge impact on Tsimshian cultural practices. This chapter considers the internal dynamics of Tsimshian life, particularly the cycles of feasting or potlatching that occurred in the winter months. The chapter that follows focuses on the best known of the Tsimshian chiefly lineages, Ligeex; it explores the people who bore this name and the politics surrounding successions to the title.

Clah's diary offers a unique view of the changing world of feasting. The richness of this source as a means to understand this changing world is evident, particularly when compared to the sources Helen Codere had to rely on in the 1950s when she traced the changing nature of Kwakwa̲ka̲'wakw potlatching.[1] She found twenty-eight reports of potlatching between 1872 and 1924, most from hostile sources such as Indian agents and missionaries who were trying to suppress the practice. Codere assumed most Europeans opposed potlatching, while Kwakwa̲ka̲'wakw were in favour of continuing the practice. Her sources did not allow her to investigate Kwakwa̲ka̲'wakw community politics but merely to track the quantity and type of goods distributed over the nineteenth and into the twentieth century. She concluded that there was an increase in potlatching over the period: "That they chose to potlatch with the proceeds of their new economic achievements and that, as a result, potlatches became grander and potlatching more extensive is hardly surprising."[2]

After investigating Tsimshian potlatching through the lens of Clah's diary, it is clear that economic conditions were not the prime factor determining the future of the Tsimshian potlatch, but the goods and foods given away at these occasions did change as a result of fashion and availability. Clah's diary offers a perspective on internal tensions among the Tsimshian over the continuing role and importance of the potlatch. During the brief years that Duncan was at Fort Simpson, he had little impact on Tsimshian ceremonial life. When he moved with some of the chiefs to Metlakatla, however, he forced the Fort Simpson Tsimshian to continue their ceremonies in the absence of key participants such as paramount Chief Ligeex. The Tsimshian decision to invite the Methodists to Fort Simpson indicates they were willing to modify their feasting system and follow the lead of Thomas Crosby. In the 1880s, when conflict between Duncan and Ridley at Metlakatla was out in the open and disillusionment with Crosby had set in at Fort Simpson, there was a revival of feasting and a renewed interest in chiefly leadership. The revival introduced innovations in feasting activities that extended to the products distributed, the acts performed, and the manner in which the Tsimshian memorialized their dead chiefs and elders. Accession to names also became increasingly controversial as high death rates and economic and political pressures disrupted lines of inheritance.

Although Clah's descriptions of daily life begin in the early 1860s, he was so preoccupied with establishing himself as a fur trader that it was not until the mid-1860s that he began to record and comment on communal affairs. The winter months from November to February, when the Tsimshian retreated to their home villages, were devoted largely to social and political consolidation. This was the time when Tsimshian publicly expressed their lineage and tribal links and their mutual obligations. These connections were most visibly manifest in their feasts. There were also lineage, clan, tribal, and village council meetings. After the arrival of Christian missionaries, church services, class meetings, and the work of secular organizations such as the Riflemen's and Firemen's associations also became part of the social calendar. In any one year, some of these forms of communal interaction would predominate over others. Some winters, feasting or potlatching reached such a pitch that there were several feasts each day; other years, there were few or no feasts.[3] During Christian revivals, the Tsimshian spent much more time in church or church meetings.

Anthropologist Christopher F. Roth points out that the matrilineage of the house "is the strongest and most naturalized level of Tsimshian social membership."[4] Unfortunately, Clah reveals little about the dynamics of his house other than its name, T'amks, to which he succeeded in the late 1860s. His references to his house tend to be implicit rather than explicit. He refers often to brothers such as Henry and Matthew Shepherd who were not biological brothers but rather clan or matrilineage brothers.[5] Clah felt no need to explain the context of everyday life and social relations.

Feasting did not occur in a social or political vacuum. Much discussion was required to fix the timing of an event, the participants, and the resources required. Feasts were held to mark a wide variety of rites of passage, including birth, marriage, death, funerals, the inheritance of a name, and the completion of a new house. These events presented crucial opportunities to enhance an individual's status, shame rivals, or both. The feasts of greatest significance to the community as a whole followed the deaths of important leaders. Confirmation of successors required public ceremonies attended by designated dignitaries. William Beynon identifies three customary potlatch feasts – mourning, memorial, and completion – that culminated in the assumption of the hereditary name.[6] In the nineteenth century, these feast cycles were the focus of political activity to maintain the hierarchical structures and internal coherence of Tsimshian life. By the latter part of the century, however, the impact of Christianity, economic change, and the colonial state had significantly undermined – but not obliterated – old social forms and structures. Many survive to this day.

Even though there were positive interactions between the Tsimshian economy and European commercial capitalism – witness the cooperation between Aboriginal people and newcomers in the fur trade – newcomers were by turns bemused, repelled, and fascinated by the practice of potlatching. They admired the materialism and competition of potlatching but bemoaned what they saw as a wasteful distribution and destruction of goods. Few, if any, fully comprehended its social, political, and economic functions. As Roth explains,

> [A]ll of the goods and activities at a feast are mobilized to signify and value the newly named person's rank and that of his lineage. Rank – established through one's own action, staged for others – is one's relationship to the wider social world; reciprocity, by contrast, is one's relationship with that world, established through interaction. A lineage chief assumes and enhances his and his lineage's political agency through the strategic deployment of goods, by negotiating an equivalence between the gifts given to guests and other goods that are never given away. Inalienable wealth is retained and a lineage's essence and capacity for meaningful social action preserved – only through the socially contingent process of paying witnesses.[7]

There was little real waste; rather, there was a realignment of goods and people, facilitating generational change. Potlatching also helped Northwest Coast societies adapt to altered circumstances, such as depopulation, political upheaval, and the impact of the global economy.

FUR TRADE ERA

Over the fifty-year period of Clah's diary, the format of feasts varied, as their ostensible purpose as Christian practices displaced what Clah called old-fashioned ways. Christianity, however, was not the only external influence on feasting behaviours. The food and goods offered at feasts varied as different products became available to the Tsimshian through an expanding trade network that linked them to the industrializing world. At the height of the liquor trade in the 1860s and into the early 1870s, Clah described most feasts as whisky feasts, even though other foods and goods were distributed. During the mid- and late 1870s and early 1880s, he calls most feasts bread and molasses feasts because hard bread or biscuits had become the primary food offering. Although the government declared potlatching illegal in 1884, it devoted few resources to stamping out the practice. Various interest groups – Indian agents, missionaries, and factions within Tsimshian communities – tried to employ the ban to their own advantage.

The first feast Clah mentions in his diary is the one he hosted on New Year's Eve in 1862 for his own Gispaxloots people (see Chapter 3). He describes it as a rice feast, even though he also distributed flour. Although the idea of presenting four hundred young men as soldiers was probably novel, acting out roles and imitating others was a pastime enjoyed by all Tsimshian. In the account of his journey through the Nisga'a hinterland in 1870, George Chismore notes that imitative theatrical displays were common. Clah's feast and display were part of a series held to claim his uncle's title as head of the lineage of T'amks. In November 1863, while Clah was living on the Nass River, Chief Niy'skinawaatk, died.[8] Clah returned to the village of Gitlaxdamks to host a feast in honour of his wife's relative. He gave away fifty pounds of rice, four gallons of molasses, and seventy pounds of flour.[9] The food distributed at both of these feasts was introduced products traded at stores.

Clah stayed on the Nass River through the winter but returned to Fort Simpson the winter of the following year, when many mortuary feasts were held, including one for the Gitando chief, Sgagweet.[10] Because Clah's trading activities in the 1860s often took him away from home, even in winter, he does not provide a continuous chronicle of events at Fort Simpson. It is, nonetheless, apparent that much feasting throughout the Northwest Coast centred on the distribution of liquor. Clah reported many Gispaxloots whisky feasts at Fort Simpson in the winter of 1866.[11]

The Gispaxloots held feasts in the absence of their primary chief, Ligeex (Paul Legaic I), who had moved to Metlakatla in 1862.[12] His house was still used by the tribe and his rank was recognized, but the holder of the head chieftainship was missing. Clah had dispatched an emissary to Metlakatla to invite Ligeex to his house raising, but Duncan had intervened to stop him from attending. It was after this feast that Duncan hoisted the black flag to indicate his displeasure with Clah's behaviour. Most of the feasts Clah reported in the 1860s were mortuary feasts to commemorate the deceased and transmit the title to an heir who, in subsequent feasts, earned the right to bear that name. On 23 November 1870, there were three mortuary feasts in the village: a Gispaxloˑots whisky feast and two rice feasts, one of them for the Ginaxangiik chief 'Wiiseeks, which was followed the next day by a "great" feast at which 60 casks of rice, 4 casks of molasses, many boxes of bread, and 160 blankets were distributed.[13]

Although Clah does not specifically say so, some of the feasts must have been what Viola Garfield calls challenge feasts, in which chiefs sought to humiliate their guests by plying them with more food and drink than they could consume, thereby shaming them and asserting their own superiority. With the advent of the liquor trade, hogsheads of rum or whisky were substituted for food at these feasts.[14] Although feasts acknowledging births, initiations, and marriages must have occurred during this period, Clah mentions only the feast held for his own son David when he took his maternal uncle's name, Gwisk'aayn (spelled *Kuskin* by Clah) in 1871 (see Chapter 3).[15] And Clah also hosted a feast for Niisyaganaat, a Gits'iis chief who, with his four companions, had saved Clah's life when his canoe overturned in October 1870.[16]

Much of the time, Clah reports the interactions at feasts without critical comment. For instance, he notes that a feast hosted by the Gitando made the top-ranking chiefs happy, while many guests expressed dissatisfaction with their gifts. He does not make a judgment as to whether the guests were justified in their complaints. His commentary runs to strong condemnation, however, of the secret society feasts that were frequent prior to Crosby's arrival. In early December 1870, Alfred Dudoward and Paul Legaic II participated in a series of these feasts: "Dancing every days an[d] every nights[.] Tsimshens eating dogs fresh [flesh]. Some eating died body[.] Canener [Cannibals]. others bre[a]cking canoes, boxs." These rituals continued into February, when frenzied participants ran around the village clearing frightened residents from their path.[17]

The Hudson's Bay Company welcomed these extravagant events because the participants bought the goods they distributed at its store. On Clah's evidence, few hosts distributed traditional foods and goods such as eulachon oil, fish, or handmade products. Most of the provisions and goods were bought from stores. After his move to Metlakatla, Duncan could not influence these rituals, although he was more effective in reducing the distribution of liquor (see Chapter 3).[18]

Clah stated in February 1871 that he would no longer participate in the chiefly system. This decision does not appear to be linked to his Christian commitment. It probably reflected his disapproval of the choice of the new Ligeex, for he had refused to support Paul Legaic II's final potlatch to succeed to the Ligeex name. (His disenchantment did not last for long, however: a year later, Clah helped with Legaic's house building.)[19] Clah returned all the goods he had received during the potlatch for his son's naming feast, which had taken place earlier that month.[20] Two days after he returned the goods, he held a feast for the village at which he gave away biscuits and molasses. He calculated that he had spent $395 over the month. The feast was preparatory to Clah cutting down the crest pole in front of his house and announcing to the Tsimshian that they should renounce the chiefly system and keep their money for themselves. Not surprisingly, this action caused some controversy in the community, even among his own relatives.[21]

Clah's conduct appears on the surface to challenge the social fabric of his society. Yet subsequent diary entries do not reflect any radical upheaval in his life. Clah wanted to indicate his disapproval of certain individuals and practices, but he did not stray beyond acceptable parameters of behaviour. His lack of support for Paul Legaic II was not a rejection of the Ligeex chieftainship, for there is no indication that he promoted a rival chiefly lineage. Although Clah was sometimes a cranky critic of Tsimshian society, he was a reformist, not a revolutionary. His day-by-day account of life belies his occasional claims to radicalism; rather, it reflects his manoeuverings inside the bounds of Tsimshian social behaviour. The destruction of the crest pole was appropriately accompanied by a feast.[22] Although he challenged the chiefly system, Clah also clearly continued to attend feasts at Fort Simpson. During the 1871-72 winter ceremonial season, Clah not only listed the many feasts that took place but also the goods he had received at them.[23]

Apart from liquor (thirty to forty gallons seem to have been consumed at feasts prior to the HMS *Sparrowhawk*'s second visit to destroy the illicit liquor trade [see Chapter 3]), the goods gifted during the season were domestic products purchased from stores, such as bars of soap, lengths of calico, and plates, cups and saucers. Traditional pelts were given away at only one large mortuary feast, and the Ginaxangiik chief, 'Wiiseeks, presented chiefly guests with 103 muskets at another.[24]

THE CHANGING NATURE OF FEASTS

The winter of 1873-74 was a time of deep division at Fort Simpson (see Chapter 7). Alfred and Kate Dudoward had returned from Victoria as dedicated Methodists, and Alfred was trying to ensure, by attending feasts, that his status in Tsimshian society was not damaged by his commitment to Christianity. The traditionalists were in disarray because many people had left to visit Metlakatla for Christmas at the height of the ceremonial season. By the following winter, Methodist missionary Thomas Crosby had made his home in the village, and the Christian forces were in the ascendance. It must have been around this time that the Tsimshian decided not to support the chiefly system, for there are no recorded mortuary feasts.[25] Wedding feasts became more significant, many of them no doubt associated with Christian marriages. Clah and Dorcas solemnized their union on April Fool's Day 1875. Clah had decided that his marriage would not be celebrated with a feast. His decision caused consternation because yet another Tsimshian institution was being challenged. The only legitimate reason left for feasting was the winter celebration, which more or less coincided with Christmas. The Christmas of 1876 was marked by feasts, now called Christmas feasts, at which people sedately consumed tea, sugar, and bread, a far cry from the raucous and violent whisky feasts of years past. Missionaries are generally given credit for this change in behaviour. Although missionaries were the instruments through which the turbulent and destructive activities associated with feasts in the 1860s and early 1870s were curbed, it was the balance of opinion among the Tsimshian that enabled radical changes to be implemented.

In 1877, Clah and his family moved to the upper Nass River where the Nisga'a continued their winter ceremonies. Clah introduced them to the Christmas feast when he invited from three hundred to four hundred people to his home on Christmas Day. In reality, the feast was a celebration to mark the completion of his house at Gitlaxdamks.[26] Three years later, however, Gitlaxdamks was almost deserted. People had moved away to Kincolith, Metlakatla, and other missions. On a visit in 1880, Clah found his wife's uncle Gwisk'aayn and his wife alone in their house.[27]

Although Clah did not maintain a winter house at Port Simpson between 1877 and 1885, he did return there regularly and, from 1880, was actively involved in Port Simpson affairs. Communal activities were now discussed at council meetings overseen by the missionary rather than at feasts and other traditionally constituted gatherings. Instead of debating accessions to chiefly and lineage names, council members debated the state of village roads. Rather than working for chiefs on their houses, men were requisitioned to work on Port Simpson's roads and taxed if they did not perform voluntary labour.[28] Although official affairs were now negotiated in this way, the old ways crept back. Throughout the 1880 Christmas season, for instance, the Port Simpson Tsimshian held mortuary feasts. Although the goods distributed were associated with Christmas feasts – tea, sugar, and biscuits – they were clearly intended to commemorate the dead.

Hundreds of people left the village on 29 December 1880 to celebrate the New Year at Metlakatla. Clah accepted this invitation enthusiastically and might have instigated the invitation as a means to undermine the traditionalists in his village, although a more likely explanation was Duncan's need to consolidate his relations with Crosby and Port Simpson Christians because he was being undermined by his own bishop and cut off from Church Missionary Society funding.[29] The villagers were invited to Christian feasts and, on New Year's Day, the Firemen's and Riflemen's bands from Port Simpson played. When the group returned to Port Simpson, those who had remained behind tried to shame them, as Clah had seven years previously, by firing cannon as they returned home.[30]

In January 1881, the Port Simpson council decided to organize the village into companies. Clah was put in charge of the Riflemen's Company and assigned the task of training them. He told the council that if they wanted a Soldiers' Company, it would need ammunition, guns, coats, hats, and everything else appropriate for a soldier.[31] Clah's involvement in community affairs began to take up increasing amounts of his time, to the detriment of his family.[32]

The following year, Clah and his family returned to Port Simpson for the winter season and for the wedding of their daughter Martha to William West. Both the Firemen's and Riflemen's bands played at the wedding feast, which was one of many feasts held that season.[33]

The Tsimshian experiment of allowing the chiefly system to erode by not replacing chiefs and other lineage heads as they died had begun to falter by 1882-83. As tensions between William Duncan and Bishop William Ridley began to disrupt life at Metlakatla, the Tsimshian had begun to reassess their decision. In early 1882, rumours circulated that several chiefs at Metlakatla were considering moving back to Port Simpson.[34] They had retained their chiefly names at Metlakatla but performed no chiefly functions. If they moved back to Port Simpson, they would resume their responsibilities. These rumours led to debate at Port Simpson about social and political structures. A meeting of chiefs and elders *(lik'agigyet)* was held in November 1883 to discuss the issue. Albert 'Alamlaxha hosted the meeting and invited his guests to indulge in what must have been the unfamiliar ritual of washing their hands with soap before drying them with a towel. They were then given a drink of water before they ate salmon and fish grease, followed by boiled herring eggs, cranberries, and blackberries. As soon as the discussion about reinstating chiefs began, however, the Christians, including Clah, walked out. Despite this lack of unanimity, mortuary and naming feasts once again became part of Port Simpson village life.[35] The decision coincided with growing apprehension among the Tsimshian and Nisga'a that the government intended to sell their lands. Well-founded rumours had begun to circulate that the government had already sold land without the Tsimshian's approval. The Tsimshian were also losing faith in Crosby as an effective advocate. The revival of strong chiefs might have been a strategy to give their community a stronger voice in negotiations rather than relying on mission or government intermediaries.[36] It is, therefore, likely that the decision to revive lineage heads and chiefdoms was done both for conservative reasons, looking back to the past, and for the pragmatic purpose of providing strong leadership in uncertain times.

In the meantime, the newly appointed Indian agent, J.W. McKay, had asked the Tsimshian to establish a council under the aegis of the government rather than the mission. Moses McDonald, Richard Wilson, Alfred Dudoward, Arthur Wellington Clah, and Thomas Crosby discussed the composition of the new council. Crosby wanted it to operate under "white law," while Clah and Dudoward (for once in agreement) argued that they should use Tsimshian law because, under white law, the Tsimshian only lost power. The council decided that one of its first tasks should be to clean up the village. Clah, as head of the Riflemen's Company, was sent around the village to enforce compliance.[37] Despite his period away from Port

Simpson and his public disapproval of so-called old-fashioned ways, Clah's status as a lig'agyet was plainly in the ascendant. He was now a man in his fifties. Ligeex, as we shall see, had been living at Metlakatla but was about to return to Port Simpson. Clah, as the head of one of the foremost lineages of the Gispaxlo'ots, was acting in a power vacuum created by the chief's absence.

THE REVIVAL OF THE LINEAGE AND CHIEFLY SYSTEM

With the revival of Tsimshian power structures, competition between the tribal groups intensified. In November 1883, the Gispaxlo'ots campaigned for Ligeex's return to Port Simpson before other groups such as the Gitando and Ginaxangiik established precedence over them.[38] When Moses Venn, another Gispaxlo'ots chief, held a feast on his return to Port Simpson, Clah gave the first speech at what might have been a mortuary feast for Venn's brother.[39] Sensing opportunity in the new climate of opinion, Clah decided to move back to Port Simpson permanently in 1885 and commenced building a house.

This house construction raises an interesting question to which there is no definitive answer. When Clah left Port Simpson in 1877, what happened to his house and the other people who were living in it? When he moved to Gitlaxdamks and then Laxk'a'ata (Canaan), it is likely that he took his immediate family with him but not his lineage relatives, although some did build their own houses at Laxk'a'ata. On returning to Port Simpson, he built a new house, which was probably a European-style frame house, because lineage plank houses were no longer being constructed.[40] Rather than seeking support from his lineage to build the house, Clah relied on his own resources and funds from Dorcas (a wife normally supported her husband's house building, even though she was not of his lineage).[41] Dorcas, annoyed with Clah, decided to withdraw her financial support. She pointed out that the blankets he intended to use to fund the building belonged to her. As a result, Clah negotiated a loan from George Williscroft, the sawmill owner at Georgetown, who supplied Clah with 3,350 feet of lumber at a cost of $34.50.[42] The erection of this house marked the beginning of Clah's long dispute with the HBC over the land on which it was built (see Chapter 6). Despite warnings from the HBC, the house was completed in mid-January 1886.[43]

Paul Legaic II, on his return to Port Simpson in 1885, also needed to build a house. As the foremost Gispaxlo'ots chief, he could call on his tribal members to help him. The house could not be built for a year, however, until the tribe had accumulated the necessary funds.[44]

As chiefs returned to Port Simpson and as names that had lain vacant were filled, the Tsimshian made major innovations in their mortuary feasts. In the past, the end of the cycle of feasts for the investiture of high-ranking persons had been marked by the raising of a crest pole in commemoration of their predecessors.[45] The poles were a record of the lineage of the deceased, carved by people who stood as "fathers" to the poles' owners.[46] Guests at the potlatch raised the pole while the owner explained the crests and their histories.[47] After 1885, stone markers or monuments were increasingly used to commemorate the deceased.[48] Ordering and delivery a gravestone required more planning than crest poles because the gravestones came to Port Simpson from Victoria by steamer and were then transported from the wharf. In January 1887, Clah wondered about the implications of supplying gravestones for all those who had died: "[S]o I think [about] w[h]ere all the friends lay. I think over half million dollar cost all them whit[e] stone."[49]

In the meantime, Clah's household was busy making biscuits for the feasting season: "[W]e make many Biscuits[.] me an[d] wife going to feast day houses everyday. Some days make 40 Biscuits, some 30[,] or 2.15 sometimes. Besides I use my own cups an[d] sarsar [saucer]. Because invitation says in every feast houses to use own in feast house to we used with oursel[v]es."[50] While feasting continued at an accelerated rate during the winter of 1887, the Tsimshian grappled with the implications of gravestones. Alfred Dudoward's mother, Elizabeth Diex, brought a large gravestone up from Victoria for the mortuary feast for Sgagweet (Paul Scoweed). Despite having been an early convert to Methodism, she came "songing old fashi [singing in the old-fashioned way]" to the accompaniment of cannon fire.[51] Alfred Dudoward, who inherited the title, and the Gitando wanted to use the occasion to elevate Sgagweet as the pre-eminent name among the Tsimshian. Both Dudoward and his mother spent many years positioning Alfred to take a leading role at Port Simpson. Dudoward's mixed heritage was both an advantage (it had given him access to newcomer networks and schooling at a young age) and a disadvantage (some

Totem poles, Fort Simpson, 1870s. BC Archives, F-07012.

Tsimshian, Clah included, viewed him with suspicion). The Gitando, led by Dudoward, planned to cut down the Sgagweet pole and replace it with a stone memorial that would elevate Sgagweet in a modern yet elaborate way. The other Tsimshian chiefs met in Paul Legaic's house and decided that the pole should not be removed but should stand alongside the stone monument. The chiefs sent Clah and John Ryan to the Gitando to convey their decision, which was challenged by the Gitando, who demanded to know how many and which chiefs were involved. One young man turned on Clah, pointing out that he had initiated the removal of crest poles. Dzagmgishaaytks, another hostile Gitando chief, reminded Clah that in the old times strangers who came to a meeting uninvited would have been enslaved. Ryan and Clah returned to report to the chiefs at Paul Legaic's house that the Gitando had decided to compromise and cut down only half the pole, leaving some of the carved crests standing.

The next day, two dozen cannon shots heralded the removal of the stone from the HBC's wharf. The Firemen's Company followed the stone along the street and continued to play as the old pole was cut in half. Blankets, coats, shirts, guns, axes, and fifty dollars were paid to those who undertook these duties. Cash amounting to more than one thousand dollars was given away, and more great feasts were promised.[52] A week later, Dudoward invited all the chiefs to Dzagmgishaaytks' house to display the $750 he had collected to pay for the $500 stone.[53] Dudoward and some other Gitando chiefs then set out to raise the status of the tribe relative to larger ones.

The revival of the lineage and chiefly system was in full flow throughout the winter. Mortuary feasts were held almost nightly. In the midst of this frenzied activity, as the Gispaxlo'ots continued to agonize over whether to replace their crest pole with a stone monument, the pole blew down in a storm. In Legaic's absence, Clah assumed responsibility for dealing with the catastrophe. The pole fell at high tide, and two canoes were used to tow it from the water. Clah felt vindicated, because he had advised replacing the pole with a memorial stone. Niisbalaas, a female Gispaxlo'ots chief, invited all Tsimshian to a feast for the fallen crests, and the Gitando watched the development with interest. Alfred Dudoward (now Sgagweet) came to Clah's house to find out what the Gispaxlo'ots would do, while his mother, who came from the Gispaxlo'ots tribe, gave unsolicited advice that the pole should be replaced by a stone monument.[54] Meetings in many Gispaxlo'ots houses followed. People debated what should be done as they waited for Paul Legaic II to return to Port Simpson from a hunting trip. When he finally arrived, they decided to have a large "Christmas feast" to reassure the Gispaxlo'ots and the Tsimshian more generally that Legaic was still pre-eminent (see Chapter 11).

Despite Clah's concerns that the revival of the old ways was turning people away from Christ, between seven hundred and eight hundred people attended the Methodist Church on Christmas Day, 1887. People dressed up for the occasion, and a number of children were baptized. Nevertheless, Clah's fears were not allayed, for he recognized that Christmas feasts did not rule out naming feasts, which were rife that season.[55] Although Clah criticized this reassertion of the old ways, he inevitably participated. The movement to reclaim names of deceased chiefs and lineage heads led some with only limited resources to make claims. One of these was David Morrison, Clah's father's brother's son (his cousin), who wanted to inherit his father's name of Niis'wa'mak.[56] As he was preparing to host a feast, he was humiliated at a Gitxaala feast. Morrison, distraught, came to Clah and probably did not leave reassured when Clah predicted that the chiefly pride displayed at the feast would not survive God's condemnation. That night, Morrison hosted a feast for chiefs at Clah's house, at which he distributed guns, coats, shirts, and blankets. Clah tried to dissuade David with the argument that he did not have the resources to support his claim: "Because in our law[,] If anyone want to be chief. Spent many thousands of dollars."[57] Ignoring Clah's counsel, Morrison held a feast the following day in Paul Legaic's house at which he offered chiefs only twenty dollars' worth of food. Two years later, Clah was still trying unsuccessfully to deflect Morrison from his determination to acquire the chiefly title as Morrison held a feast for Nisga'a guests for his newly built house at Laxk'a'ata (Canaan).[58] This suggests Morrison was asserting a stronger claim to the land through his father than the one Clah held through his paternal line.

THE SALVATION ARMY AND THE ANTI-CHIEF MOVEMENT
Even as Clah simultaneously denounced and participated in the resurgence of the old ways, another, stronger, anti-chief movement appeared in Port Simpson – the Salvation Army. It is difficult to unravel the religious, social, and power politics at work, but it is clear that there was strong antipathy

between chiefs such as Alfred Dudoward, who were working to expand their power base, and members of the Salvation Army such as Paul Brentzen (a Gispaxloʼots Eagle) and his wife, who were opposed to the chiefly system: "[A]ll Salvation stand outside singing an[d] pray morning an[d] evening. Salvation keep speak in the street to stop big feast. stop Brand [?] heart spend you mon[e]y for Big feast[.] that make god angry."[59] Henry Tate, Clah's son, who was closely aligned with the Salvation Army, criticized Clah for having a foot in each camp, condemning feasts while participating in them. He advised Clah that he should return to his early Christian commitment as described in William Duncan's book.[60]

The conflict between the Salvation Army and the chiefs reached a climax in December 1892, during the last Christian revival of Crosby's tenure at Port Simpson. In the first days of the new year, a chief, Maalmgoobn (spelled *Mellam-cooper* by Clah), who had been preparing a grand feast in memory of a son and had had a gravestone carved in the shape of a sea lion for the memorial, shot himself because he believed the Christians would prevent his potlatch.[61] Then, when negotiations between the Methodists (ironically, supported by the chiefs) and the Salvation Army were underway for the use of the hall for services, Dudoward (Sgagweet) and his brother-in-law Albert McMillan (ʼWiiseeks) arranged for the Salvation Army to be locked out. The Gits'iis tribe supported the lockout because the Salvationists had stopped a gravestone-raising feast for their deceased chief. Plans for the erection of another twelve gravestones were now in jeopardy. The Salvation Army had alienated chiefs in all the tribes, and they were calling for the Salvationists' removal from the village.[62]

As various groups in the community mobilized against feasts, an invitation arrived from the Nisga'a chief, Mountain, for a gravestone-raising potlatch at Kincolith. A large group of people came together to decide whether to accept the invitation, and they once again decided to quash the chiefly and lineage system.[63] The next winter, at a follow-up meeting at Ligeex's house, the chiefs and lineage heads decided, perhaps not surprisingly given the composition of the group, to reinstate chiefs and prohibit the Salvation Army from undermining them.[64] Yet not all the chiefs were of one mind. Niishoʼot (Albert Nelson), who had attended Mountain's ceremony, invited guests to the Riflemen's Hall to apologize for breaking Port Simpson's rules.[65] A few weeks later, Niisbalaas called her people together to instruct them not to commemorate her when she died.[66]

Government and missionaries impinged in various ways on Tsimshian internal politics – primarily by banning potlatches but also by passing laws that defined "Indianness." Dudoward was the son of a Tsimshian mother and French Canadian fur trader. Under the Indian Act of 1876, he was not legally recognized as an Indian. Over the years, Clah made several references to Dudoward's mixed descent and implied that it was inappropriate for a so-called half-breed to be participating in secret society rituals. Some official action must have been taken to define Dudoward's status in 1890, because the Tsimshian discussed throwing him out because he had Canadian citizenship and was, therefore, no longer a member of their community.[67] From Clah's perspective, Dudoward should have renounced his citizenship; Dudoward, however, could not change his racial identity, as defined by Canadian law.

In December 1888, Clah wrote that his wife, Dorcas, also felt that she had been barred from Tsimshian citizenship during the revival of the potlatch. She had apparently been excluded from a feast for high-ranking women, which had made her feel something of an alien at Fort Simpson: "[M]y wife vexed me this morning. she plame [blame] herself at for married me[.] she wants married at Nasiki [Nisga'a] chief. she telling me that my hearts very full darkness. some she said that I got mouse in my heart and my belly[.] she telling me everything bad. she wish to move of at nass river were she belongs. [She says, ']I am not citizen in this place.'"[68] The re-emergence of the Tsimshian hierarchical system was accompanied by a heightened sense of Tsimshian identity; both were strengthened by government moves to alienate Tsimshian land and bring the Tsimshian under direct state control.

THE LAW AGAINST THE POTLATCH

The revival of feasting among both the Tsimshian and the Nisga'a occurred after the Canadian government had amended the Indian Act in 1884 (proclaimed 1 January 1885) to ban the potlatch. As historian Robin Fisher notes, the law was impractical and impossible to enforce. The first person arrested under the amended Act, in 1889, was Kwakwaka'wakw, but the presiding judge dismissed the case and condemned both the law and its application.[69] By the 1930s, however, when anthropologist Viola Garfield was undertaking fieldwork, the impact of the ban had become evident.[70] What has not been generally recognized in debates about the suppression of the potlatch is the strength of anti-potlatch forces within indigenous communities. In 1891, anti-potlatch zealots tried unsuccessfully to embroil the Methodist missionaries in their campaign. The Gispaxlo'ots chief, Xpi'lk (Lucy Wright), invited all the chiefs' wives to a feast in the Riflemen's Hall. Matthew Shepherd and Matthew Johnson approached Dr. Albert Edward Bolton, the mission doctor and justice of the peace, to stop the feast, pointing out it was against the Queen's law. When Bolton refused to act, they went to Robert H. Hall, the HBC officer and magistrate at Port Simpson. He fobbed them off onto Crosby. Despite Shepherd and Johnson's threats that they would prevent him from preaching if he did not stop the feast, Crosby did not intervene.

Clah reported that Crosby and "all leaders Elders [im]prisoned last night for falling." It is unlikely that he meant they were physically imprisoned; however, the next day, a Sunday, Bolton led the church service in Crosby's stead. Bolton recorded in his diary that Crosby had asked him to take over because the leaders had asked him to remain silent for acceding to the potlatches.[71] It is not clear why Shepherd and Johnson took exception to this particular feast. Both were Gispaxlo'ots, and Johnson, at least, had contributed handkerchiefs from his own store to Xpi'lk's resources. This suggests it was not merely anti-potlatch sentiments that motivated him.[72] Viola Garfield, who used Matthew Johnson as an informant in the 1930s, noted that he had been Crosby's assistant and had been instrumental in persuading some Tsimshian "to sign a statement about thirty years ago, disavowing all native customs."[73]

Xpi'lk's feast was followed the next day by another women's feast, this time in the Ginaxangiik tribe, and hosted by the wife of chief Albert McMillan, 'Wiiseeks. She distributed shawls and provisions. On the same day, there was a large wedding feast for six hundred people at which thirty-four boxes of biscuits were given away.[74] That no attempt was made to stop these feasts indicates that the anti-potlatch movement at the time was not universal, but confined to the Gispaxlo'ots. Not long after, however, having been thrown into turmoil by the sudden death of Paul Legaic II, the Gispaxlo'ots also returned to potlatching.

Although Crosby avoided directly confronting the Tsimshian about their feasting, he did employ other strategies that suggest he remained uncertain about what were and were not acceptable celebrations. In March, a steamer from Victoria delivered a large gravestone for the Gits'iis after seven months' delay. It was rumoured that Crosby had asked the provincial government to hold up delivery to avoid a large potlatch during the Christmas celebrations.[75]

On the Nass River, conflicts over potlatching were more prolonged and fraught than at Port Simpson, partly because some Nisga'a chose to live in villages where missionaries had no influence and where the whole range of potlatch activities remained a vital part of winter life. Others were caught up in Anglican and Methodist rivalries.[76] In 1886, for instance, Justice A.C. Elliot sent a circular to chiefs on the Nass River to inform them that they could be jailed for six months for holding a potlatch.[77] Because the law banning the potlatch did not recognize the broad range of activities that fell under the umbrella of the Chinook Jargon term *potlatch,* people were uncertain about which activities had been outlawed. In 1898, a Nisga'a chief wrote to Victoria to ask for clarification of the law. He explained that the missionary James McCullagh had reported him and a number of other chiefs for raising a war party against missionaries who had persuaded another chief to give up potlatching: "If we are not allowed to potlatch we will stop. Tell us exactly how the law stands. If we are allowed by law to potlatch[,] and you say so[,] we will do it. Mr McCulloch [sic] says if we get a little boy or girl and make a present[,] or [if] a friend makes a present. Or if anybody dies and a present is made to the survivor, he will summon and fine us. Is this right?"[78] McCullagh's attempts to curtail feasts met with little success. When Clah arrived on the Nass in 1891, he found another missionary, the Methodist teacher Stone, trying to drum up support for an anti-potlatch petition. Clah pointed out to Stone that a man-of-war had not been able to stop potlatching two years previously, and he suggested that he should negotiate directly with the potlatchers.[79]

At Port Simpson, feasts continued unabated, although Tsimshian were fully aware of the law. At one feast, Dudoward assured people they would not be jailed for potlatching.[80] In the winter of 1891-92, Clah despaired and complained that Tsimshian had abandoned Christianity for naming feasts: "If any brother or uncle die[,] start big feast. Take uncles name or brothers name. [F]irst we take Jesus name when we baptized. Now we change in the wicked name."[81] But Clah never consistently stood against the "old-fashioned ways." As he bemoaned the plethora of naming feasts, he and other senior Gispaxlo'ots were planning a large memorial stone for all the Ligeexs, a stone that would ensure that the title remained pre-eminent among the Tsimshian. In 1902, when the young, female Ligeex died with no immediate heir, the Tsimshian went through another long succession controversy.

Even though feasting seems to have been in abeyance at Port Simpson throughout the late 1890s – when the town council, headed by a chief, became the focus of village politics – mortuary feasts and other feasts once again became common in the early years of the twentieth century. In 1903, Clah recorded that his son Albert, as heir to his deceased Nisga'a maternal uncle, had succeeded to the Gitlan Wolf crest chiefly name of Gwisk'aayn. At the time, Albert was living with his parents at Port Simpson, not at Gitlaxdamks, the home of his mother's family. A member of the Wolf crest (laxgibuu) came to Clah's house in November to invite Albert to host a feast before he became their chief. Clah voiced no concerns over his son taking his uncle's name. Two days later, Albert held a snow feast, a trad-itional Wolf Clan feast, at which he served berries with eulachon grease, dried salmon, and rice mixed with sugar and black currants.[82] After Albert's death in 1913, his nephew William Beynon (son of Rebecca Wellington and William Beynon Sr.) succeeded to the title at Port Simpson. Viola Garfield provides a full description of the snow feast based on Beynon's account: "Before dawn on the morning of the feast day[,] several men of the clan went howling through the village[,] giving the wolf call" before messengers were sent out with invitations. At the feast, guests were given ice cream instead of the traditional foods. After the meal and dances, the chief rose to explain the feast's mythological background, thanked the guests for at-tending, and announced he would take the title of his late uncle. Speeches by Wolf Clan chiefs followed, food and handkerchiefs were distributed, and dances concluded the celebration.[83]

It is clear that the Tsimshian as a group never made a unanimous or irrevocable decision to give up the old ways. In years when reformers who wanted radical change held power, mourning and commemorative feasts were in abeyance at Port Simpson. But resolutions to give up potlatching and the chiefly system never withstood the Tsimshian's need to ensure that social and political structures survived, regardless of the other changes taking place in their lives. Even a diehard reformist such as Clah was not prepared to place himself and his family at a disadvantage by turning his back on feasts that would establish their place in the Tsimshian hierarchy. Feasts could be rebadged "Christmas feasts" or "Christian marriage feasts," but no one, including the missionaries, was willing or able to ban feasts altogether. Even Tsimshian who had grown up away from Port Simpson – for instance, William Beynon and George Kelly, who became Ligeex – were drawn back into the "social life of names."[84] It was much easier to reconcile Christian beliefs within a Tsimshian system than to cut loose from the system altogether. Some of the people who benefitted the most from the changes introduced by colonialism were also strong adherents of the old ways: the old ways reinforced their status among their people and gave them a platform from which to negotiate with the colonial world. On the other hand, it became increasingly difficult to fill chiefly titles as the population was decimated by smallpox and other infectious diseases. Lineages either had to adopt people or call on associated lineages to ensure that heirs were available.[85] As often as not, an appropriate person could not be found, or he or she would refuse to take on the social and financial obligations of the title.

11

Ligeex, Chief of the Gispaxlo'ots

Ligeex was a Heiltsuk (Bella Bella) name with origins in the early sixteenth century. The first Ligeex was the son of a high-ranking Gispaxlo'ot Eagle Clan mother and a Heiltsuk chief. The name became the pre-eminent chiefly title of the predominant tribe of the Tsimshian. Ligeex and his tribe, the Gispaxlo'ots, controlled trade on the Skeena River and access to the eulachon fishery near the mouth of the Nass River. The sea otter trade, which was established after Captain James Cook's visit to the Pacific Northwest, threatened this supremacy because other tribal groups had better access to the sea otter grounds. The Ligeex in the late eighteenth century partly overcame this disadvantage by entering into strategic marriages, but it was not until the end of the sea otter trade and the establishment of the land-based fur trade that Ligeex was again able to establish ascendancy.[1] Soon after the Hudson's Bay Company established its trading post on the Nass River in 1831, Ligeex married his daughter to one of its officials, Dr. John Kennedy, and further cemented his ties with the company by facilitating the move of its trading post to his land on the Tsimshian peninsula. Although Clah would have known this Ligeex, it was his heir who was his contemporary. This was the man who was christened Paul Legaic and joined William Duncan at Metlakatla in 1862. His heir also took the name Paul Legaic, and he was succeeded by Martha Legaic and George Kelly.[2]

Much has been written about Ligeex by anthropologists and historians, making the title the best known among the nineteenth-century Tsimshian.[3] Ligeex, the individuals who held the name, and the title itself, figured significantly in Clah's life and in his diary. Clah's account of the lives, deaths, and successions of the three men and one woman who held the Ligeex name during his adult life shed light on issues relating to feasting and politics in Tsimshian society. Knowledge of Ligeex to date has been gleaned primarily from Tsimshian adawx, many of which were collected by William Beynon for Marius Barbeau and for his own research. Some of these adawx are reproduced in Barbeau's *Tsimshian Narratives*. Susan Marsden and Robert Galois use these oral histories extensively in their article on the fur trade in the late eighteenth and first half of the nineteenth century. Viola Garfield collected accounts of Ligeex's activities from informants in the 1930s, including a detailed description of a feast held by Paul Legaic II. Garfield's ethnographic descriptions have been employed by others, including Jay Miller. There are also documentary sources for Ligeex in the Hudson's Bay Company Archives and in William Duncan's reports of his first decade on the Coast. These sources have been used by Duncan supporters such as Henry Wellcome and John Arctander.[4] Clah's first-hand account adds significant details to our knowledge of the place of Ligeex in nineteenth-century Tsimshian politics. Of course, Clah was no disinterested observer. He was deeply implicated in the politics of the Gispaxlo'ots and the Tsimshian, and it is fascinating to see how he related to the different Ligeexs. He was influenced not only by his personal likes and dislikes and his kinship links but also by his evolving attitude to the chiefly system and his changing status in Tsimshian society. Clah's observations document the influence of missionaries and colonialism on the Ligeex lineage and status, particularly the process of succession as the lineage became depleted through deaths and a lack of interest on the part of potential heirs.

In 1892, after the death of Paul Legaic II, Clah recalled there had been five Ligeexs up to that time: "5 head chiefs. legaic [Ligeex] who die[d] years[,] and some died many years. Before whit[e] people came up, one last year. one buried skeenah river 200 two hundred years ago[.] that I not see, one old legaic die 300 three hundred years, one Doctor kennedys Father in law died Port Simpson 52 years ago. 4 legaic buried Fort simpson, one buried Metlekatlah."[5] Clah's knowledge of the earlier Ligeexs is obviously a bit hazy. In another diary entry, he claims there were nine Ligeexs, the richest of whom was the one who had his portrait painted on a cliff face near the mouth of the Nass River.[6] The history of this Ligeex and the circumstances leading to his assertion of his pre-eminence by having his face and most prized coppers painted on the cliff face has been recorded by William Beynon.[7] The Ligeexs who figure in Clah's diary are Paul Legaic I (d. 1869), Paul Legaic II (Ligeex from 1869 to 1891), Martha Legaic (1891-1902), and George Kelly (1907- 33). Between the death of Martha and the succession of George Kelly, a panel of four men was appointed by the Gispaxlo'ots to act in the Ligeex's place.[8]

PAUL LEGAIC I

Clah's relationship with the man who became Paul Legaic I was burdened by underlying tensions. Clah was a cousin of Legaic on his father's side, "my dear father his nephew."[9] During the fur trade era, Clah needed Ligeex's patronage to trade on the Skeena River (see Chapter 3), yet he found Paul Legaic's alcohol-fuelled and imperious and violent behaviour abhorrent. After Legaic became a Christian, Clah was better disposed towards him, even though Legaic bowed to William Duncan's demand that he no longer participate in Gispaxlo'ots affairs. Duncan was also impressed by Legaic's transformation. The man who was the first among the chiefs of Fort Simpson, who had threatened and verbally abused Duncan, and who had dominated trade on the Skeena River not only had become a pliant convert, he had also withdrawn from the chiefly system to live at Metlakatla as a Christian man. H.G. Barnett argues that Legaic was caught in a difficult situation in 1862. Although he had outmanoeuvred the previous incumbent's younger brother in his bid to become chief, the disappointed rival never forgave him and worked persistently to undermine Legaic's prestige and standing among the Tsimshian. Barnett interprets Legaic's ultimately futile confrontation with Duncan over the initiation ceremony of his daughter as but one in a series of humiliations. He claims further that a council of Gispaxlo'ots elders had agreed that Legaic should give up his leadership role and move to Metlakatla but retain his rank and privileges. Those who did not know of this secret meeting saw Legaic's capitulation as the act of a traitorous chief abandoning his people.[10] Although Barnett provides a plausible explanation for Paul Legaic's overnight transformation from a drunken bully to a God-fearing Christian, he does not present any evidence to support his argument.

Clah writes that he accompanied Legaic on a trading expedition up the Skeena River in May and June 1862. It was on this trip that Legaic sought revenge and compensation from the Gits'ilaasu (Kitselas) for the murder of one of his uncles. On their return, the two men found a smallpox epidemic raging at Fort Simpson. Legaic went to Metlakatla on 5 July to ask Duncan if he could join the mission, and Duncan welcomed him into his own house. By 21 July, Legaic had not only moved to Metlakatla, he had also requested baptism, which he received on 20 April 1863. He was christened Paul Legaic.[11] In September, when smallpox threatened Metlakatla, Legaic fled the scene.[12] His only male relative died of the disease and, in a state of panic, Legaic burned his ceremonial (halait) objects. By December, however, he had decided to settle at Metlakatla and had started to build a house.[13] When Clah visited Legaic in late December to invite him to his feast at Fort Simpson, Legaic – with Duncan's strong backing – refused. Duncan recorded Legaic's response to Clah, "My canoe was full of people when it capsized ... & all the people lost but myself[.] I swam to Mr Duncan's place[,] & here I will remain[,] & here die."[14]

Clah might not have known of the secret deal that Barnett refers to because he had not yet succeeded to the T'amks name (the feast to which he invited Legaic was part of his succession series) and, therefore, was not senior enough to attend such a high-ranking meeting. It is also possible that if such a meeting did take place, it occurred while Clah and Legaic were away trading on the Skeena. The diaries of both Clah and Duncan, however, strongly suggest that smallpox drove Legaic to Metlakatla. Although Legaic claimed that he had reformed his behaviour after the move, his wife was not convinced that he had given up drinking and gambling and asked Duncan to keep an eye on him while she was away from the mission. Legaic explained away his past bad behaviour as a reaction to the murder of his father when he was a boy, "this lead him to a savage life."[15] Although Legaic had withdrawn from active participation in Tsimshian potlatching, he would have preferred to have seen the system dismantled. Duncan believed Legaic was jealous of those chiefs at Fort Simpson who were still accumulating and displaying their property. Legaic, however, had not gone to Metlakatla as a poor man – he still owned slaves, coppers, and other forms of wealth.[16] Even after Legaic's baptism, Duncan expressed reservations about his conversion, "Here is that notorious Legaic – a Christian at least by name & I have hope, a Christian at heart. It is wonderful to see the change in him since the day he came with a furious band to stop me in my school work, driving out the scholars & only prevented from murdering me by a friendly Indian watching his movements & standing ready to shoot him should he strike me."[17]

PAUL LEGAIC II

Legaic's abandonment of Fort Simpson and the Gispaxlo'ots must have caused consternation and a jockeying for position among his lineage and tribal group, and the situation was exacerbated by his death from tuberculosis in 1869. Paul Legaic was succeeded by a man from his lineage who adopted his Christianized name, Paul Legaic. As the round of mortuary and commemorative feasts began at Fort Simpson, the Gispaxlo'ots tried to retrieve tribal property (including coppers) from Paul Legaic I's house at Metlakatla. Duncan barred their way, however, and the feasts had to begin without it.[18] Clah recorded that feasts were conducted in Ligeex's Fort Simpson house for days at a time. Whisky feasts were held from 20-22 October; the following day, a bread and molasses feast was held by the "Kighcage" (possibly the Kaigani Haida from Alaska) for the Tsimshian. Feasting resumed in November, when two American and two British flags were hoisted to mark a bread feast at which calico, soap, and nine boxes of bread were distributed. Another whisky feast followed.[19] Paul Legaic II spent the summer amassing provisions and held a big whisky feast in November 1870. Secret society feasts for the nulim (Dog Eaters) and xegedem (Cannibals) followed in December, and the new Legaic was inducted into the nulim society.[20] Paul Legaic II invited the Gitxaala, who arrived in four canoes and spent five hours dancing in Ligeex's house. Then the Tlingit chiefs arrived. The celebrations continued into February and culminated in a large feast at which Paul Legaic II gave away all his property, including elk skins, 60 coppers, and 710 blankets (presumably, some of these had been recovered from Legaic I's house at Metlakatla). Most of the Gispaxlo'ots applauded Legaic – with the notable exception of Clah, "Now everybody laughing to me. Because I not to [do] as this same as everyone else."[21]

This series of feasts appears to be identical with those described by Viola Garfield in *Tsimshian Clan and Society* and reproduced in many other studies. Garfield's discussion of these ceremonies offers insights that flesh out the meaning of Clah's narrative. Ligeex began the series by inviting the Gispaxlo'ots to a feast to outline his plans and obtain their support. After discussing subsequent feasts and the guests to be invited, Ligeex then hosted members of his father's lineage to seek their support. The main potlatch was given the following year. Messengers, accompanied by lesser chiefs, were sent out with invitations. Niis'wa'mak was sent to the Gitxaala. As Clah notes, four canoe loads of Gitxaala attended the feast. While the messengers were away, Ligeex and the Gispaxlo'ots prepared the food and entertainment. As visitors arrived by canoe, they were greeted by Ligeex's sister, accompanied by Gispaxlo'ots women in ceremonial costume who danced and sang on the beach. Ligeex's sister metaphorically threw her guardian spirit to the visiting chief, who then wrestled with it and threw it back. Only then could he and his retinue land. Ceremonies and a feast followed, and more took place the next day, including a challenge feast at which Ligeex "boasted of his greatness and belittled the achievements of his guests." Food and dancing continued until Ligeex and the Gispaxlo'ots concluded the festivities by distributing their accumulated property. Legends and names associated with Ligeex's crest were announced, and copper shields he owned were displayed and named. Finally, the gifts left for the Gispaxlo'ots were distributed among themselves.[22]

Throughout February 1872, Legaic hastened to complete a new house in time to commemorate the third anniversary of the death of Paul Legaic I. Although the weather was stormy and the construction was rushed, resulting in accidents and injuries, Legaic achieved his goal.[23]

Having been elevated to head chief of the Gispaxlo'ots, Paul Legaic II soon followed his namesake's footsteps to Metlakatla. His motivations are not clear, but there are clues. Following his succession, Legaic had been humiliated at a feast when another Gispaxlo'ots chief, Xpi'lk, was recognized ahead of him. Although Legaic had acquired the Ligeex title, it seems that he had not asserted his own pre-eminence among the Tsimshian. He had also given an official undertaking that he would no longer participate in potlatches. A move to Metlakatla extricated him from a difficult situation. Legaic's departure from Port Simpson was clouded by controversy, for he not only left the Gispaxlo'ots without effective leadership, he also dismantled the Ligeex house and took it with him to Metlakatla against the specific instructions of his predecessor.[24]

The Gispaxlo'ots were once again without a resident head chief. In 1882, community leaders debated the merits of replacing Legaic. Moses McDonald (Niisnawaa), head of the Port Simpson council, asked Clah – who was a senior Gispaxlo'ots lineage head at the time, even though he was not living permanently at Port Simpson – whether his people would accept William Kelly as their head chief. Clah returned with a firm no from the Gispaxlo'ots, who did not want the Ligeex name reassigned.[25]

A couple of years later, Paul Legaic II made a surprise return from Metlakatla to reclaim his position. His decision to return might have been driven by the dissension between Duncan and Ridley rather than a strong urge to regain his chiefly role.[26] His tribe was relieved to have the headship occupied because the Gitando and the Ginaxangiik were vying to replace the Gispaxlo'ots as the pre-eminent tribe at Port Simpson. To celebrate his return, two cannon were fired, a red flag was hoisted on the beach, and fifty women dressed in the garb of women from the Interior walked the streets. Their faces were painted red and black, and they were dressed in marmot and marten skins, which were also tied around their heads. George Pemberton, Legaic's brother-in-law, in imitation of the Hagwilget, greeted him in a fur shirt and with a gift of two coppers.[27]

Legaic came with a young wife, Oyhis, and frequent demands on the Gispaxlo'ots for material support. The tribe required a year to accumulate the funds to build their new house. The Gispaxlo'ots also had to pay off a twelve-dollar debt that Legaic owed at Metlakatla, and Oyhis expected them to provide money for her to buy food:

> Legaic wanted his people give some mon[e]y everyday to him. But stoped[.] don't give him any help. Legaic and his wife use too much money for buying Grub[.] use too much Bread[.] one meal 3 teaspoonfull of sugar in one small cup. 2 persons drink 2 tea pots full of tea water in 10 minut[e]s. 10lbs of sugar in 2 weeks[.] [W]hen they short in grub[,] his wife walk round the houses ask If anybody will help in sugar or bread. People give them food. But they use too much[.] legaic his [he's a] good in gunsmith[.] he makes mon[e]y for work. But his young wife spented too much.[28]

The return of Ligeex had clearly proved to be a mixed blessing.

Legaic's house was thirty-five feet long, twenty-one feet wide, and eleven feet high. It required six thousand feet of lumber at a cost of eighty-four dollars. As plans were drawn up for the house (like Clah's, it would stand on land claimed by the HBC), there were discussions among the Tsimshian about cutting down the old Ligeex crest pole and replacing it with a stone monument to commemorate the previous five Ligeexs. Clah notified Paul Legaic I's widow about the decision.[29] In the meantime, however, the pole fell during a storm, removing the matter from the hands of mere mortals (see Chapter 10).[30] Nonetheless, the fate of the old pole remained a live question as late as 1889: "[H]ave me[e]ting for sawing pieces of the old pole belongs old legaic[,] head king of tsimshen. Batrick Spoochs [Patrick Russ] says, ['][D]on[']t Dutch [touch] any[.] Belongs old people."[31] Planning for the new stone memorial continued and was made more urgent with the sudden death of Paul Legaic II.

THE DEATH OF PAUL LEGAIC II AND THE POLITICS OF SUCCESSION

Legaic had been suffering from fainting spells or fits for some time. On 8 January 1891, the Riflemen invited Legaic to their hall. After an hour, he went outside to smoke his pipe and did not return. The alarm was raised in the middle of the night, and people went out with lamps into cold, dark conditions to look for him. It was raining, the tide was coming in, and strong easterly winds were blowing. When it became clear that Legaic was lost or dead, Niisho'ot (Albert Nelson of the Gitzałaał) and Niisyaganaat (Herbert Wallace of the Gits'iis) were assigned to take possession of the body. It was found at 4 o'clock in the morning.[32]

The politics of succession broke out the moment Legaic was reported missing. Because there was no viable candidate in Legaic's own lineage, several contenders stepped forward. The most aggressive and persistent was Alfred Dudoward, chief of the Gitando. Clah noted that during the search for the body, Dudoward told the Gitando that when it was found they should claim it and place it in the Gitando chief's house. William Beynon's informant, William Pierce, gave him a similar account of the Gitando's ambitions.[33] Clah claimed Henry Tate found the body but then called a Gitando to help him:

> Henry taite [Tate] first seen hands up the water[,] Bodys underneath. henry taite calling one of the Alfreds people Named Albert Nes-gitle-was-nos[,] singing[,] ["][C]all friends. we found Body of Paul legaic.["] all the people running out on water fetch the Body on Beach. all the men an[d] women. Swim[m]ing[,] crying for the Kings death. all cried. Back [pack, that is, carry] the body on shoulders[,] walk up the his house. all

his people of leagaic singing out. war sing [song] called showesk. after 5 minut[e]s Alfred an[d] all his people withe him. Kitan-doo [Gitando] one man black his face. he carr[i]ed Eagle war knive. 2 feet long[,] 2 inch wide named Skalas-skalas. one name Jam-kis—hytaks [Dzagmgishaaytks][,] he says lock the door. Sing at war sing showesk all Spach-latch [Gispaxlo'ots] men stand round Paul legaics Body. they think Kitan-doo [Gitando] people take the body of King legaic out.[34]

By forcefully positioning themselves to prepare Legaic's body for burial, the Gitando hoped to pave the way for Dudoward, as head of the Eagle Clan, to inherit the Ligeex name. Had Dudoward succeeded, he would have held the chieftaincy of both the Gitando and Gispaxlo'ots. Clah's account emphasizes his own role in outwitting the Gitando. He does not mention Xpi'lk, who, according to Beynon, took charge in the Ligeex's absence.[35] Clah advised the Gispaxlo'ots to pay their tribesmen for their efforts in looking for Paul Legaic II's body with new coats, shirts, pants, and stockings to replace their wet clothes. They were also given forty new rifles worth $800, two hundred blankets worth $250, and clothes to the value of $150. An additional three hundred blankets worth $400 were presented to the chiefs who undertook to make Legaic's coffin. Dudoward and the Gitando countered by distributing $277 in cash, $200 worth of provisions, and other offerings that totalled $3,000.

In addition to this bidding war, the Riflemen's and Firemen's companies vied for the honour of escorting Legaic's body to the burial ground. Both companies assembled in the dead of night; they were dressed in their uniforms and had their band instruments in readiness for their part in the solemn procession. Clah suggested that the Firemen illuminate the streets with oil lamps.[36]

In the morning, Paul Legaic I's widow and daughter, Sarah, arrived from Metlakatla to witness the proceedings, while Niisho'ot and Niisyaganaat argued over who would make the coffin and the fence around the grave. The Gispaxlo'ots decided that Niisyaganaat would be responsible for the coffin, and Niisho'ot for the fence. Niisho'ot believed he had a stronger claim because Legaic had been his brother's son. He then bought a silver handle for the coffin that Niisyaganaat's people, the Gits'iis, refused to accept until Clah intervened. The Firemen and Riflemen continued to compete for the honour of carrying the coffin. Clah insisted that the

funeral ceremony should take place in the church rather than at the Soldiers' Hall.

According to William Beynon, a feast was planned to mark the elevation of Paul Legaic II's niece Martha to the chieftaincy (he had no nephews).
Without informing the Gitando, messengers were sent out with groundhog
skins to invite the chiefs of the tribes. As soon as the messengers returned,
a drum roll summoned the guests to Ligeex's house. After the preliminary
welcome, Xpi'lk announced that Martha would take the Ligeex name. As
the Gispaxlo'ots distributed their wealth to those in attendance, the Eagle
Clan of the Gitando entered the feast house with their own gifts. Xpi'lk
announced the new Ligeex to them, while another Gispaxlo'ots chief,
Niis'awalp, reprimanded the Gitando for not following correct protocol
(they should have distributed their wealth through Ligeex's tribe).[37]

Clah recounts a different version of the Gitando strategy to undermine
the Gispaxlo'ots' plans. With the support of their close allies the Ginanaxan-
giik, the Gitando demanded that the mourning feast be delayed. When
that failed, they tried to enlist Thomas Crosby's support. Clah quickly
intervened in an effort to forestall the missionary's interference:

> I said to him[,] ["][I]s it so to you not come in our feasting[.] the almighty
> God sent Christian alround [all around] the world to walk in rough
> places[,] and God sent down His Son from heaven clean all our Bad
> ways.
>
> Because you Say you not see our feast. feast is not kill nobody. not hurt
> you[.] why you fraiden [afraid] to eat food in our feasting house[?]["] so
> I ask him again. ["]will you come or not[,] also[,] If you not come in our
> invitation. may be our people have Council today or tomorrow about you.
> you mine [mind] that.["]

Nonetheless, both Crosby and magistrate Bolton decided to attend the
feast, not just as observers but also as active participants. The Gispaxlo'ots
elders held that the Ligeex succession should have the imprimatur not only
of the Tsimshian but also of the church and the Queen. Crosby represented
the church, and Bolton, as a justice of the peace, the Crown: "[H]e give
power in Spahlots [Gispaxlo'ots][.] he put his hand upon New Legaic.
Beside 4 elders legaic['s] head men who taken care [of] legaic['s] power."[38]

The final commemorative feast for the new Ligeex was held the following December.[39]

Although temporarily stymied by the Gispaxlo'ots, Alfred Dudoward had not given up his ambition to become the pre-eminent chief at Port Simpson. He held a feast at which he bound members of his lineage to support him.[40] There were also unfinished discussions about the monument for all Ligeexs, past and present, which had been interrupted by Paul Legaic's death and tussles over the succession. Meetings were held in December 1891 to discuss where the memorial should be placed. The sizeable sum of $370 had been collected to pay the stonemason, who would bring the memorial by steamer from Victoria.[41] On 8 January, the stonemason, James Fisher, arrived. Not everyone approved of the image he had carved of Paul Legaic I, which was in profile: "[W]e not satisfied because one eye. I want him to make full face." The widow of Paul Legaic I and her daughter, Sarah, were summoned from Metlakatla to give their opinion. Fisher must have been relieved when Sarah agreed that the face should be in profile.[42] As Sarah and the Gispaxlo'ots planned a commemorative feast, the Gitando began a bidding war to place money at the base of the monument. This attempt to once again undermine the Gispaxlo'ots possibly harked back to older traditions such as placing a copper shield or burying a slave at the base of a crest pole.[43] The monument was eventually erected. Crosby attended but, much to Clah's disgust, did not give his blessing. The inscription on the memorial (which still stands) reads,

> In memory of the 1st Legai [sic], a head chief. Died a long time ago. Before the white man came. Also three other head chiefs named Legai, also Paul Legai, a head chief of the Tsimpsean Nation, who died a Christian at Port Simpson, B.C., January 7th, 1891. Aged 45. Paul Legai said the day he died to his people: "One thing I hope I would like to die in a lonely place so no one would see me and I hope my people would not find me for five hours for I think I would be in Heaven by that time." His body was found eight hours after. God gave him longer than he hoped for.[44]

Historian Ronald Hawker points out that this memorial fulfills the function of a crest pole, commemorating lineage ancestors as well as the recently deceased.[45]

Martha Legaic, George Kelly, and the End of the Ligeex Line

The succession of Martha Legaic, as she became known, solved a pressing problem for the Gispaxlo'ots by overcoming rivals put forward by Sgagweet and the Gitando. But she was by no means an ideal choice for a position that carried so much status and responsibility.[46] As a sixteen-year-old girl, she was obviously too young and inexperienced to make decisions alone. Instead, an advisory group of elders decided where she should go, who she should contact, and how she should behave. In November 1891, it was suggested she should be put under the guidance of a "wise old woman," but this unnamed person lacked the resources to feed and support the chief and her social obligations.[47]

It was not until late 1898 that a new house was built for Martha Legaic. The project became embroiled in a debate over whether the old house should be pulled down. Those Gispaxlo'ots who did not wholeheartedly support Legaic were not inclined to contribute to the house raising. Conflict also erupted when John Tate carved an eagle flagstaff for the house. Christians wanted to cut it down because they feared it would trigger a series of potlatches. The Indian agent, Charles Todd, was summoned from Metlakatla to mediate the dispute.[48]

Thomas Crosby's attempt in November 1896 to enlist Martha Legaic as head of the Christian Band of Workers and the Epworth League reflected the limits of her autonomy. The Gispaxlo'ots council vetoed her participation on the grounds that, as chief of all the Tsimshian, she should not be associated with a particular Christian faction.[49] Several years later, Legaic decided of her own volition to join the Band of Christian Workers, thereby committing herself to a Christian life. The Gispaxlo'ots disapproved of her association with the organization and passed a resolution that she cut her ties with them. This she refused to do. Clah accused Martha of doing evil, but it is not clear if "evil" refers to her refusal to conform to tribal decisions or some other objectionable behaviour. Some Gispaxlo'ots thought she was being disloyal, and there was talk of removing her from the tribe.[50] She survived as Ligeex, however, and repented of her "bad behaviour" in early 1902, just a few months before her unexpected death on the Nass River.[51]

Martha Legaic's passing precipitated a new crisis for the Gispaxlo'ots that took five years to resolve, albeit without the frenzied rivalry of previous developments. Viola Garfield notes that with the end of the Ligeex lineage, a chief had to be drawn from either another lineage in the Ligeex house or a related house. Pending a final decision, four lineage heads were selected to serve as an interim council to represent Ligeex. Although Clah had played a central role in the arcane politics surrounding Martha's elevation, by 1902 he had little influence on events, either because of his age or because the four-person council kept the negotiations secret. In the winter following Martha's death, the Gispaxlo̱ots pondered who should be the next Ligeex. George Kelly and Sarah Legaic were two options. Dudoward was still interested, but the Gispaxlo̱ots made it clear they did not want him. He argued that Sarah Legaic should be excluded from consideration because her mother was a commoner.[52] George Kelly had been adopted by Dudoward's mother, Elizabeth Diex (Lawson), the sister of his natural mother. At some point, Diex had moved from the Gispaxlo̱ots to the Gitando, where Dudoward had become Chief Sgagweet, and Kelly was in the house of Sgagweet but a different branch. Diex still claimed rights in the Gispaxlo̱ots, and Kelly was eventually adopted into the Gispaxlo̱ots. He was brought to Port Simpson in 1902 as the heir apparent, but he did not succeed to the Ligeex title until 1907.[53] Garfield, who met and interviewed George Kelly when he was old and blind, discovered that he had spent most of his life in Victoria and knew little of Tsimshian culture. She regarded him as a rather pathetic figure who was valued for his position rather than his contribution to Gispaxlo̱ots status. At his death in 1938, another council was elected to represent what a century before had been the great chief of the Tsimshian, Ligeex.[54]

The story of Ligeex, from the heyday of the fur trade – when a young man took the opportunities offered to build up his own and his lineage's status among the Tsimshian and neighbouring peoples and to dominate trade and monopolize relations with the HBC – to the nadir of an absent incumbent in the twentieth century, reflects the changes experienced by the Tsimshian over a century. It illustrates the complex influence of colonialism and the way its subjects became enmeshed in its processes. Disease, low reproduction rates, alcohol abuse, violence, and processed foods accompanied the imposition of a colonial state apparatus and the introduction of new religious and moral codes, and they, in turn, influenced the gradual eclipse of Ligeex. But it was primarily furs, gold, and fish that initially invigorated and then decimated the local trading system on the

Northwest Coast, which ultimately determined the history of Ligeex and the Tsimshian. In the fur trade era, Ligeex was able to enhance his status among the Tsimshian, neighbouring peoples, and newcomer traders by generating wealth, but once that wealth dissipated, Ligeex's status shrank to a point where the name retained significance only for the Gispaxloots. Yet even the clan and tribe who held the name could not find an heir willing to burden themselves with the financial obligations of the title. As late as 1891, there were Tsimshian who were willing to sacrifice much to attain the title, but by 1902 there were no direct heirs and fewer incentives to shoulder the responsibilities of the name. There was also a strong anti-chief putsch at Port Simpson that included influential Gispaxloots such as Matthew Johnson and which might have discouraged wider interest in the Ligeex name. While other Tsimshian chiefly lineages continued to function in the twentieth century, Garfield claims the Gispaxloots not only failed to fill the Ligeex name, they stopped fulfilling the financial and social reciprocal obligations of Ligeex, thus damaging their relationship both *to* and *with* the wider social world.[55]

12

Old Age: The End of Voyaging

By the 1890s, when he was in his sixties, Clah thought of himself as an old man. His grey hair proclaimed his age, as did the hair of his old acquaintance, James Hamilton Moffat, which he described as "whit[e] as sheeps hair."[1] Although middle age was associated with wisdom among the Tsimshian, old age does not seem to have been revered: "Old Ices [Ha'is] 75 years old[.] he was with me[.] he work as too old man. [M]y fathers relation works like 2 year [old] boy."[2] But even those who were not senile were ridiculed: "Some heathen people laugh at 3 of us[:] old man Arthur Wellingon Clah[,] an[d] one Named Neokhs, one Named Wykh. [T]hee says old men good for not[h]ing[.] no use to keeped them [a]live in our place."[3] Clah, while acknowledging that he and his two old companions were virtually blind, believed they were wiser.[4]

AN OLD MAN'S VIEWPOINT

Clah's strategy for dealing with his decline in status and influence was to reiterate his important role in the recent history of his people. He took to referring to himself as "Saint Clah" and "Duke Wellington"; he described himself as the man who fought the heathens, the first among his people to find Jesus, the man who looked after the poor, and the man who had preached the word of God far and wide. He realized that his "Report book," as he began to call it, might establish his place in history. In fact, he was writing that history: "[N]orth west coast History[.] reported Saint Clah Arthur Wellington. First man believe Jesus amongs[t] the heathen indians friends. I telling all yours when I believe the gospel from our lord Jesus Christ."[5]

Arthur Wellington Clah as an old man (note the indentation in his forehead,
an injury sustained during a fight in Victoria in 1855 with Baptiste Bottineau).
BC Archives, F-08904.

The diary, which had begun as a tool to improve his written English
and as a means to learn the Gregorian calendar and the days of the week,
quickly became a daily record of Clah's life and a moral accounting of the
Tsimshian and Nisga'a. Over the last decade or two of his life, the diary
developed an extra function as a running historical commentary centred
on Clah's achievements. No one else is acknowledged in the fight against
heathenism. Perhaps Clah was influenced by the hagiographic biographies
of William Duncan, which marked Clah out as the man who taught
Duncan Sm'algyax, who saved him from the wrathful Ligeex, and who had

been the first to see the Christian light. Clah willingly adopted the role of first Christian and expanded it to first Tsimshian preacher. Because Clah was always such an individualist, he mentions no disciples and no converts.

Clah thought of himself as the great voyager, in terms of distances travelled, places visited, and his evangelical journeys. These claims are well supported by his daily entries, for he had indeed made many journeys. However, he grossly exaggerated his achievements by failing to acknowledge that many others had also undertaken long journeys and preached the word to remote villages. Clah's later diaries reveal a rather vain old man reprising his life.

Clah had kept his writing hidden from prying eyes, but once he came to believe he was recording a history for posterity, he sought affirmation and support from missionaries. In 1898, Paul Legaic I's widow asked Clah to show his diary to her granddaughter, "I said to her, [']I never give my writed [writing] to anybody till finished an[d] Brented [printed] in Book[.] now [then] you read.[']"[6] Yet a few months earlier, Clah had told the Anglican priest William Collison about his diary and asked him to write in it. Perhaps he remembered Collison's reference to Clah's relationship with Duncan during a sermon in 1894: they were "2 men clean the road for me an[d] for yours ... Now he has get in [is getting] old man Arthur Wellington Clah."[7] Clah asked S.S. Osterhout to write a foreword for his 1901 journal, and another diary and some notes found their way into the papers of Methodist minister George Raley, who was at Port Simpson from 1906 to 1914. A typescript of "Reminiscences of Arthur Wellington Clah" was produced by the Reverend Lashley Hall, and it became the great ambition of the elderly Clah to see the history encapsulated in his diary published.[8]

As Clah became less physically able and as his world shrank from the halcyon days of fur trading and gold prospecting to his potato patch at Laghco and community politics at Port Simpson, the diary became the focus of his life. He lived out his fantasies in the autobiographical commentaries that he included alongside many of his daily entries. As his eyesight failed, maintaining the diary became a struggle. From the mid-1890s, he frequently complained of sore eyes. On trips to Victoria, he visited doctors who gave him ointments and drops, which do not seem to have provided much relief and certainly did not improve his sight. In August 1900, Clah described himself as half blind. Two years later, he was more explicit, "My eyes half pline [blind][.] I see day like smok[e] But I doneet [don't] stop written [writing]."[9] As Clah's eyesight declined, his writing became increasingly illegible. In the entries for 1900, when he first complained of being half blind, the writing is large, sloping down the page. The entries for 1906 are difficult to decipher. Firm in the belief that God was supporting his endeavour, Clah struggled on. The decision to stop writing must, therefore, have been traumatic.

Clah's later reminiscences contrast "new" people, that is, contemporary people, with the old people he knew in his youth. These entries are not so much nostalgia as a matter of fact. He dwells less on the violence of the fur trade era, which concerned him so much as a younger man, and more on how people lived before they gained access to new technologies and foods. In December 1900, Clah criticized the citizens of Port Simpson for not keeping the township clean, unlike the old people, who, he implies, were more energetic and industrious. The old people had used stone axes and hammers (which they had to sharpen every few months) and wooden nails to make the wooden boxes they used for storing fish and meat, which they ate with wooden spoons. Clah was conscious of the dramatic changes in the Tsimshian diet. The old people had drunk cold water, not hot tea and coffee. They had never encountered sugar, molasses, rice, or bread, and when they did start using sugar, they only had a small teaspoon, in contrast to the huge quantities of sugar consumed by contemporary people.[10]

The most depressing contrast between old and new people was the fall Clah perceived in the standard of living. Contemporary Tsimshian were largely dependent on a money economy and were not able to earn enough to sustain themselves. They could no longer exist on a diet of traditional foods – eulachon grease, dried fish, seaweed, and berries – but needed money to buy provisions such as sugar, flour, bacon, coffee, and tea. They also needed money to purchase guns, axes, and other tools. They had to buy lumber from the sawmill to build their houses and, although Clah does not mention it, by the early twentieth century some used gasoline launches rather than hand-hewn canoes for freighting and transport.[11] All these things had driven Aboriginal people into wage labour. Their mobile lifestyle was now determined more by employment opportunities than the seasons.[12] Families no longer had the time or, perhaps, the inclination to collect and store enough food to get them through the winter months. As a result, when their food reserves ran low, they had to leave their winter villages in January to hunt and fish. Until the eulachon and herring arrived in March, they had no money to buy food. Tsimshian still collected Indian foods, as Clah referred to them, which they could trade among themselves, but stores operated on the basis of cash rather than barter.

James McDonald argues that "the bulk of the reproduction of Tsimshian labor power and society was accomplished outside the capitalist relations of production. After fishing season, fishermen returned to their fish-drying camps and re-entered a very differently organized production cycle."[13] This labour pattern influenced the Tsimshians' relationship with the canneries. Neither McDonald nor Rolf Knight, while investigating wage labour participation, consider the wider implications of wage labour on the Tsimshian economy. Clah, although unable to articulate an analysis of what was happening to the Tsimshian, observed the economic and psychological impact of wage labour on his society. Although people could still fish, hunt, and collect foods, these foods no longer constituted their whole diet, nor could they be used in the money economy to buy processed foods. Clah, on one of the occasions he was living alone at Laghco, walked to Port Simpson with two kettles of crabs he hoped to sell for money he could use to buy store foods. He was embarrassed that poverty had forced him to accept a low price.[14]

Clah noted similar changes in the fortunes of the Nisga'a: "I walk up Killaghtamax [Gitlaxdamks] village. The place half empty, use[d] to be big place. [F]irst time I take my wife in that tribe[,] good many people[:] strong tribe and rich people to all tribes on [N]ass river[.] [N]ow tribe very poor. [P]eople very near all out. [G]o easy places the young people."[15] Clah implies that only the poor old people have remained in the village, while the young have deserted it for an easier life, probably in villages such as Kincolith near the mouth of the Nass or, perhaps, further afield.

Clah's failing sight and physical frailty profoundly restricted his activities. He found it increasingly difficult to walk long distances and to see where he was going in dim light. In March 1894, Clah joined Thomas Crosby on the *Glad Tidings* for an evangelical trip up the Nass River. They stopped first at Kincolith. The next day, they left the boat at Red Bluff and made their way up the river, pulling a sleigh on the ice. Clah could not keep up with the rest of the party: "[F]riends left me behine [behind] them 2 miles becau[s]e ... old man. I cannot walk very fast."[16] Later in the year, however, he hiked four miles up the mountains in search of elusive gold, carrying a pack on his back that weighed between fifty and seventy pounds. It included tools, clothes, and ammunition, but no food. He might have been slow, yet he still had the strength to undertake this taxing journey. In the next few years, he ventured less often from home.

Although Clah was no longer as agile as he had once been, he could still sail and paddle his canoe in his sixties and seventies, relying on his wife and daughters to guide him when the light was dull. He had never been a successful hunter; now he could not hunt at all. Even on the rare occasion when he joined a hunting party, he stayed at the camp while the younger men went in search of game. In 1895, for instance, Clah went to the hunting grounds near Klemtu (China Hat) with Henry Wesley and his brother Charles. While the brothers went out trapping each day, Clah watched over the camp. He kept his courage up through prayer each night. On the long, arduous journey back to Port Simpson, Clah fell on rocks in the dark of night and injured himself. He thanked God he did not die. The three men returned to Port Simpson in November, after fifty-nine days away.[17]

Failing sight not only made Clah more prone to accidents, it also affected his ability to orient himself, even in familiar places. On a visit to Metlakatla in 1895 to visit Albert, who was boarding at the school, Clah could not find his way in the dark and had to call on his son to guide him.[18] In former days, Clah had easily negotiated the notorious coastal fogs, even on long canoe journeys. The elderly Clah became lost in the fog at Laghco early one morning while on the shore collecting crabs and devilfish: "[V]ery near lost myself in first daylight[.] very low tide. I get up[.] I go down to take crabs an[d] devel [devil] fish[.] it was very thick fogging walk down mile tide[.] come back I [t]ry go home. I coden [couldn't] fin[d] no way. I walk round 2 hours[.] I have hear small Black crow speaking. So I go where he speaks[.] he found small Creek[.] now I follow the creek an[d] I get up the house[.] 4 hour walk round thick fog all day."[19] Clah also lost his old sure-footedness; he fell in his canoe and split his head open in a fall on the Balmoral wharf.[20]

By the early 1890s, Clah's son, Albert, was at school in Metlakatla, his daughter Rebecca had moved to Victoria with her Welsh husband, William Beynon, and his daughter Martha was widowed. There was no able-bodied male in the immediate family until Martha married Henry Wesley on 18 December 1894. The arrival of a younger man had an immediate impact on the family's ability to procure food. Six days after the marriage, Clah and Wesley went hunting together. A few months later, the men went on the fifty-nine-day trip to Klemtu. Wesley was a more successful hunter than his father-in-law had been in his prime. Clah was well pleased with the new addition to his family. At Laghco, just a few months after Martha and Henry's marriage, he noted that Henry Shepherd, his kinsman and member of his house, was too slow at collecting food, while Henry Wesley was "not one day empty[.] he bring everything we eat."[21]

The advent of a new son-in-law brought other changes to the pattern of family life. Instead of going to the Nass River each spring to fish for eulachon and make grease, the family now spent the spring hunting and fishing on Stephens and Dundas islands. They traded seaweed, herring spawn, and dried fish for eulachon grease. During the first spring after his marriage, Wesley helped Clah build the long-awaited house at Laghco, to which they moved in April.[22] Clah and Dorcas had spent a month each year over six years clearing the land at Laghco. Spurred on by the knowledge that their house would finally be built, they devoted three months to working on the garden in 1895. Meanwhile, Wesley hunted and caught halibut, which the family smoked. In June, Clah embarked on the second of two trips to introduce his son Albert to his "grandfather's generation's" hunting grounds near Klemtu. The previous year, Albert had accompanied Clah and Shepherd on a similar journey during the summer holidays.[23] Although Clah claimed rights to the hunting grounds that dated back six hundred years – when earlier generations had fished, hunted sea otters and land animals, and collected seagull eggs from the rocks – he was unfamiliar with the area. A passing canoe of Gitg'a't (from Hartley Bay) identified the islands for Clah and advised him to come earlier in the season because the gull eggs were all finished. He followed that advice in 1895, returning home with three hundred eggs.[24]

WILLIAM DUNCAN AND CLAH MEET FOR THE LAST TIME

Apart from visits to Victoria to see his daughter and to pursue his land claims, the only extended journey Clah took as an old man was to New Metlakatla on the invitation of William Duncan. Given the two men's long association and Clah's innate curiosity, it is surprising that he did not visit the mission until twenty years after its establishment. Duncan sent a message to Clah in April 1906: "[N]ews from Alaska. My Brother William

Duncan wanted me Before he die."[25] Duncan, who was a year younger than Clah and would outlive him by two years, realized that there might not be another opportunity for the two old men to get together.[26] At the end of 1906, Albert returned from a trip he had taken to New Metlakatla as part of Port Simpson's marching band. He bore a gift of ten dollars from Duncan to Clah: "[T]hat makes my heart very cry when I got 10 dollars in my hand."[27] The following year, Clah set out to visit his old friend.

Long ago, Clah had passed by Annette Island on a canoe trip to Sitka, but the island had altered out of all recognition since the establishment of the industrious mission community. When Duncan and the Metlakatlans had migrated to the island, it had been unoccupied. The previous inhabitants – Tlingit – had left. According to some sources, the Tlingit had given the Tsimshian permission to move onto their land, but it was the US government that had made the official decision to allow the Tsimshian to build a community on the island.[28] The immigrants from British Columbia built a village with a church and other public buildings and a cannery. Despite his age, Duncan continued to rule the community with an iron hand, although there were increasingly vocal complaints about his inability to delegate authority and to keep up with changing times.

Clah left Port Simpson on 16 November by steamer and reached Ketchikan, Alaska, on the same day. He went immediately to the adjoining Aboriginal village of Saxman to see Edward Marsden, a Tsimshian man who had left the Duncan fold to become a Presbyterian minister independent of Duncan's control. Clah stayed for the Sunday service and dinner but refused Marsden's invitation to remain for two weeks. He reached his destination two days later and was greeted by Duncan and a few friends before he retired to his nephew's house. Over the following days, Clah caught up with old friends. Unfortunately, his diary does not recount his conversations with Duncan; it merely reiterates their early history.

Clah was well looked after during his stay at New Metlakatla. He lists all the generous offers of money he received and the invitations he had from friends and relatives to join them for dinner. William Duncan gave him five dollars for his return ticket, and others gave him money to buy food. Even the captain of the steamer to Ketchikan waived his fare. Clah certainly enjoyed being feted as Duncan's early assistant. After visiting the Sunday school, he was prevailed upon to talk about old times and how he had first preached the gospel – one of his favourite topics. On another occasion, a community meeting was called at which Clah was asked to reminisce about Duncan's arrival on the Northwest Coast and his early proselytizing.[29] Clah enjoyed playing the role of the wise and knowledgeable old man. His reception in Alaska reflects an important distinction between his own people at Port Simpson and those who had followed Duncan from one mission settlement to the next. At New Metlakatla, the people wanted to retrieve the stories of early Christianity on the Coast. At Port Simpson, although there were many professed Christians, there were others who still valued their pre-Christian beliefs and customs and resented Clah's denigration of their "old ways."

Clah's visit to New Metlakatla coincided with the US Thanksgiving holiday and a ferocious storm. Many people trying to get back to the island for the holiday were frustrated by high winds and furious seas. News came from the Mainland that buildings had been blown down and trees uprooted. On the island, people could not sleep for they were worried their houses might blow away. Shingles fell from the church roof, and boats smashed on the beach. Duncan's cleverly engineered water supply, fed by a mountain spring, was destroyed as rocks dislodged and blocked the flow of water. As at Port Simpson, firewood was in short supply, forcing citizens of the village to sail long distances to collect it. During the storm, many were stranded, unable to return. By the time Clah left Metlakatla, the storm had abated, and he was able to take his leave after a three-week visit.[30]

LAGHCO

The trip to New Metlakatla was no doubt a welcome interlude in Clah's now humdrum life. In the past, he had always welcomed new experiences and places, but by the turn of the twentieth century he moved mostly between Port Simpson and Laghco with occasional forays to Victoria, the Skeena River canneries, and the hunting and fishing grounds on the offshore islands. At Port Simpson, he continued to take an interest in community politics, but as an observer rather than as an active participant. And, of course, he kept up his running battles over land with the HBC and with Victoria bureaucrats and lawyers. Many days, however, were spent alone or with his wife at Laghco.

Dorcas still worked at the canneries, but she also spent many weeks each year on the arduous task of weeding, preparing the ground for planting, seeding, and harvesting their crop of potatoes and other vegetables.

She also travelled with her daughter's family when they went to the off-shore islands. These trips suggest that although Clah could no longer contribute to hunting and fishing activities, Dorcas was able to participate more actively in women's food-gathering pursuits.

From late fall through the winter, Clah collected wood at Laghco with his family. He was still able to chop, saw, and load the firewood into his canoe. But he occasionally complained of weakness and was conscious that he lacked the stamina of old. During particularly cold winters, Dorcas would go to Laghco to check their store of potatoes, but there was little she could do to stop them from freezing and spoiling. Laghco beach provided a good supply of clams in late winter and early spring that could be eaten fresh or dried. Later in the season, while the younger men went hunting, these foods were supplemented by herring spawn, halibut, dogfish, cod, and rock cod caught offshore. In 1898, Wesley and Albert returned with one hundred mink and six land otters.[31]

Clah was always at home for the spring season; he often stayed on at Laghco when the rest of the family moved away. It was a novel experience being quite on his own, and not one he really relished. It seems to have been the fate of older Tsimshian to be left in nearly deserted winter villages while their families spent the better part of the year as migratory workers. In 1901, while alone at Port Simpson, Clah decided to do a census of the people left in the village. He found five old women on Rose Island and on the mainland, four old women and six old men. There were also a few children left behind with their elderly relatives. Apart from the constable and hotel manager and their wives, the only able-bodied adults in the village were at the HBC's fort.[32] All the able-bodied Tsimshian were away fishing and working in canneries, some as far afield as Vancouver.

In May, Clah and Dorcas, sometimes with the help of other family members, began planting potatoes and other vegetables. On Saturdays, Dorcas would go to Port Simpson to attend the Salvation Army services, while Clah stayed home. By June, Dorcas and the rest of the family had travelled to the canneries on the Skeena River. Once the fishing season was under way, Clah would join the family on the Skeena to help with the fishing. For many years, Henry, Martha, and family worked for the Carlisle cannery at the mouth of the Skeena, while Albert worked at Balmoral. After the cannery fishing ended, either in July or August, depending on the fish runs, the families dispersed. Following the end of the commercial fishing season, the family usually journeyed up the Skeena to fish on their own behalf and smoke the catch. Sometimes they fished on the coast.[33] While Wesley and Albert were away, Clah and Dorcas harvested their potatoes and other vegetables at Laghco in October. In 1907, Clah proudly reported that they had produced two tons of potatoes, half a ton of turnips, and forty heads of cabbage from their half-acre garden.[34]

Clah usually spent Christmas at Port Simpson. Christmas was not celebrated with the same anticipation and festivities as it had been during the early years of the Methodist mission. After 1900, it barely rates a mention in Clah's diary. Clah bemoaned the lack of interest in the holiday and walked out early in the morning to greet people and wish them a happy Christmas, only to discover that no one was about. The lack of interest in Christmas suggests that rivalries among the different religious denominations had more to do with politics than religion. On Christmas Day, 1900, the Port Simpson constable arrested two Salvation Army men for singing in the streets, even though there was no one about to hear them.[35] New Year's Eve and Day tended to be a more celebratory and boisterous occasion. Bands performed, and some years the Methodists held Watch meetings.

The Wellington Family

In 1902, 1903, and 1904, Clah spent part of the winter with his daughter Rebecca's family in Sidney on Vancouver Island. Travelling there meant negotiating new forms of transport: tramcars and trains. On his trip in 1905, Clah stayed at hotels. He arrived by steamer in Vancouver, where he faced the unfamiliar task of looking for accommodation. The first places he tried were reserved for Chinese. A Heiltsuk chief he met at the waterfront took him by the hand to a hotel, but it was full. Another acquaintance eventually found him a hotel room for twenty-five cents a night and fifteen cents for a meal.[36] In Victoria, he stayed at the Occidental Hotel for three nights before he took the train to Sidney. Rebecca and her children likewise visited her parents on extended stays. In between visits, they kept in touch by mail, sending one another food packages – Clah and Dorcas sent fish oil and dried fish south, while Rebecca sent store foods north.

Clah's immediate family becomes more visible in his diary once he reached old age because he spent much more time with them than he had in earlier times. When he travelled, it was with his family to the canneries or hunting grounds. Unfortunately, proximity to his wife and adult children and grandchildren did not result in more fulsome descriptions of their activities or personalities. Dorcas and Clah's marriage continued to be punctuated by arguments. Dorcas felt the isolation at Laghco keenly and resented the hard work in the garden: "[M]y wife told me this morning that she keep thinking[,] who wants paid her work hard every day and every years cleaning land[?]" Clah replied that God would notice and reward her.[37] Although Clah indicated he also worked in the garden, it is likely Dorcas undertook most of the hard labour, for women rather than men were saddled with this new form of work. Some of Dorcas and Clah's altercations were more explosive: "[M]y wife crying[,] for she wants go back Clquah callams [Lax Kw'alaams]. I told her to sawing firewood first to used when go home. she says[,] [']this place just like prison[.'] she like Salvation army very bad. she made 2 beds[:] one for her, one for me. she speaks very rough to me."[38]

The youngest of Dorcas and Clah's daughters, Fanny, had died at the age of nineteen in 1894. She had been living in the Crosby Girl's Home at Port Simpson. After four weeks' suffering from a sore neck, she was sent home, but died three days later. She received a Christian funeral attended by mourners dressed in black.[39] Fanny was the last of the Wellington children to die prematurely, but the family continued to suffer the loss of a number of grandchildren.

Martha's two daughters by William West, Emma and Miriam, also spent periods at the Girl's Home, but Martha withdrew Emma after the matron criticized her for being a single mother.[40] Clah expressed a great deal of affection for Rebecca's oldest child, William Beynon Jr. He stayed with his grandparents at Port Simpson and often accompanied them around Victoria, no doubt acquiring much of the underlying knowledge that would make him such an effective ethnographer of the Tsimshian later in life. The most tragic death among the grandchildren was that of Arthur Wesley, who died in July 1909. He had also spent a lot of time with his grandfather. One day, Clah playfully reprimanded Arthur for firing a gun while they were travelling in a canoe. The boy handed the gun to his grandfather, who threw it into the water, causing it to discharge. Incredibly, the bullet ricocheted off a stone and hit young Arthur in the chest.[41] He died of complications nine months later, leaving his twice-widowed mother with two daughters and a son.

Information about Clah's life is sparse between 1909, when he ceased keeping his diary, and his death in 1916. He outlived his son Albert by three years and might have outlived Dorcas as well.[42] How and under what circumstances his dim eyes finally closed is not known. We can only speculate that the Riflemen's and Firemen's bands escorted his coffin to the church, where he was remembered as one of the first Tsimshian Christians, and on to the cemetery. Did the next lineage head of T'amks host memorial feasts following Clah's death? We will never know because the daily record of Port Simpson life stopped with Clah.

Conclusion

Arthur Wellington Clah sailed with the winds of change that defined his life with varying results. Sometimes, as in his early adherence to Christianity and his success as a fur trader, the navigation was clear and he reached his destination. At other times, he was buffeted by variable winds that sent him in circles. However hard he paddled, there seemed to be no way forward. There were times when Clah found himself moving against the communal current. He often felt he was carrying the evils of his world upon his strong shoulders – all those unreformed people who continued the "old-fashioned" ways instead of following Clah's lead to salvation and a moral life. Through his daily diary entries, he mapped the many different routes he and his people took over fifty years. Clah found the route to salvation but not to a prosperous and easy life. Many of his children and other close family members did not survive the journey, while Clah manoeuvred his canoe into the relatively calm but unsatisfactory backwaters of old age.

This investigation of Clah's voyages focuses on their colonial context. The cumulative experience of these journeys transformed him from an enthusiast ready to absorb new experiences and grab new opportunities to a disillusioned old man who felt disempowered, dispossessed, and betrayed by a Queen, and later King, of England who should have protected Tsimshian interests. Christianity, which many view as an integral part of European colonization, was not experienced as such by Clah. Christianity gave Clah reassurance when he felt downhearted or overwhelmed by the many tragedies of his life. It gave him strength and hope. He lauded himself as the first Tsimshian Christian, but he did not perceive Christianity as a foreign import. Christianity existed independently of the institutions and individuals who carried it to the Tsimshian. It was a body of knowledge and beliefs available to anyone. There were people – mostly missionaries and ministers – who had expert knowledge, but they and their churches neither owned nor controlled Christianity. Clah grew angry at missionaries' demands for money because he considered them an unwarranted tax. Unlike exchanges of property in the potlatch, the money demanded by priests neither put them under a system of mutual obligation nor guaranteed they would take responsibility for the welfare of their parishioners. Nonetheless, Clah continued to respect their religious knowledge. As an old man, he could see that these men were implicated in the colonial project, but they were still men of God. He could attend a church service held by Thomas Crosby or one of the other ministers even though he resented their material demands and their inability to ameliorate the impact of colonialism.

Clah's attitude to the servants of the colonial state – Indian agents, lawyers, judges, and politicians – was similar. He continued to hope they would help solve his problems, particularly his land disputes, rather than seeing them as part of the state that was undermining his rights. Even Peter O'Reilly, who, as Indian reserve commissioner, was clearly playing a role in dispossessing the Tsimshian of their land, could still be claimed by Clah as a friend and someone who might act on his behalf to fix his problem. His attitude towards Euro-Canadians appointed to positions of authority was influenced by the way Tsimshian authority operated. When individuals inherited positions within the Tsimshian house and chiefly system, their responsibilities and influence increased without destroying previous relationships. These changes over a lifetime are well illustrated in Clah's attitude towards Alfred Dudoward. Dudoward was a rebellious youth when Clah was a young man trying to establish himself among the HBC fur traders. By the time Clah was an old man with no resources in the 1890s, Dudoward was a well-established businessman with stores and a trading boat and well on the way to becoming the most influential chief and community leader at Port Simpson.

Clah could see that the positions and influence of the Euro-Canadians he met on the goldfields followed similar trajectories. As mature men, they held positions of power and the accoutrements that went with them: offices, servants, and large houses. Just as Clah would make direct approaches to influential people in his own community, and just as others would come to him to negotiate on their behalf, Clah went directly to the men he knew in Victoria. He sought out their homes and knocked on their doors. He did not distinguish between a judge or senator's office and his private abode. He never caught on to the idea of making appointments and was frustrated when people sent him away with a suggestion that he return at a more convenient time.

Historians, political scientists, and other scholars analyze historical events on the Northwest Coast in the latter half of the nineteenth century and the early part of the twentieth century in terms of colonialism, a term Clah did not know and never used. He did have a notion that the Coast was not unique, and he had a concept of the British Empire. Even when it was evident to him that decisions affecting his life were being made in Victoria and Ottawa, he still invoked Queen Victoria and King Edward as the source of authority and the English, rather than the Canadians, as the people responsible for whittling away his rights.

Loss of land was the prime concern of the Tsimshian and Nisga'a during the colonial period. This process began with land pre-emptions and was greatly accelerated by O'Reilly's allocation of reserves. Close analysis of Clah's diary brings out the complexities of the land issues confronting Aboriginal peoples. Formalizing colonial control over land pitted Aboriginal communities and individuals against one another as they fought to maintain access and authority over the little land that remained available to them. Clah's conflict with the Nisga'a over the land at Laxk'a'ata (Canaan) on the Nass River graphically illustrates these tensions. The bureaucratization of land holdings also highlighted ambiguities in land ownership dating back to the fur trade era. Clah's running battle with the HBC is an example of how a trading relationship based on negotiated exchanges and goodwill morphed into an unequal fight over control of land after the trade died and the colonial state formalized its land tenure system. By this time, there were other outside interests vying for access to land at Port Simpson, particularly when it was mooted as a terminal port for a railway line. In 1907, the Port Simpson Improvement Company of Seattle dealt speculatively in Port Simpson land, which had already been divided into town lots. In 1909, there were 370 acres of land, which were divided into lots ranging from 160 to 170 acres, costing between $160 to $400 each. John

Flewin, who figures frequently as the town constable in Clah's diary, owned twenty-five acres across the bay, which he put up for sale for $80-$175.[1] By contrast, Clah, who would have willingly sold his house and land to the HBC, could not do so.[2]

Clah remained so focused on his immediate interests that the broader picture of land alienation is not fully addressed in his diary. He did, however, participate in meetings about the issue at Port Simpson, occasionally acting as a scribe for groups of petitioners and signing petitions against the reserve system.

Clah operated much better as an entrepreneur than as a wage labourer. Wage labour, which limited initiative and had poor financial returns, was another symptom of the colonial system. The legislative framework that the state developed to protect canneries and curtail Aboriginal fishing was another aggravation for Aboriginal fishers, who had profitted from control of their own marine resources prior to the industrial production of canned salmon. These racially biased laws emphasized their subservient status. When the Tsimshian confronted politicians and bureaucrats in Victoria over their land claims and a right to treaties, they were patronized and belittled as incompetent children who did not deserve the rights of full citizenship.

The gold rushes introduced a new racial hierarchy to the province. Clah both observed it, particularly the treatment of Japanese and Chinese miners and workers, and experienced it. In 1897, when he was sleeping on the deck of a steamer to Port Simpson from Victoria (as, no doubt, he had often done on his many voyages), a crew member woke him up and ordered him to make way for a white passenger: "[O]n str Boscowitz. When I was sleep[,] the bad sail man come to me wake me up. he says, [']get up you. move your bed and all you had on a boat steamer[.] a whit[e] man wants take you[r] place to sleep with. come come get up.['] so I move. Same another that make my hearts bad[,] that makes me no sleep. walk inside ship all night."[3] Clah's anger and humiliation are obvious in this last line. He did not record such incidents during the era of the fur trade. The rough and tumble of the days before formal colonization was never as shameful and humiliating as the institutionalized racism of the colonial era. In the confrontation with Baptiste Bottineau that Clah describes in the first pages of his diary, Clah and his brother fight back; they do not meekly make way for a white man see (Chapter 3). They had a personal relationship with the people who attacked them that survived the altercation. By contrast, the old man of 1897 had no way of redressing racial laws or the racist behaviour of strangers.

The establishment of New Metlakatla was partly a response to colonial interference in Tsimshian lives. Duncan was lucky that his falling out with the Anglican Church in Canada coincided with the imposition of reserves on Tsimshian territory, for one of the main motivating forces of the move was not loyalty to Duncan but the wish to escape from the "slavery" of land dispossession and wage labour. Had Clah been able to convince the Port Simpson Tsimshian to move to Alaska, he would have escaped Canada for the same reasons.

Clah did not realize until he was an old man that the Tsimshian had been manoeuvred into a non-negotiable position by the colonial state. Even when the realization came, he kept working towards reconciliation with the system. He always thought that if he could only enlist the help of those with influence and power, he could find a satisfactory pathway that would protect him and his family. It did not work out that way. Clah's long voyage ended with many regrets. Yet he could also look back with satisfaction on his achievements.

Appendix 1
Clah's Trade Records for 24 and 25 December 1865

Skeenah River December 24th 1865

Hookometh
2 Beavers large   1½ gal rice, 4 gal molasse[s]
1 martin [marten]

Thooket
2 martins   3 half gal rice, 1 half gal molasses

Kmases
1 martin   2 half gal rice, 1 gal molasses

Nahcotsnahoh
1 mink   for gil powder

Skeenah River December 25th 1865

Bought [from] Dowelask [h]is wife
1 martin   6½ ftm [fathom] 26 in[ch] cotton
1 do martin   2 paper vermillion

Naw Quah
6 martins   3 ee 3 pts plue [blue blanket]

Cutshepah
1 large Beaver   ½ gal rice

Pecusk
1 martin   20 leafs tobacco

Thanemkit
1 martin   20 leafs tobacco

Ahletax
2 minks   6 inch yellow soap

Quahege
1 martin   1 squ[are] headed axe

Ahtadahad
1 martin   3½ gal rice
2 Beaver   3½ gal molasses

Dowclask
1 martin   3½ gal molasses, 3½ gal rice
4 martins   2 ee 3 pts plew plkts [blue blankets]

Quahtge
1 martin   1 axe sq. headed

Source: Wellcome Library, Arthur Wellington Clah, Diaries and Papers, WMS Amer 140-64.

Appendix 2
Key People in Clah's World

Lucy Addosk (Adooskw) — Clah's mother-in-law.

Catherine (Kitty) Armour — Nisakx's (Martha McNeill's) niece.

Matthew Baillie Begbie — Chief justice of British Columbia.

Rebecca Beynon — (Née Wellington) Clah's second oldest daughter, who married a Welsh sea captain, William Beynon.

William Beynon Jr. — Rebecca Beynon's oldest son. He became a Gitlaan chief, Gwisk'aayn, after his uncle Albert's death. He was a primary informant for anthropologists Marius Barbeau and Viola Garfield and became an ethnographer.

Albert Edward Bolton — Medical missionary at Port Simpson in the 1890s.

Paul Brentzen — Gispaxlo'ots titleholder and active member of the Salvation Army.

George Chismore — A medical doctor who accompanied Clah on a journey up the Nass River and along the grease trail to the Skeena River.

William Collison — CMS missionary who worked at Metlakatla, Massett, and Kincolith.

H.E. Croasdaile — Established a cannery on the Nass River in 1881.

Thomas Crosby — Methodist missionary who came to Fort Simpson in 1874 and remained until 1897.

Robert Cunningham

CMS lay missionary who became an HBC employee, then trader and cannery owner. Married a Tsimshian, Elizabeth Ryan.

Alfred Dudoward

The son of a French Canadian HBC employee and a Tsimshian woman, Diex. Became Gitando chief Sgagweet and had aspirations to the Ligeex name. He and his wife, Kate, invited the Methodists to Fort Simpson in 1874.

William Duncan

CMS lay missionary who arrived at Fort Simpson in 1857, moved to Metlakatla in 1862, and to New Metlakatla in 1887.

Alfred Green

Methodist missionary at Laxgalts'ap (Greenville).

James Grey or Gray

Miner who later pre-empted land on upper Nass River and operated a small cannery in 1891.

John Kennedy

HBC surgeon and clerk at Fort Simpson from 1831 to 1839 and from 1843 to 1847. Chief trader at Fort Simpson in 1847-48 and 1849-52. He married a daughter of Ligeex.

James Alfred Hall

An Anglican minister who was briefly at Metlakatla in Duncan's absence in 1877.

R.H. Hall

An HBC clerk from 1877 to 1887 and a junior chief trader at Port Simpson from 1887 to 1892.

Matthew Johnson

Head of a Gispaxlo'ots Killer Whale house. He was actively involved in Port Simpson politics in the 1890s and 1900s and was one of four Gispaxlo'ots who formed a council to lead the tribe after Martha Legaic's death.

George Kelly

Became Ligeex in 1907. He had been adopted by Alfred Dudoward's mother, Elizabeth Diex/Lawson.

Martha Legaic

Was appointed Gispaxlo'ots chief at age sixteen. She died in 1902.

Paul Legaic I	Was Ligeex in the 1850s and 1860s. He moved to Metlakatla in 1862 and was baptized by William Duncan. He died in 1869.
Paul Legaic II	Became Ligeex after Paul Legaic I. He also lived at Metlakatla, but returned to Port Simpson. He died in 1891.
Sarah Legaic	Was Paul Legaic I's daughter. She lived at Metlakatla with her mother. They both remained good friends of Clah.
William John Macdonald	Senator from 1871 to 1915.
James McCullagh	CMS missionary at Aiyansh on the upper Nass River.
Joseph W. McKay	Justice of the peace and Indian agent.
Albert McMillan	Ginaxangiik chief who assumed both 'Wiiseeks and 'Alamlaxha names.
Donald McNeill	Son of William Henry McNeill and his first wife.
Martha McNeill (Nisakx)	Clah's wife's aunt. She was married to a Nisga'a chief, Saga'waan, before living with and later marrying the HBC trader and factor William Henry McNeill. Dorcas Wellington eventually inherited land in Victoria that had been owned by the McNeills.
Mary McNeill	A daughter of William Henry McNeill and his first wife.
William Henry McNeill	An HBC trader and factor who undertook two tours of duty at Fort Simpson. He married Nisakx and moved to Victoria after his retirement. He died in 1875.
David Morrison	Clah's cousin on his father's side who assumed the name Niis'wa'mak.
Mountain	Nisga'a chief Saga'waan and Dorcas' uncle.
Albert Nelson (Niisho'ot)	A Gitzaxłaał chief.
Nisakx	See entry for Martha McNeill.
Niy'skinwaatk	A hereditary name in Dorcas' house held by her uncle (Nisakx's brother) and then

	her brother (see Martha McNeill). Both men were known as George Niy'skinwaatk.
Peter O'Reilly	A gold commissioner and magistrate. He was Indian reserve commissioner from 1880 to 1898.
S.S. Osterhout	Methodist missionary at Port Simpson in the late 1890s.
Henry William Pierce	Clah's nephew by adoption. He became an ordained Methodist minister and missionary.
William Pollard	The first Methodist missionary at Fort Simpson who baptized four Wellington children.
I.W. Powell	Superintendent of Indian affairs in BC from 1872 to 1889.
William Ridley	Anglican bishop of Caledonia based at Metlakatla.
Patrick Russ	Gispaxlo'ots titleholder Spooxs.
Elizabeth Ryan	A Tsimshian student of Duncan who married Robert Cunningham. She drowned in a boat accident in 1888.
Sgagweet	Gitando chiefly name, which was held by Paul Sgagweet (died 1887) and later inherited by Alfred Dudoward.
Henry and Matthew Shepherd	Members of Clah's house of T'amks.
Harry Swanson	Married Clah's granddaughter Miriam.
A.P. Swineford	Governor of Alaska in the late 1880s.
Henry Wellington Tate	A son of Clah. Although not part of his primary family, there is evidence he was brought up in the Wellington household. It is possible his mother was Habbelekepeen, with whom Clah had a brief marriage. Tate married Isabella Cameron who, after his death, married Sam Bennett. Tate was an informant of the anthropologist Franz Boas, recommended by Clah.
Charles Todd	Indian agent based at Metlakatla in the 1890s.

Robert Tomlinson	CMS missionary at Kincolith and a Duncan ally.
A.W. Vowell	Gold commissioner at Cassiar, a stipendiary magistrate, Superintendent of Indian Affairs from 1890, and Indian reserve commissioner from 1898 to 1911.
Wallace	Clah's brother.
Herbert Wallace	A Gits'iis chief, Niisyaganaat, and informant to William Beynon and anthropologist Marius Barbeau.
Albert Wellington	Clah and Dorcas' youngest son. He became chief Gwisk'aayn and married Maggie Booth.
Andrew Wellington	Clah and Dorcas' second surviving son. Died when he was nine years old.
David Wellington	Clah and Dorcas' oldest surviving son. Died when he was thirteen years old.
Dorcas (Catherine, Datacks)	Clah's wife from a Nisga'a chiefly family. Her brother was Niy'skinwaatk and sister, Nisakx (Martha McNeill). She had two other sisters named Lucy Yatze (Yads) and Emily Barton in the diary.
Fanny Wellington	Clah and Dorcas' daughter. Died when she was eighteen years old.
Martha Wellington	Clah and Dorcas' oldest daughter. See Martha Wesley.
Mary Elizabeth Wellington	Clah and Dorcas' daughter. Died when she was thirteen years old.
Rebecca Wellington	Clah and Dorcas' daughter. See Rebecca Beynon.
Arthur Wesley	Clah and Dorcas' grandson. Died at age twelve from a gunshot wound.
Henry Wesley	Martha Wellington's second husband. Died in 1905.
Martha Wesley	Clah and Dorcas' oldest surviving child. She married William West in 1881. He died in 1888, possibly murdered. She married Henry Wesley in 1894.

'Wiiseeks	Ginaxangiik chief. See Albert McMillan.
George Williscroft	A newcomer who was married to a Tsimshian woman and owned a sawmill in Georgetown.
Lucy Wright (Xpi'lk)	Married to James Wright and inherited the chiefly name Xpi'lk.

$\mathcal{N}otes$

INTRODUCTION

1 Arthur Wellington Clah, Diary, 31 March 1902, Wellcome Library, WMS Amer 140, 1-72 (hereafter Clah Diary). Reproduced as written.

2 Ibid., 30-31 December 1903.

3 R.M. Galois, "Colonial Encounters: The Worlds of Arthur Wellington Clah, 1855-1881," *BC Studies* 115-16 (1997-98): 105-47; Susan Neylan, *The Heavens Are Changing: Nineteenth-Century Protestant Missions and Tsimshian Christianity* (Montreal and Kingston: McGill-Queen's University Press, 2003), Chap. 6; Susan Neylan, "'Eating the Angels' Food': Arthur Wellington Clah – An Aboriginal Perspective on Being Christian, 1857-1909," in *Canadian Missionaries, Indigenous Peoples: Representing Religion at Home and Abroad,* ed. Alvyn Austin and Jamie S. Scott (Toronto: University of Toronto Press, 2005), 88-110; Peggy Brock, "Building Bridges: Politics and Religion in a First Nations Community," *Canadian Historical Review* 24, 2 (2000): 67-96; Peggy Brock, "Two Indigenous Evangelists: Moses Tjalkabota and Arthur Wellington Clah," *Journal of Religious History* 27, 3 (2003): 348-66; Peggy Brock, "New Christians as Evangelists," in *Missions and Empire,* ed. N. Etherington (Oxford: Oxford University Press, 2005), 132-52.

CHAPTER 1: THE LIFE AND TIMES OF ARTHUR WELLINGTON CLAH

1 Hilary Stewart, *Cedar: Tree of Life to the Northwest Coast Indians* (Vancouver: Douglas and McIntyre, 1984), 45-50.

2 See, for example, Andrew R.C. Martindale and Susan Marsden, "Defining the Middle Period (3,500 to 1,500 BP) in Tsimshian History through Comparison of Archaeological and Oral Records," *BC Studies* 138 (Summer 2005): 13-50.

3 Margaret A. Ormsby, *British Columbia: A History* (Vancouver: Macmillan, 1958), 11, and Robin Fisher, *Contact and Conflict: Indian-European Relations in British Columbia, 1774-1890,* 2nd ed. (Vancouver: UBC Press, 1992), 1-2.

4   Jean Barman, *The West beyond the West: A History of British Columbia* (Toronto: University of Toronto Press, 1996), 35-37; Ormsby, *British Columbia,* 57.

5   This settlement was known as Fort Simpson until about 1880, when it became Port Simpson. This raises problems in nomenclature. I use both names. I refer to Fort Simpson when I discus events prior to 1880 and to Port Simpson after that date. Today, the community is known by its Tsimshian name, Lax Kw'alaams.

6   Ormsby, *British Columbia,* 66-68.

7   G.R. Newell, "William Henry McNeill," *Dictionary of Canadian Biography Online,* http://www.biographi.ca/EN/ShowBio.asp?BioId=39274&query=mcneill.

8   G.P.V. Akrigg and Helen B. Akrigg, *British Columbia Chronicle, 1847-1871: Gold and Colonists* (Vancouver: Discovery Press, 1977), 2.

9   Governor James Douglas, Vancouver Island, to Sir George Grey, 1 March 1856, British Columbia Archives (BCA), Letters, Secretary of State, C/AA/10.1/3.

10   *British Colonist,* 23 June 1860 and 26 June 1860; Grant Keddie, *Songhees Pictorial: A History of the Songhees People as Seen by Outsiders, 1790-1912* (Victoria: Royal BC Museum, 2003), 69.

11   Barry M. Gough, *Gunboat Frontier: British Maritime Authority and the Northwest Coast Indians, 1846-1890* (Vancouver: UBC Press, 1984), 85.

12   Dianne Newell, *Tangled Webs of History: Indians and the Law in Canada's Pacific Coast Fisheries* (Toronto: University of Toronto Press, 1993), 3.

13   See Susan Neylan, *The Heavens Are Changing: Nineteenth-Century Protestant Missions and Tsimshian Christianity* (Montreal and Kingston: McGill-Queen's University Press, 2003), 181-86, for a more detailed account of the Bini and the oral traditions associated with him.

14   See Alfred Crosby, *Ecological Imperialism: The Biological Expansion of Europe, 900-1900* (Cambridge: Cambridge University Press, 2004); Cole Harris, "Voices of Disaster: Smallpox around the Strait of Georgia in 1782," *Ethnohistory* 41, 4 (1994): 591-621.

15   There likely were earlier epidemics, but they have not been recorded. Helen Meilleur claims that smallpox arrived on the Coast in the eighteenth century but does not present any evidence. See *A Pour of Rain: Stories from the West Coast Fort* (Vancouver: Raincoast Books, 2001), 203. Harris deduces that smallpox reached the Georgia Strait to the south in 1782 from the east, but he does not comment on whether it travelled north along the Coast. See "Voices of Disaster."

16   Robert Boyd, *The Coming of the Spirit of Pestilence: Introduced Infectious Diseases and Population Decline among the Northwest Coast Indians, 1774-1874* (Seattle: University of Washington Press, 1999), 193-200.

17   An example of this approach is Peter Carsten's *The Queen's People: A Study of Hegemony, Coercion, and Accommodation among the Okanagan of Canada* (Toronto: University of Toronto Press, 1991).

18 Margaret Seguin, "Introduction: Tsimshian Society and Culture," in *The Tsimshian: Images of the Past, Views for the Present,* ed. Margaret Seguin, 2nd ed. (Vancouver: UBC Press, 1993), ix, and Viola E. Garfield and Paul S. Wingert, *The Tsimshian and Their Arts* (Seattle: University of Washington Press, 1966), 5-6. Although all these groups are known to speak Tsimshian languages, in the following chapters I use *Tsimshian* to refer to Coast Tsimshian and *Nisga'a* to refer to peoples domiciled on the Nass River.

19 See R.M. Galois, "Colonial Encounters: The Worlds of Arthur Wellington Clah, 1855-1881," *BC Studies* 115-16 (1997-98): 105-47, for a detailed account of the seasonal movements and activities of the Tsimshian.

20 Christopher F. Roth, "'The Names Spread in All Directions': Hereditary Titles in Tsimshian Social and Political Life," *BC Studies* 130 (2001): 69-92.

21 The nine Tsimshian tribes at Metlakatla were Gitando, Gitzaxłaał, Gits'iis, Gitlaan, Gispaxlo'ots, Giluts'aaẅ, Ginax'angiik, Ginadoiks, and Gitwilgyoots. See Susan Marsden, ed., *Na Amwaaltga Ts'msiyeen: The Tsimshian, Trade, and the Northwest Coast Economy* (Prince Rupert, BC: School District No. 52, 1992); Galois, "Colonial Encounters," 111; Tsimshian Chiefs, *The Tsimshian Trade and the Northwest Coast Economy* (Prince Rupert: Prince Rupert School District 52, 1992), 70; and Jay Miller, *Tsimshian Culture: A Light through the Ages* (Lincoln: University of Nebraska Press, 1997), 17-18.

22 Among many Tsimshian, *smʼoogit* referred to the heads of houses, but at Lax Kw'alaams it referred to the head of a whole tribe – that is, the head of the highest ranking house in the tribal group. The term *lik'agyet* referred to other house heads. Roth, "The Names Spread in All Directions," 37.

23 William Beynon, "Secret Societies," 1939, BCA, Marius Barbeau Northwest Coast Files (MBNCF), MS-2101, Reel A1413, B-F-7.6; M.-F. Guedon, "An Introduction to Tsimshian World View and Its Practitioners," in *The Tsimshian: Images of the Past, Views for the Present,* ed. Margaret Seguin (Vancouver/Seattle: UBC Press/University of Washington Press, 1993), 149-153; Miller, *Tsimshian Culture,* 19.

24 Guedon, "An Introduction," 155. Garfield claims there were two secret societies – the Dog Eaters and the Dancers – that were open to all Tsimshian, while the Cannibal, Fire Thrower, and Destroyer "were acquired as personal, hereditary prerogatives and not as societies." See Garfield and Wingert, *The Tsimshian Indians,* 45.

25 *Potlatch* is a Chinook Jargon word and a gloss for a wide range of ceremonies and dances. See Philip Drucker, *Indians of the Northwest Coast* (New York: McGraw-Hill, 1955), 125-29. Oral histories collected in the twentieth century by Marius Barbeau and William Beynon in *Tsimshian Narratives* describe both warfare and potlatching rivalries. Clah only started using the term *potlatch* in the 1880s; prior to that decade, he always wrote about feasting, dancing, and giving away property. He did not use a single term to describe these wide-ranging activities.

26 Fisher, *Contact and Conflict*, 207.

27 Patterson, "Neshaki: Kinfolk and Trade," *Culture* 10, 2 (1990): 16, and Miller, *Tsimshian Culture*, 136.

28 Dorcas had at least one stillbirth, during which she nearly died, that I have not included. Arthur Wellington Clah, Diary, 16 September 1869, Wellcome Library, WMS Amer 140, 1-72 (hereafter Clah Diary). Galois includes two stillbirths in his list of Clah and Dorcas' children. See "Colonial Encounters," 147.

29 Clah Diary, 23 September 1867.

30 Canadian Museum of Civilization, Hull, Quebec, Barbeau Northwest Coast Files, B-F-24.5, and BCA, Wilson Duff Papers, GR-2809, Tsimshian file 85, "Gispaxlo'ots Personal Names."

31 Clah Diary, first entry as written. Galois suggests Kaelle-ca-con is Laghco, a place where Clah would later buy land and build a house. Galois, "Colonial Encounters," 106.

32 Ibid., preliminary pages before 1858 entry.

33 Ibid., first entry. These names are reproduced as Clah wrote them. Throughout the diary, Clah refers to other people as brothers, but it is not clear whether they are biological brothers who share the same parents or clan brothers. Galois suggests, based on personal communication with Susan Marsden, that Clah was adopted and that his biological father was from Gits'ilaasu. Clah was raised by Guyagan, an Eagle of the Gispaxlo'ots, who was killed around 1838. The diary refers only to Krytin as Clah's father.

34 Ibid., 20 June 1860. "Recent Tsimshian Warfare (1868)," informant Charles Barton, recorded by Marius Barbeau in *Tsimshian Narratives 2: Trade and Warfare*, edited by George MacDonald and John J. Cove (Ottawa: Canadian Museum of Civilization, 1987), 236-38. It was while he was in the south that Clah received news that his brother Wallace had been killed. Clah spells *Ligwanh* in a number of different ways, for example, *Lycun, Lyquna, Layqun,* and *Leequan.*

35 Clah does not mention this incident, but the HBC journal and Duncan's diary both refer to it. It happened just before Duncan arrived at Fort Simpson and before Clah started his own diary. William Duncan Journal, 2 November 1857, BCA, William Duncan Papers, MS-2758, Reel A01715; Fort Simpson (Nass) Post Journal, 13 September 1857, Hudson's Bay Company Archives, B.201/a/8.

36 Clah Diary, 1858.

37 William Duncan Journal, 2 June 1858. Duncan calculated that 650 Tsimshian had left for Victoria that season.

38 Clah Diary, 24 June 1860.

39 Keddie, *Songhees Pictorial,* 77-78.

40 Clah to William Duncan, 2 December 1862, University of British Columbia Library, William Duncan Papers, Correspondence – Letters received, 1862, MG 29 H 15, microfilm. Duncan reported in his diary that, based on Clah's letter, there had been

360 deaths from smallpox at Fort Simpson, and only 2,079 people remained in the village. William Duncan Journal, 3 December 1862. These figures are not entirely accurate. Clah's letter states there were:

Kashepahlock [Gispaxloʼots] 291 alive and 13 dead
Kanahhancac [Ginaxangiik] 280 alive and 32 dead
Kathantoo [Gitando] 166 alive and 32 dead
Cattallak or Shepasth [Gitxaala/Ts'ibasaa?] 332 alive and 35 dead
Catches [Gits'iis] 152 alive and 25 dead
Cathlane [Gitlaan] 260 alive and 38 dead
Killowchow [Gitlutsaaw] 174 alive and 38 dead
Ketchelahle [Gitzaxłaał] 115 alive and 15 dead
Kinahdoyeks [Gitnadoiks] 146 alive and 42 dead
Cathwellakoch [Gitwilgyoots] 153 alive and 31 dead
Total at Fort Simpson 2,069 alive and 301 dead
Tsimshian communities outside Fort Simpson:
Kathchellash [Kitselas on Skeena River] 80 alive and 32 dead
Unnamed place 84 alive and 17 dead
Catchemhyalom [Kitsumkalum] 91 alive and 13 dead

41 Clah Diary, 11 July 1862. This plant has not been identified.
42 Ibid., 21 June 1862.
43 Keddie, *Songhees Pictorial*, 81. Small numbers of northerners continued to visit Victoria, but the large annual migrations stopped with the smallpox epidemic.
44 Clah Diary, 7 October 1869, "[S]he die for her own work. She has running to every one whites an[d] Indians is not our work but her is fault. She had bad diseases."
45 Ibid., 7 May 1869.
46 Ibid. Clah describes Paul Legaic as his father's nephew.
47 Galois, "Colonial Encounters," 139n127.
48 Ibid. Clah uses the name at the beginning of the first diary, when he presumably did not hold the name.
49 Clah Diary, 31 December 1862 and 1 January 1863.
50 Ibid., 20-22 October 1869 and 10 February 1871. I use the Christian name and contemporary spelling of *Ligeex* when I refer to a particular person who holds the Ligeex name, for example, Paul Legaic I or Paul Legaic II. When I refer to the position in a general sense, I use the current orthography of *Ligeex*.
51 Jan Hare and Jean Barman, *Good Intentions Gone Awry: Emma Crosby and the Methodist Mission on the Northwest Coast* (Vancouver: UBC Press, 2006), 40-41, and Neylan, *The Heavens Are Changing*, 115-17.
52 Meilleur claims in her autobiographical account of Port Simpson that, in the absence of men, the women and children survived on snacks. They only prepared full meals when the men were at home. Helen Meilleur, *A Pour of Rain*, 287-88.

53   See Newell, *Tangled Webs*.

54   Clah stayed with the Beynon family when he visited Victoria, and his daughter spent extended periods at Port Simpson with her children. He rarely mentions his son-in-law.

55   Clah Diary, 26 January 1894. This resulted in a falling-out between the two sisters as Martha was a member of the Methodist Church.

56   Neylan, *The Heavens Are Changing*, 53-63; E. Palmer Patterson, *Mission on the Nass: The Evangelization of the Nishga* (Waterloo, ON: Euchalon Press, 1982); and Peggy Brock, "'Building Bridges': Politics and Religion in a First Nations Community," *Canadian Historical Review* 24, 2 (2000): 90-91.

57   W.H. Pierce, *Thirteen Years of Travel and Exploration in Alaska,* edited by Professor and Mrs. H. Carruth (Lawrence, KS: Journal Publishing Company, 1890) and *From Potlatch to Pulpit: Being the Autobiography of the Rev. William Henry Pierce, Native Missionary to the Indian Tribes of the Northwest Coast of British Columbia,* edited by J.P. Hicks (Vancouver: Vancouver Bindery, 1933).

58   Ralph Maud, *Transmission Difficulties: Franz Boas and Tsimshian Mythology* (Burnaby: Talonbooks, 2000), 11.

CHAPTER 2: KEEPING ACCOUNT

1   Molly McCarthy, "A Pocketful of Days: Pocket Diaries and Daily Record Keeping among Nineteenth-Century New England Women," *New England Quarterly* 73, 2 (2000): 284-85, quoting William Cobbett, *Advice to Young Men and (Incidentally) to Young Women in the Middle and Higher Ranks of Life* (1830); Robert Fothergill, *Private Chronicles: A Study of English Diaries* (London: Oxford University Press, 1974), 11-37.

2   McCarthy, "A Pocketful of Days," 280, 291.

3   Fort Simpson (Nass) Post Journal, 23 May 1855, Hudson's Bay Company Archives, B.201/a/8. It was noted that four hundred canoes had left for Victoria in the past two months, thus denying the HBC's own trading post this trade.

4   This was a common format for nineteenth-century diaries; therefore, it is not necessarily proof that the journal was Clah's original model. See McCarthy, "A Pocketful of Days," 286-87.

5   William Duncan Journal, 20 and 26 December 1860, British Columbia Archives (BCA), William Duncan Papers, MS-2758. Edward was named for Rev. Edward Cridge.

6   R.M. Galois, who is annotating the first diary, suggests that the first two diaries were copied from entries Clah made elsewhere (personal communication with author). See also R.M. Galois, "Colonial Encounters: The Worlds of Arthur Wellington Clah, 1855-1881," *BC Studies* 115-16 (1997-98): 105-47. I am not convinced this is correct because Clah clearly states he bought the first book on 27 September 1859.

7   The Wellcome Library has catalogued sixty-two diaries and several books in which Clah kept his financial dealings. See WMS Amer 140, 1-72 (hereafter Clah Diary). There is also a diary that seems to be a partial copy of the 1906 diary in the BC Archives, George Henry Raley Papers, 98208-50, H/D/R13/C52.

8   Clah Account Book, 16 June 1863, Wellcome Library, Arthur Wellington Clah, Diaries and Papers, WMS Amer 140-64.

9   Clah Diary, 6 April 1885. A few months later, Clah noted, "Mr McCollar [McCullagh] this same man lost his Sunday last Spring priest his very good society [CMS] man. One time he lost his Sunday 14 Nov 1885."

10   Ibid., 10 February 1885. The *Ayers American Almanac* was published by Dr J.C. Ayers and Co.

11   These boxes were made in many different sizes. They were used to store ceremonial paraphernalia and to boil food. See Hilary Stewart, *Cedar: Tree of Life to the Northwest Coast Indians* (Vancouver: Douglas and McIntyre, 1984) for a comprehensive discussion of cedar's many uses. Stewart's *Indian Fishing: Early Methods on the Northwest Coast* (Vancouver: J.J. Douglas, 1977) describes the use of bentwood boxes for cooking.

12   Clah Diary, 6 March 1872.

13   Ibid., 15 May 1871.

14   Ibid., 2 April 1881.

15   Thomas Mallon, *A Book of One's Own: People and Their Diaries* (New York: Tickner and Fields, 1984), 6; Stuart Sherman, *Telling Time: Clocks and English Diurnal Form, 1660-1785* (Chicago: University of Chicago Press, 1996), 106-7.

16   Clah Diary, 20 August 1900. The writing in this diary is large and slopes down the page.

17   It is possible, although unlikely, that Clah continued his diary after 1909.

18   Ibid., 13 March 1866. On 29 July 1875, he bought a watch for ten dollars, and on 15 September of the same year he took payment in cash and a damaged watch. In August 1879, he bought a watch for ten dollars and immediately settled a twenty-dollar debt with a Tsimshian.

19   Ibid., 5 September 1888 and 1 January 1891.

20   Franz Boas mentioned meeting a watchmaker at Port Essington in 1888 who travelled around repairing Indian watches. His account suggests that many Tsimshian had watches by the late 1880s. See Franz Boas, *The Ethnography of Franz Boas,* compiled and edited by Ronald P. Rohner (Chicago: University of Chicago Press, 1969), 95.

21   BCA, William Duncan Papers, MS-2758, Reel 1720, 16697-16703. This seems to be a translation from Sm'algyax into English, hence its poor grammar.

22   Sherman, *Telling Time,* 35.

23   Clah Diary, 1 July 1866 and 2 September 1870.

24   Ibid., 12 September 1887.

25 Ibid., 9 February 1872

26 Ibid., 18 November 1873. William Duncan's *Metlahkatlah: Ten Years' Work among the Tsimsheean Indians* (London: Church Missionary House) was published in 1869 and then reissued as *The British Columbian Mission, or Metlahkatlah* in 1871.

27 Clah Diary, 6 October 1882. Missionary J.B. McCullagh gave Clah "W. Duncans History book" to read.

28 Ibid., 28 January 1891.

29 Ibid., 19 October 1907.

30 See R.M. Galois, "Colonial Encounters: The Worlds of Arthur Wellington Clah, 1855-1881," *BC Studies* 115-16 (1997-98): 108.

31 For example, see Jamie S. Scott and Gareth Griffith, eds., *Mixed Messages: Materiality, Texuality, Missions* (New York: Palgrave Macmillan, 2005) and Peggy Brock, "Setting the Record Straight," in *Indigenous Peoples and Religious Change,* ed. Peggy Brock (Leiden: Brill, 2005), 107-28.

32 Clah criticized missionaries for travelling on Sundays, for lying, and for always asking their congregations for money. In a diary entry of 20 June 1869, for example, he criticizes Duncan for travelling on Sunday, and on 21 December 1891 he complains, as he does on many occasions, that Thomas Crosby, the Methodist missionary at Fort Simpson, is always asking for money: "[W]e p[b]laming thomas Crosby keep asking collection mon[e]y everyday."

33 In 1884, a Haida man tried to borrow Clah's diary to show it to a "China chief": "[A] hydah indian named Alek came from massit [Massett] take my Journal to shew my writen to China Chiefs. I woulden let him carry out as I allow anyone Readed. so the hydah caught matt [got mad]. I told him I lay down his Name on my Book. Clah Diary, 13 July 1884.

34 Barbeau briefly describes other Tsimshian oral accounts. See Marius Barbeau, *Tsimshian Narratives 2: Trade and Warfare,* ed. George MacDonald and John J. Cove (Ottawa: Canadian Museum of Civilization, 1987), 552.

35 Andrew R.C. Martindale and Susan Marsden, "Defining the Middle Period (3,500 to 1,500 BP) in Tsimshian History through Comparison of Archaeological and Oral Records," *BC Studies* 138 (2003): 13-50. See also Susan Marsden and Robert Galois, "The Tsimshian, the Hudson's Bay Company, and the Geopolitics of the Northwest Coast Fur Trade, 1787-1840," *Canadian Geographer* 39, 2 (1995): 169-83, and Susan Marsden, "Adawx, Spanaxnox, and the Geopolitics of the Tsimshian," *BC Studies* 135 (2002): 101-35.

36 Clah Diary, 13 November 1876.

37 C.M. Barbeau, "Review of *Tsimshian Mythology* in *American Anthropologist*," 19, 4 (1917): 552.

38 Galois, "Colonial Encounters."

39 William Beynon's mother was Rebecca, Clah's daughter. Beynon's father, also William Beynon, was a Welsh captain of steamers that went up and down the Northwest Coast.

40 William Beynon, *Potlatch at Gitsegukla: William Beynon's 1945 Field Notebooks,* edited by Margaret Anderson and Marjorie Halpin (Vancouver: UBC Press, 2000) and "The Tsimshians of Metlakatla, Alaska," *American Anthropologist* 43, 1 (1941): 83-88; Marjorie Myers Halpin, "William Beynon, Ethnographer: Tsimshian, 1888-1958," in *American Indian Intellectuals,* ed. Liberty Mercer, Proceedings of the American Ethnonological Society (St. Paul, MN: West Publishing, 1976), 141-56.

41 Maud notes that Boas approached Clah as a possible informant on Tsimshian culture: "My friend, George Hunt, of Fort Rupert, Vancouver Island writes me that you are interested in preserving the traditions of your people." This letter was passed on to Henry Tate, who worked for Boas for a number of years. Ralph Maud, *Transmission Difficulties: Franz Boas and Tsimshian Mythology* (Burnaby: Talonbooks, 2000), 11.

42 Barbeau, "Review of *Tsimshian Mythology,*" 553, 561.

43 Sherman, *Telling Time;* Fothergill, *Private Chronicles;* Thomas Mallon, *A Book of One's Own;* and McCarthy, "A Pocketful of Days."

44 See Karin Barber, ed., *African Hidden Histories* (Bloomington: Indiana University Press, 2006), especially Stephan F. Miescher's, "'My Own Life': A.K. Boakye Yiadom's Autobiography – The Writing and Subjectivity of a Ghanian Teacher-Catechist," 27-51, and Ruth Watson's, "'What Is Our Intelligence, Our School Going and Our Reading of Books without Getting Money?' Akinpelu Obiseasan and His Diary," 52-77. Susanne and Lloyd Rudolph have written extensively about the diary of Amar Singh. See Susanne Rudolph and Lloyd Rudolph, eds., with Mohan Singh Kanota, *Reversing the Gaze: Amar Singh's Diary – A Colonial Subject's Narrative of Imperial India* (Boulder, CO: Westview Press, 2002), and Susanne Rudolph and Lloyd Rudolph, "Becoming a Diarist: The Making of an Indian Personal Document," *Indian Social and Economic History Review* 25, 2 (1988): 113-32. See also Tiyo Soga, *The Journal and Selected Writings of Rev. Tiyo Soga,* edited by Donovan Williams (Cape Town: A.A. Balkema, 1983). There is increasing interest in related genres, such as autobiographies, in which the author and the subject of the writing are the same person, and life histories, which are often written by an author not the subject of the book but based on oral accounts of the subject.

45 Lloyd Rudolph, "Self as Other: Amar Singh's Diary as Reflexive 'Native' Ethnography," *Modern Asian Studies* 31 (1997): 168.

46 Ibid., 150.

47 For example, Clah Diary, entries for March 1902.

48 Sherman, *Telling Time,* 31, 35.

49 Clah Diary, 17 January 1885.

50 Ibid., 16 February 1889. William Duncan moved his mission to Alaska after the CMS removed him from their society. The Tsimshian believed that people followed Duncan across the border because the Canadian and British Columbian governments were taking their land under the guise of allotting reserves. The United States was

presented to them as the land of freedom, a place where they would be paid properly and could own land.

51 Leland Donald, *Aboriginal Slavery on the Northwest Coast of North America* (Berkeley: University of California Press, 1997).

Chapter 3: The Fur Trade Era

1 Arthur Wellington Clah, Diary, Book 140-1, Wellcome Library, WMS Amer 140, 1-72
(hereafter Clah Diary).

2 Arthur Wellington Clah, Diary and Notes, British Columbia Archives (BCA), George
Henry Raley Papers, 98208-50, H/D/R13/C52. Peter Quintal (Quantal in Clah's
diary) was the son of Francois Dubois Quintal, born in Quebec, and a Tsimshian
woman, Mary. See Jan Hare and Jean Barman, *Good Intentions Gone Awry: Emma
Crosby and the Methodist Mission on the Northwest Coast* (Vancouver: UBC Press,
2006), 48-49.

3 Published account of visit to Fort Simpson, no author or date (c. 1860s), William
Duncan, Journal, No. 3, 1856-59, 7 October 1857, BCA, William Duncan Papers,
MS-2758, Reel A1720.

4 Clah Diary, May 1856. Baptiste Bottineau had travelled through Fort Simpson the
year before on his way to the Stikine River in search of gold; therefore, Clah and he
might have met before this fight. Fort Simpson (Nass) Post Journal, 9 May 1855,
Hudson's Bay Company Archives (HBCA), B.201/a/8.

5 Clah Diary, 1 November 1859.

6 Clah Account Book, 1 November 1859-72, Wellcome Library, Arthur Wellington
Clah, Diary and Papers, WMS Amer 140-63 (hereafter Clah Account Book).

7 New Westminster was established on the Mainland in 1859 by the Royal Marines.
G.P.V. Akrigg and Helen B. Akrigg, *British Columbia Chronicle, 1847-1871: Gold and
Colonists* (Vancouver: Discovery Press, 1977), 157.

8 Fort Simpson (Nass) Post Journal, 13 September 1857, B.201/a/8; William Duncan
Journal, 2 November 1857. In May 1862, Duncan noted that Clah told him he had
been attacked by drunks on the Nass River and had shot at them, wounding a woman
in the ankle. William Duncan Journal, 10 May 1862. Although Clah mentions heavy
drinking on the Nass, he does not describe being attacked or any shooting. Clah
Diary, 5-6 May 1862.

9 Barry M. Gough, *Gunboat Frontier: British Maritime Authority and the Northwest
Coast Indians, 1846-1890* (Vancouver: UBC Press, 1984), 92.

10 Quoted in Charles Lillard, *Seven Shillings a Year: The History of Vancouver Island*
(Ganges, BC: Horsdal and Schubart, 1986), 143.

11 William Fraser Tolmie, *The Journals of William Fraser Tolmie: Physician and Fur
Trader* (Vancouver: Mitchell Press, 1963), 290, entry for 2 September 1834.

12 Fort Simpson (Nass) Post Journal, 12 and 20 October 1856. It was not only the Tsimshian and neighbouring peoples who drank and fought: HBC employees were often incapacitated by liquor. See, for example, Fort Simpson (Nass) Post Journal, 20 September 1856 and 19 December 1856.

13 Clah Diary, 8 December 1862.

14 William Duncan Journal, 14 April 1863, and Fort Simpson (Nass) Journal, 14 April 1863. Captain Pike only found 36 gallons of alcohol and two casks of mixed spirits on the *Langley*, but 221 gallons of spirits were found off-loaded from the schooner at Kitimat, and another 60 gallons were hidden in bushes on an island. J.W. Pike to the Collector of Customs, New Westminster, 20 April 1863, University of British Columbia Library, William Duncan Papers, Correspondence – Letters received, 1863, MG 29 H 15, microfilm. The *Petrel* was taken over by the HBC and used as a trading schooner.

15 Peter Murray, *The Devil and Mr. Duncan: The History of the Two Metlakatlas* (Victoria: Sono Nis Press, 1985), 72-74.

16 Clah Diary, October and November 1860. He was paid fifteen dollars per month.

17 Ibid., 20 October 1862, and Gough, *Gunboat Frontier*, 92.

18 Clah Diary, 31 March–1 April 1871; BCA, William Duncan Papers, MS-2758, Reel A1719, 15791-15806.

19 Clah Diary, 23-26 April 1871.

20 Ibid., 5, 18, 31 October 1871.

21 Ibid., 8 December 1862.

22 Ibid., 17 April 1863.

23 Viola Garfield, *Tsimshian Clan and Society*, Publications in Anthropology, vol. 7, no. 3 (Washington: University of Washington, 1939), 167-340, 208. Jonathon R. Dean notes a mortuary rum feast was held at Fort Simpson in 1837. See "'Those Rascally Spackaloids': The Rise of Gispaxlots Hegemony at Fort Simpson, 1832-40," *BC Studies* 101 (1994): 60.

24 Clah Diary, 1 and 3 January 1871.

25 See "Recent Tsimshian Warfare (1868)," informant Charles Barton, recorded by Marius Barbeau, in *Tsimshian Narratives 2: Trade and Warfare*, ed. George MacDonald and John J. Cove (Ottawa: Canadian Museum of Civilization, 1987), 236-38, for an account of the whisky feast and subsequent violence.

26 Clah Diary, 13 June 1867 and 30 April 1868; Governor Frederick Seymour, "Report and Journal of Visit of Governor Seymour to the North West Coast in HMS *Sparrowhawk* 1869," University of British Columbia Library, Rare Books and Special Collections.

27 Clah Diary, 1 June 1868; Seymour, "Report and Journal."

28 Akrigg and Akrigg, *British Columbia Chronicle*, 375-76.

29 Clah Diary, 22 November 1871 and 25 December 1872.

30 William Duncan Journal, 23 December 1872.

31   Clah Diary, 20 September 1873.

32   Viola E. Garfield, "The Tsimshian and Their Neighbours," in *The Tsimshian Indians and Their Arts,* ed. Viola E. Garfield and Paul S. Wingert (Seattle: University of Washington Press, 1966), 30.

33   Leland Donald, *Aboriginal Slavery on the Northwest Coast of North America* (Berkley: University of California Press, 1997), 34.

34   Richard Somerset Mackie, *Trading beyond the Mountains: The British Fur Trade on the Pacific, 1793-1843* (Vancouver: UBC Press, 1997), 285.

35   R.M. Galois, "Colonial Encounters: The Worlds of Arthur Wellington Clah, 1855-1881," *BC Studies* 115-16 (1997-98): 119n45, lists trips to Victoria in February-April 1862, June–August 1863, and May–July 1864.

36   Also spelled *Laxhlgu'alaams.* Tsimshian accounts emphasize this connection, while colonial accounts ignore it. For example, see Tolmie, *Journals of William Fraser Tolmie,* for a first-hand colonial account. Susan Marsden and Robert Galois' "The Tsimshian, the Hudson's Bay Company, and the Geopolitics of the Northwest Coast Fur Trade, 1787-1840," *Canadian Geographer* 39, 2 (1995): 169-83, gives a detailed account of the pre-eminence of Ligeex and the Gispaxlo'ots in the fur trade and Ligeex's links with the HBC. Dean uses HBC journal entries to dispute this reading. See Dean, "These Rascally Spackaloids," 41-78.

37   Clah Diary, 14 May–12 June 1862.

38   E. Palmer Patterson, "Neshaki: Kinfolk and Trade," *Culture* 10, 2 (1990): 13-24.

39   Clah Diary, 13 March 1863.

40   Ibid., 21 April 1863. The Fort Simpson (Nass) Post Journal records that Nisakx brought 315 marten, bear, and beaver skins and 6 otter skins, plus some salmon. She then continued on to Metlakatla, where the bishop baptized her.

41   Clah Diary, 5 October 1863; Fort Simpson (Nass) Post Journal, 7 and 10 October 1863. The Hudson's Bay Company Archive's Biographical Sheets list Moffatt as chief trader at Fort Rupert in 1863. He moved to Fort Simpson in 1864. See http://www.gov.mb.ca/chc/archives/hbca/biographical/m/moffatt_hamilton.pdf.

42   Patterson suggests that, through the influence of Nisakx and her family, the HBC trading post, which had been moved away from the Nass River in 1834, was re-established. See Patterson, "Neshaki," 20-21.

43   Clah Diary, 14 July 1863, 19 June 1864. The trip to Victoria took nineteen days; the following year, it took twenty days.

44   Ibid., 15 July 1864; Fort Simpson (Nass) Post Journal, 15 July 1864.

45   Murray, *The Devil and Mr. Duncan,* 82-83; Clah Diary, 29 July 1863. Hamilton Moffatt complained in 1863 that William Duncan was more of a threat to his trade than the whisky schooners. Helen Meilleur, *A Pour of Rain: Stories from the West Coast Fort* (Vancouver: Raincoast Books, 2001), 147-48.

46   Clah Diary, 21 November 1865.

47   Ibid., 30 November 1865.

48 Ibid., 3 December 1865.

49 Ibid., 10 January–5 February 1866.

50 Ibid., 8 February 1866; William Duncan Journal, 8 February 1866.

51 Clah Diary, 13 February 1865; Fort Simpson (Nass) Journal, 13 February 1865.

52 Clah Diary, 17, 21, 23, 24 February 1866, and Clah Account Book, 20 February 1866.

53 See Galois, "Colonial Encounters," 117 and 120, for useful charts that tabulate Clah's trading trips.

54 Clah Diary, 26 August 1864.

55 Meilleur, *A Pour of Rain,* passim.

56 Clah Diary, 26-27 April 1870. In one entry, Clah says he hired twelve men; in another, he says he hired twenty.

57 Ibid., 2 May 1870.

58 Ibid., 24 January 1872.

59 Galois, "Colonial Encounters," 121. Galois observes that these outposts were not successful.

60 Clah Diary, 24 May 1867.

61 Ibid., 3 May 1867.

62 Clah Account Book, 29 July 1867:

My new wife trading

4 beaver	1 fancy silk hadkef	$2.00
3 prime minks	3 bunch sea beeds [weed?]	00.75
1 lynx	4 yds yellow flannal	3.00
	1 pal skirt	4.00
		$9.75

63 Clah Diary, 18 November 1866, 9 September 1867, and 18 September 1867.

64 Ibid., 31 October 1867.

65 Ibid., 18 September 1867.

66 Ibid., 30 January 1869.

67 Ibid., 8 March 1869.

68 Ibid., 14 April 1869.

69 Ibid., 10 January 1869.

70 See Chapter 9 for a discussion of Clah's dreams about missionaries.

71 Clah Diary, 18 October 1866.

72 George Chismore, "From the Nass to the Skeena," *Overland Monthly* 6, 35 (1885): 449-50.

73 Ibid., 457-58.

74 Ibid., 449, 457-58.

75 Ibid., 450.

76 Ibid., 453. Chapter 8 offers a more detailed account of this performance.

77 Ibid., 454.

78   Ibid., 455.

79   Neil J. Sterritt et al., *Tribal Boundaries in the Nass Watershed* (Vancouver: UBC Press, 1998), 202.

80   Chismore, "From the Nass," 456.

81   Clah Diary, 6-7 July 1870.

82   Chismore, "From the Nass," 457.

83   Clah Diary, 15-16 July 1870.

84   Stuart Sherman, *Telling Time: Clocks and English Diurnal Form, 1660-1785* (Chicago: University of Chicago Press, 1996).

85   The United States bought the Russian territories in 1867.

86   Clah Diary, 28 July 1870.

87   Ibid., 20-21 August 1870.

CHAPTER 4: CHASING GOLD

1   See, for example, Robin Fisher, *Contact and Conflict: Indian-European Relations in British Columbia, 1774-1890,* 2nd ed. (Vancouver: UBC Press, 1992); Rolf Knight, *Indians at Work: An Informal History of Native Labour in British Columbia, 1858-1930,* 2nd ed. (Vancouver: New Star Books, 1996).

2   William Duncan, "Account of a Visit to Fort Simpson," n.d. (c. 1868), British Columbia Archives (BCA), William Duncan Papers, Reel A1720.

3   Arthur Wellington Clah, Diary, 7 and 8 January 1869, Wellcome Library, WMS Amer 140, 1-72 (hereafter Clah Diary). On another occasion, Clah complained that Cunningham was sleeping with many women, including Clah's wife. Elizabeth Cunningham was in a canoe with the Reverend Harold Sheldon and three other people when it capsized and all but one boy were drowned on the Skeena River in 1888. Clah Diary, 23 February 1888.

4   R. Geddes Large, *The Skeena River of Destiny* (Vancouver: Mitchell Press, 1958), 31.

5   Clah Diary, 11 February 1871: "[A]lso Mrs Cuningham went back at Mission. Take everything down who belong her man Cuningham Leave company all together. says Built store mouth Skeenah an of [and up at] Ackwelget [Hagwilget]."

6   Large, *Skeena River of Destiny,* 31. New English place names appear in Clah's diary as Europeans extended their activities into the hinterland. Clah adopted these names without comment, even though there were pre-existing Tsimshian names. In 1871, when services for miners were established at the mouth of the Skeena River, Port Essington and Woodcock's Landing became frequent destinations, as did the Forks and Hazelton upriver. See William Henry Collison, *In the Wake of the War Canoe,* edited by Charles Lillard (Victoria: Sono Nis Press, 1981), 202. Port Essington was named by George Vancouver. It was an autumn camp of the Tsimshian called Spa-ukshut. Cunningham and Hankin pre-empted land at the camp site to establish a store. Woodcock's Landing was named after the man who opened an inn there. In

1876, a cannery was established by the North West Commercial Co. It later became Inverness Cannery. See Large, *Skeena River of Destiny*, 30-31.

7 *Daily Standard*, 21 January 1871, located at the end of the Clah Diary, 140-8.
8 Clah Diary, 11 May 1871.
9 Ibid., 23 May 1871.
10 Ibid., 26 May 1871.
11 Ibid., 11 May–3 June 1871.
12 Ibid., 31 July and 1 August 1871.
13 David Riccardo Williams, "Peter O'Reilly," *Dictionary of Canadian Biography Online*, http://www.biographi.ca.
14 Clah Diary, 5-6 January 1872.
15 Ibid., 7 April 1872.
16 Ibid., 25 April–25 May 1873.
17 Ibid., 1 July 1873 and 19-20 July 1873.
18 Ibid., 6 August 1873.
19 Stephen Redgrave, Journals and Sundry Papers, 1852-75, BCA, E/B/R24A; Victor G. Hopwood, "Thomas McMicking," *Dictionary of Canadian Biography Online*, http://www.biographi.ca.
20 W.H. Pierce, *Thirteen Years of Travel and Exploration in Alaska*, edited by Professor and Mrs. H. Carruth (Lawrence, KS: Journal Publishing Company, 1890), 11. The tone of this account was, no doubt, partly the result of the editorial intervention of the Carruths.
21 It is possible that the editors coloured the narrative with their own prejudices.
22 Clah Diary, 1 June 1887. This meant that Clah could not get a job at Treadwells.
23 Pierce, *Thirteen Years*, 63. In his journal, Redgrave listed the costs of basic provisions: flour, eighty dollars a barrel; beans, forty dollars for a hundred pounds; sugar, sixty cents a pound; tea, three dollars a pound; and bacon, seventy cents a pound. See Redgrave, Journal and Sundry Papers, 5 May 1875.
24 Clah Diary, 15-26 June 1875.
25 Ibid., 12-14 July 1875.
26 Ibid., 9 January, 22 February, and 1 March 1876.
27 Ibid., 28 September 1875.
28 Ibid., 7 September 1875.
29 Ibid., 7 August 1886.
30 Ibid., 9 October, 1875. One of these lawyers was David, whom Clah was to call on many years later in Victoria, when he was Justice David, for help resolving his land disputes. "Judge Seleven" was probably the gold commissioner for Cassiar, J.H. Sullivan. Cook eventually paid Clah two hundred dollars in gold dust.
31 On 25 April 1976, Clah noted that he had bought land at Laghco from Anchleg for $600; however, on 19 May he paid Nes-kemass $700, which also covered Nes-kemass'

labour. The next, day Clah went to Laghco to see the land he had bought. Presumably, the first sale fell through, while the second went ahead. See Chapter 6 for more details on Clah's land dealings.

32   Clah Diary, 29 June 1881.
33   Ibid., 6 September 1879.
34   Ibid., 9 August 1879.
35   Ibid., 17 February 1881.
36   BC Sessional Papers, No. 5, 1881, 849, BCA, Microfilm D-24, Reel 1.
37   Clah Diary, 13 June 1881.
38   BC Sessional Papers, No. 5, 1881, 849, microfilm D-24, reel 1, BC Archives.
39   Clah Diary, 4-5 July 1881.
40   Ibid., 12 May 1887.
41   Pierce, *Thirteen Years,* 65.
42   Clah Diary, 30 June 1886.
43   Ibid., 6-21 July 1886.
44   Ibid., 4 June 1887.
45   Ibid., 14 August 1886.
46   Ibid., 23 July 1887.
47   Redgrave, Journals and Sundry Papers, 5 May 1875.
48   Clah Diary, 3 July 1887.
49   Ibid., 29 August 1887.
50   Ibid., 12 September 1887.
51   Ibid., 23 September 1887.
52   Ibid., 9-19 August 1888.
53   Ibid., 15 September 1888.
54   Argillite is a sedimentary rock similar to slate and shale but with no slate cleavages. Haida are well known and excellent carvers of black argillite, as were Tsimshian.
55   Clah Diary, 8 August 1887 and 24-25 September 1888.
56   Ibid., 21-30 April 1885.
57   Ibid., 1 May 1885.
58   Ibid., 15 June 1885.
59   Neil J. Sterritt et al., *Tribal Boundaries in the Nass Watershed* (Vancouver: UBC Press, 1998), 215; Clah Diary, 30-31 August and 6 September 1880. Surviving Tsetsaut became integrated with Nisga'a in the late nineteenth century. See Gordon B. Inglis et al., "Tsimshian of British Columbia since 1900," in *Handbook of North American Indians,* vol. 7, *Northwest Coast,* edited by Wayne Suttles (Washington, DC: Smithsonian Institution, 1990), 289.
60   Clah Diary, 28 January 1885.
61   Ibid., 28 July 1893 and 28 August 1893.
62   R.M. Galois argues that Clah bought land at Laghco and, later, on the Nass because he had a falling out with Crosby, who intervened in his dispute with Peter Quintal

and the other men he had bought out after they built their boat at Dease Lake. See "Colonial Encounters: The Worlds of Arthur Wellington Clah, 1855-1881," *BC Studies* 115-16 (1997-98): 142. The quarrel might have been a contributing factor, but it is unlikely that Clah would have moved from Fort Simpson if he believed it would damage his economic situation.

63 Clah Diary, 7 November and 1 December 1877.

64 Lands Administration Division file 1273/79, BCA, Correspondence Files Relating to the Administration, Management, Conservation, and Development of Crown Lands and National Resources, British Columbia Lands Branch, GR-1440, Reel B2663; Kittacdamix Petition Re Redgrave Taking Up Land, 12 February 1879, BCA, GR-1440, B266 File 283/79; Clah Diary, 1 July 1879; Henry Schutt to W. Duncan, 4 November 1879, BCA, William Duncan Papers, MS-2758, Correspondence Received, 1876-80, Reel A1706. Despite Clah's dispute with Redgrave, he travelled with him and associated with him at the goldfields that year. Clah Diary, 9-11 and 30 June 1879. This dispute is discussed in Chapter 6.

65 Clah Diary, 8 August 1887.

66 Ibid., 13 and 28 June 1878 and 19 July 1878. Because Clah also spells *Linton* as *Linden*, it is not clear which is the correct spelling.

67 Andrew died on 13 September 1882, David on 27 February 1883, and Ida on 1 January 1883. No date is given for Maggie's death, but it was also at this time. Clah Diary and Clah Account Book, Wellcome Library, Clah Diaries and Papers, WMS Amer 140-67. Clah heard about his grandsons' deaths from his daughter Martha when he returned from Juneau on 20 October 1887. It is not clear whether they were both her children or whether one was Rebecca's.

68 Clah Diary, 13 September 1882.

69 Clah first heard of West's death on 6 March 1888. Martha and William West were married on 26 December 1881. Arthur Wellington Clah, Diary and Notes, n.d., BCA, George Henry Raley Papers, 98208-50, H/D/R13/C52; Clah Diary, 26 December 1881.

70 Clah Diary, 4 May 1883. There are two versions of this diary. The reference to the deaths of Ida and Maggie are in Vol. 67.

CHAPTER 5: FOOD PRODUCTION AND WAGE LABOUR

1 Nancy J. Turner, *Food Plants of British Columbian Indians,* Part 1, *Coastal Peoples* (Victoria: BC Provincial Museum, 1975), 20-21.

2 Arthur Wellington Clah, Diary, 13 March 1865 and 7 March 1887, Wellcome Library, WMS Amer 140, 1-72 (hereafter Clah Diary).

3 Ibid., 1 April 1887.

4 Ibid., 24 March 1886.

5 Ibid., 21 March 1866

6 Ibid., 12 March 1892. Eight canoes took twenty tons of fish in one tide and thirty-three tons in the next tide.

7   Hilary Stewart, *Indian Fishing: Early Methods on the Northwest Coast* (Vancouver: J.J. Douglas, 1977, 124). On one occasion, when Clah was travelling with Chief Niishoʼot (Albert Nelson) and his son from Port Simpson to Metlakatla, they passed a herring spawning area. Niishoʼot directed Clah and his son to cut hemlock branches to place in the sea to harvest the herring. Clah Diary, 29 March 1894.

8   Clah Diary, 19 March–3 April 1889.

9   Stewart, *Indian Fishing*, 149.

10 Clah Diary, 30 March 1892. Andrew Martindale and Irena Jurakic suggest that an extended family of about thirty people could produce a year's supply of eulachon and salmon in two to three months. Clah does not indicate how many family members were involved in eulachon production. See Martindale and Jurakic, "Northern Tsimshian Elderberry Use in the Late Pre-Contact to Post-Contact Era," *Canadian Journal of Archaeology* 28, 2 (2004): 254-80, 257.

11 Turner, *Food Plants of British Columbian Indians*, 34.

12 Clah Diary, 28 March 1992.

13 George Chismore notes that, to suit European tastes, the HBC had grease made from fresh rather than decomposed fish. The grease was odourless and used for cooking and as a substitute for cod liver oil. George Chismore, "From the Nass to the Skeena," *Overland Monthly* 6, 35 (1885): 451.

14 Clah Diary, 25 May 1887.

15 Dianne Newell, *Tangled Webs of History: Indians and the Law in Canada's Pacific Coast Fisheries* (Toronto: Toronto University Press, 1993), 13.

16 Clah Diary, 9 April 1892.

17 Ibid., 22 May 1876 and 29 September 1881.

18 Ibid., 26 December 1898.

19 Ibid., 17 June 1897.

20 Ibid., 20-21 February 1871.

21 Ibid., 16 November 1907.

22 Reserve Commissioner (Peter O'Reilly) to the Superintendent of Indian Affairs, Ottawa, 25 March 1882, Department of Indian Affairs, Records of Joint Reserve Commission Letterbook, British Columbia Archives (BCA), GR-0933, Reel B1391, Vols. 1273-1283; Statement by Rev. A.E. Green in an appendix to Methodist Missionary Society, *Letter from the Methodist Missionary Society to the Superintendent General of Indian Affairs Respecting British Columbia Troubles* (Toronto: Methodist Missionary Society, 1889), 15. In a letter dated 3 April 1886, Green claimed that Grey took possession of his land "by means of a bogus paper" and later received a Crown grant based on false representations. Extract of a letter from Rev. A.E. Green, BCA, Department of Indian Affairs, RG 10, Vol. 3700, File 16,686, Reel B290. Green claimed that Snow, Grey, and Robinson had rented land from the Nisga'a, but O'Reilly reported

that they had pre-empted land that was later converted to Crown grants by the provincial government.

23 Clah Diary, 22 October 1886, Peter O'Reilly, Minutes of Decision. Snow might have split from his wife, who seems to have been a white woman – she was forced out of Greenville when it was declared a reserve. She moved to Kincolith in 1886.

24 O'Reilly to Superintendent of Indian Affairs, 25 March 1882. Grey claimed that he had pre-empted in 1874 the land that was issued as a Crown grant on 3 January 1878.

25 Thanks to the anonymous reviewer for this reference.

26 Clah Diary, 17 November 1873, 20 February 1874, 12 May 1878, 11 June 1878, 26 August 1878, April 1884, 31 May 1890, and 15 July 1891.

27 Ibid., 6 March 1879. In some sources (for example, Green's correspondence) the name is spelled *Robinson,* in others (for example, O'Reilly's letter) it is *Robertson.* Clah uses both spellings.

28 A.E. Green, *Letter from the Methodist Missionary Society,* 15.

29 Clah Diary, 6 June 1880; 8, 12, 14 July and 9 August 1880.

30 W.M. Ross, "Salmon Cannery Distribution on the Nass and Skeena Rivers of British Columbia, 1877-1926" (Bachelor's essay, University of British Columbia, 1967), 15.

31 Clah Diary, 11, 13 August 1881.

32 Ibid., 8 November 1881.

33 Ibid., 26 December 1881.

34 Ibid., 25, 30, 31 January 1882. The dispute between Duncan and Ridley is documented in many publications, including, Peter Murray, *The Devil and Mr. Duncan: The History of the Two Metlakatlas* (Victoria: Sono Nis Press, 1985); Jean Usher, *William Duncan of Metlakatla: A Victorian Missionary in British Columbia,* National Museum of Man Publications in History, No. 5 (Ottawa: National Museum of Man, 1974); and Henry S. Wellcome, *The Story of Metlakahtla,* 2nd ed. (New York: Saxon, 1887). These issues are discussed in later chapters.

35 Clah Diary, 6 May 1882.

36 Ibid., 24 December 1882.

37 Ibid., 10 March and 12-17 April 1883.

38 Ibid., June–July 1883.

39 James A. McDonald, "Social Change and the Creation of Underdevelopment: A Northwest Coast Case," *American Ethnologist* 21, 1 (1994): 167.

40 Ross, "Salmon Cannery Distribution," 40; Newell, *Tangled Webs,* 51.

41 Clah Diary, 9-23 July 1884.

42 Ibid., July and August 1884.

43 Ibid., 27 August 1884.

44 Ibid., 1-16 September 1884.

45 Ibid., 8 August 1891. Chinese men were also hired to supervise and record the men's catch as they delivered them to the cannery.

46 Ross, "Salmon Cannery," Appendix, 4-7.

47 Clah Diary, 9 May 1889 and 21 January 1890. These licences were not a success and were modified in response to cannery owners' (rather than Aboriginal) complaints in 1892. Newell, *Tangled Webs*, 69-70.

48 Douglas Harris, *Fish, Law, and Colonialism: The Legal Capture of Salmon in British Columbia* (Toronto: University of Toronto Press, 2001), 66.

49 Clah Diary, 2 June 1890. McDonald argues that cannery owners preferred paying wages to ensure that the fishermen and their families stayed with the company for the season. McDonald, "Social Change," 167-69.

50 Clah Diary, 19 July 1899.

51 Newell, *Tangled Webs*, 78.

52 Clah Diary, 13 September 1891. Paige Raibmon, *Authentic Indians: Episodes of Encounter from the Late-Nineteenth-Century Northwest Coast* (Durham: Duke University Press, 2005).

53 Raibmon, *Authentic Indians*, 76-77; G. Thomann, *American Beer: Glimpses of Its History and Description of Its Manufacture* (New York: US Brewers' Association, 1909), Chap. 10.

54 Raibmon, *Authentic Indians*, 81; Clah Diary, 31 August 1891.

55 Clah Diary, 13-20 September 1891.

56 Ibid., 5 September–5 October 1899.

57 Ibid., 29 September 1891.

58 Ibid., 16-17 May 1893.

59 F.W. Howay, "Potatoes: Records of Some Early Transactions at Fort Simpson, B.C.," *The Beaver*, Outfit 259 (March 1929): 155-56. Howay notes that while the Haida grew the potatoes, the Tsimshian acted as middlemen, selling the potatoes to the HBC. Rolf Knight, *Indians at Work: An Informal History of Native Labour in British Columbia, 1858-1930*, 2nd ed. (Vancouver: New Star Books, 1996), 168; Helen Meilleur, *A Pour of Rain: Stories from the West Coast Fort* (Vancouver: Raincoast Books, 2001), 84-85. Potatoes were used to distill alcohol as well as for food. John Davidson Darling, "The Effects of Culture Contact on the Tsimshian System of Land Tenure during the Nineteenth Century" (Master's thesis, University of British Columbia, 1955), 26.

60 Meilleur, *A Pour of Rain*, 86-88.

61 Lugeneth is probably Ligwiniis, a high-ranking Gitlaanok of the Wolf Clan.

62 For instance, in January 1882, Clah had a cargo of half a ton of potatoes. Clah Diary, 20 January 1882. In 1886, he claimed he had sold fifteen thousand pounds of potatoes for fourteen dollars. Clah Diary, 22 September 1886.

63 Ibid., 7 May 1897.

64 Ibid, 21 June 1898.

65 Ibid., 23-24 October 1891.

66 Ibid., 24 May 1892.
67 Ibid., 6 February 1891.
68 Ibid., 11 and 13 February 1891.
69 Ibid., 29 May 1893. Todd was following provincial government policy when he allocated only ten acres. Paul Tennant, *Aboriginal Peoples and Politics: The Indian Land Question in British Columbia, 1849-1989* (Vancouver: UBC Press, 1995), 44; Cole Harris, *Making Native Space: Colonialism, Resistance, and Reserves in British Columbia* (Vancouver: UBC Press, 2002), 74-75.
70 Clah Diary, 15-16 October 1894.
71 Martindale and Jurakic, "Northern Tsimshian Elderberry Use," 258.
72 Clah Diary, 31 August 1870 and 6 April 1889.
73 See, for example, Martindale and Jurakic, "Northern Tsimshian Elderberry Use," 274; Jo-Anne Fiske, "Colonization and the Decline of Women's Status: The Tsimshian Case," *Feminist Studies* 17, 3 (1991): 509-35.
74 Andrew Martindale, "Tsimshian Houses and Households through the Contact Period," in *Household Archaeology on the Northwest Coast,* ed. E. Sobel, A. Trieu Gahr, and K.M. Ames (Ann Arbor: International Monographs in Prehistory, 2006), 143.

CHAPTER 6: LAND MATTERS

1 Arthur Wellington Clah, Diary, 4 August 1888, Wellcome Library, WMS Amer 140, 1-72 (hereafter Clah Diary).
2 Swineford was district governor of Alaska from 1885 to 1889.
3 Peter Murray, *The Devil and Mr. Duncan: The History of Two Metlakatlas* (Victoria: Sono Nis Press, 1985), 198, 209-10.
4 Letter to A.W. Clah from A.P. Swineford, 23 September 1887, British Columbia Archives (BCA), MS-0271.
5 Kenneth Brealey, "Travels from Point Ellice: Peter O'Reilly and the Indian Reserve System in British Columbia," *BC Studies* 115-16 (1997-98): 231.
6 Although the conflicts over land were played out after British Columbia joined the Dominion, coastal peoples continued to view Queen Victoria as the ultimate authority and someone they might be able to deal with rather than impersonal governments in Ottawa and Victoria.
7 Viola E. Garfield and Paul S. Wingert, *The Tsimshian and Their Arts* (Seattle: University of Washington Press, 1966), 14. See also Douglas Harris, *Fish, Law, and Colonialism: The Legal Capture of Salmon in British Columbia* (Toronto: University of Toronto Press, 2001).
8 Marjorie Halpin and Margaret Seguin, "Tsimshian Peoples: Southern Tsimshian, Coast Tsimshian, Nishga, and Gitksan," in *Handbook of North American Indians,* vol. 7, *Northwest Coast,* ed. Wayne Suttles (Washington, DC: Smithsonian Institution, 1990), 267. These winter villages had originally been located on the lower Skeena

River. By the time they moved to Port Simpson, one tribe, Gitwilksibaa, had become extinct.

9   R.M. Galois, "Colonial Encounters: The Worlds of Arthur Wellington Clah, 1855-1881," *BC Studies* 115-16 (1997-98): 139.

10   Clah Diary, 29 November 1877. When cross-examined by Robert Tomlinson about his Nass River houses, Clah made it clear that his house at Aiyansh was not his, but his wife and children's, ibid., 27 January 1879. Galois, "Colonial Encounters," 142n142. Galois claims the land belonged to Clah's wife, although he does not offer any evidence.

11   Clah Diary, 26 August 1878.

12   I.W. Powell to Chief Commissioner of Lands and Works, 1 October 1879, BCA, British Columbia Lands Branch, Correspondence Files Relating to the Administration, Management, and Development of Crown Lands and Natural Resources, GR-1440, Reel B2663, File 1273/79.

13   Petition, 14 February 1879, BCA, GR-1440, Reel B2664, Files 342/81 and 383/79.

14   For a detailed discussion of the history of reserves in British Columbia, see Cole Harris, *Making Native Space: Colonialism, Resistance, and Reserves in British Columbia* (Vancouver: UBC Press, 2002).

15   Paul Tennant, *Aboriginal Peoples and Politics: The Indian Land Question in British Columbia, 1849-1989* (Vancouver: UBC Press, 1995), 34-35, 40-41; Harris, *Making Native Space,* 35-36, 68.

16   See Peggy Brock, "The Historical Dispossession of Indigenous Lands in Western Australia and British Columbia," *Studies in Western Australian History* 23 (2003): 157-65.

17   Reserve Commissioner to Superintendent General of Indian Affairs, 8 April 1882, BCA, Department of Indian Affairs, Records of Joint Reserve Commission, GR-0933, Letterbooks 1871-1919, Reel B1391, Vols. 1273-1283.

18   Clah Diary, 30 June and 1 July 1879. Vowell took over from Powell as Indian superintendent for British Columbia in 1890 and became Indian reserve commissioner in 1898. See Harris, *Making Native Space,* 219.

19   Ibid., 23 August 1879.

20   Ibid., 13 October 1881.

21   Ibid., 23 August 1878.

22   Methodist Missionary Society, *Letter from the Methodist Missionary Society to the Superintendent General of Indian Affairs respecting British Columbia Troubles* (Toronto: Methodist Missionary Society, 1889), vi.

23   Ibid., 43-45.

24   Clah Diary, 7 October 1881.

25   Ibid., 10 October 1881.

26   Ibid., 19 October 1881.

27 Crosby received a letter from Vowell dated 27 September 1881 that advised him of O'Reilly's visit as O'Reilly was about to leave Victoria. A.W. Vowell to T. Crosby, 27 September 1881, University of British Columbia Library, Thomas Crosby Fonds, Correspondence 1881-82, Box 1-10.

28 Reserve Commissioner to Superintendent General of Indian Affairs, Ottawa, 25 March 1882, BCA, Department of Indian Affairs, Records of Joint Reserve Commission, GR-0933, Letterbooks, 1870-1919, Reel B1391, Vols. 1273-83.

29 Clah Diary, 20-21 October 1881.

30 Ibid., 21-22 October 1881.

31 Arthur Wellington Clah to Commissioner of Crown Lands for British Columbia, 11 March 1883, BCA, British Columbia Lands Branch, Correspondence Files Relating to the Administration, Management, and Development of Crown Lands and Natural Resources, GR-1440, File 496/83. The note added to this letter by the Indian superintendent states: "This man has houses and land claims scattered up & down the River at various places. Cannot hold land without Special authority of Governor in Council."

32 Clah Diary, 16, 18 April 1887.

33 Harris, *Making Native Space*, 205; Statement of Rev. T. Crosby, Appendix, Methodist Missionary Society, *Letter*, 4.

34 Clah Diary, 24 March 1888; Methodist Missionary Society, *Letter*, iii.

35 Methodist Missionary Society, *Letter*, 44.

36 J.P. Planta, "Report of the Commission to the Northwest Coast Indians by JP Planta: Relating to the Commission Appointed to Enquire into the State and Conditions of the Indians of the North-West Coast of British Columbia, 22 February 1888," BC Sessional Papers, 22 February 1888, BCA, Microfilm D-24, Reel 5, 17-18; Brealey, "Travels from Point Ellice," 212. Planta accepts the Nisga'a view that Tsimshian had no rights to land on the Nass River without considering Tsimshian claims regarding land usage on the Nass River.

37 Clah Diary, 13-14 March 1884. It is not clear if these threats were carried out. In 1888, the Kincolith Nisga'a told Fisheries officials they owned the river, refused to buy fishing licences, and claimed that any licence fees belonged to them. See Harris, *Fish, Law, and Colonialism*, 63.

38 Planta, "Report," 431; O'Reilly Report Re Reserve No. 10. Rights to Stoney Point and other Nass River reserves were still in dispute in 1916 when the McKenna-McBride Royal Commission held hearings. See, BCA, Department of Indian Affairs, GR-0123, RG 10, Vol. 11019, p. 651.

39 Clah Diary, 23 April 1887.

40 Meeting at Port Simpson with McKay 8 December 1883, University of British Columbia Library, Thomas Crosby Fonds, Box 1-7.

41 Clah Diary, 15, 17 December 1885.

42   Ibid., 15-16 December 1885; R.H. Hall to A.W. Clah, 15 December 1885, and A.W. Clah to R.H. Hall, 14 January 1887, UBC Library, Thomas Crosby Fonds, Box 1-9.

43   Paul Legaic to R.H. Hall, 14 January 1887, UBC Library, Thomas Crosby Fonds, Box 9.

44   Gispaxlo'ots to Superintendent Powell, 4 November 1882 and 8 March 1883, UBC Library, Thomas Crosby Fonds, Box 6.

45   William Beynon manuscript, Reel 3, No. 214, informant W.H. Pierce, UBC Library.

46   Gispaststi [Gispaxlo'ots] Band, Port Simpson, to Royal Commission, 16 October 1915, BCA, GR-0123, RG 10, Vol. 11019, p. 656. Jonathon R. Dean claims that, according to HBC journal entries, Chief Niisho'ot had established, ahead of Ligeex, a house at Fort Simpson in November 1834 (he died during the smallpox epidemic of 1836). See Dean, "'Those Rascally Spackaloids': The Rise of Gispaxlots Hegemony at Fort Simpson, 1832-40," *BC Studies* 101 (1994): 52.

47   William Fraser Tolmie, *The Journals of William Fraser Tolmie: Physician and Fur Trader* (Vancouver: Mitchell Press, 1963), 287; Memorandum from W.F. Tolmie, with excerpt from his diary, 20 July 1834 and A. Munro to Board of Commissioners on Indian Land Claims and Reserves in British Columbia, 9 October 1876, BCA, GR-1440, RG 10, Reel B02950, Vol. 3699, File 16682.

48   I.W. Powell to Thomas Crosby, 16 September 1881, BCA, GR-1440, RG 10, Reel B0290, Vol. 3699, File 16682.

49   J.A. Grahame to W. Pollard, March 1874; W. Pollard to P. O'Reilly, 13 July 1874; W. Pollard to P. O'Reilly, 11 August 1874; extract from Indian Superintendent Powell's Report, 26 August 1879; I.W. Powell to T. Crosby, 16 September 1881; G. Blenkinsop to I.W. Powell, 27 September 1881. All in BCA, GR-1440, RG 10, Reel B0290, Vol. 3699, File 16682.

50   Clah Diary, 29 December 1885.

51   Ibid., 12 January 1886.

52   Ibid., 24 August, 8 and 31 October, and 11 November 1898. It was later claimed by the Gispaxlo'ots that Charles Todd, the Indian agent, had used misrepresentation to persuade people to sign papers giving away a portion of the Port Simpson lands. Clah was a signatory of the submission to the commission. Gispaststi [Gispaxlo'ots] Band, Port Simpson, to Royal Commission, 16 October 1915.

53   Clah Diary, October-November 1907.

54   Ibid., 21, 23 December 1907; January 1908; and 20 October 1909. W.T. Kergin to Arthur Wellington Clah, 25 January 1909, BCA, George Henry Raley Papers, 98208-50, H/D/R13/C52, Arthur Wellington Clah, Diary and Notes.

55   Anonymous, "Port Simpson," BCA, Marius Northwest Coast Files, MS-2101, Reel A1413.

56   Clah Diary, December 1889.

57   Ibid., 8 January 1892.

58 Ibid., 29 August 1892, 22 September 1893, 20 December 1895, 15 February 1896, and 22 July 1896. Despite the poor quality of the land, Clah was allocated only ten acres in line with provincial policy.

59 Sylvia Van Kirk, "Tracing the Fortunes of Five Founding Families in Victoria," *BC Studies* 115-16 (1997-98): 148; Cecil Clark, *The Best of Victoria: Yesterday and Today* (Victoria: Victorian Weekly, 1973). Shoal Bay had previously been known as McNeill Bay. I thank Sylvia Van Kirk for her assistance in locating documents relating to Nisakx, particularly her will, and for making available her genealogy of W.H. McNeill's family.

60 E. Palmer Patterson, "Neshaki: Kinfolk and Trade," *Culture* 10, 2 (1990): 21. Nisakx is usually spelled *Neshaki* in the contemporary records. According to William Duncan, McNeill had not married Nisakx because of "feelings of shame she being so far beneath him." William Duncan Journal, 15 April 1862, BCA, William Duncan Papers, MS-2758.

61 This transaction is confirmed in a letter from lawyer Charles Wilson to Roderick Finlayson and J.C. Prevost, 20 February 1891, BCA, Victoria Supreme Court Probate/Estate Files, GR-1304, Reel B09319, File 1485/99.

62 Clah Diary, 4 May 1891.

63 Ibid., 18 October 1892.

64 BCA, Victoria Supreme Court Probate/Estate Files, GR-1304, Reel B09319, File 1485/99.

65 Clah Diary, 1 November 1892.

66 Ibid., 21 October 1894, copies of power of attorney given to Donald H. McNeill for D.W. Clah, L. Yatze, and E. Barton filed 18 May 1894, BCA, Victoria Supreme Court Probate/Estate Files, GR-1304, Reel B09319, File 1485/99.

67 Clah Diary, 22 July 1895.

68 Ibid., 20-21 July 1895.

69 Ibid., 22 July 1895; deposition sworn on 31 October 1895, BCA, Victoria Supreme Court Probate/Estate Files, GR-1304, Reel B09319, File 1485/99.

70 It took another nine months to collect the necessary signatures to revoke the power of attorney. Clah Diary, 7 April 1896.

71 Ibid., 27 July 1895.

72 Ibid., 3 August 1895. It is not clear when Clah next visited Bridgeman, who on that occasion gave him back papers, signed before Queen's council, that gave more power to Chief Ligeex. Ibid., 9 December 1896.

73 Langley and Martin to Attorney General, 22 March 1899, enclosing an earlier letter to the attorney general of 15 June 1898, BCA, Victoria Supreme Court Probate/Estate Files, GR-1304, Reel B09319, File 1147/98, 1485/99.

74 Clah Diary, 20 October 1899 and 23 June 1900.

75 Ibid., 22 August 1807.

76 Tennant, *Aboriginal Peoples*, 39-41.

CHAPTER 7: BECOMING A CHRISTIAN

1   Arthur Wellington Clah, Diary, the end of diary Number 33, July 1887, Wellcome Library, WMS Amer 140, 1-72 (hereafter Clah Diary).
2   It is, of course, possible that Clah did attend a Christian service or meeting in 1855.
3   Clah Diary, first volume of the Diary (140-1), entry for 1858.
4   William Duncan Journal, 17 May 1858, British Columbia Archives (BCA), William Duncan Papers, MS-2758. Galois notes that Bishop George Hills in Victoria, in January 1860, was impressed by Clah's literacy and his knowledge of Christianity. See R.M. Galois, "Colonial Encounters: The Worlds of Arthur Wellington Clah, 1855-1881," *BC Studies* 115-16 (1997-98): 135-36.
5   Clah Diary, July 1861
6   Ibid., February 1862.
7   Ibid., April 1862.
8   Ibid., 21 June 1862.
9   Ibid., 28 July 1862.
10 See, for example, ibid., 1 August 1863 and 11 January 1864.
11 Ibid., 24 February 1864.
12 Ibid., 25 December 1892.
13 See, for example, ibid., 25 September and 25 October 1870.
14 Ibid., 14 October 1867. Galois suggests this reflected Tsimshian views that social discord reflected a lack of spiritual harmony. See "Encountering Colonialism," 137.
15 Clah Diary, 30 April 1868.
16 Ibid., 1 January 1869.
17 Ibid., 27 August 1866. See also 18 August 1865 and 28 September 1869.
18 Ibid., 26 February 1868.
19 William Duncan Journal, 10 July 1868.
20 For example, Duncan travelled to Fort Simpson to preach on a Sunday. Clah Diary, 20 June 1869. Clah noted many times that Crosby travelled on Sundays as he moved about the Coast and rivers preaching.
21 In 1869, while trading from the *Petrel,* Clah had to make do with praying on Sunday. Ibid., 7 February and 11 April 1869.
22 Peter Murray, *The Devil and Mr. Duncan: A History of the Two Metlakatlas* (Victoria: Sono Nis Press, 1995), 112.
23 Duncan Journal, 14 January 1874. In his diary, Clah writes that there were thirteen canoes that went to Metlakatla. See entry for 23 December 1873.
24 Each New Year's Day, Duncan gave a feast for the village people, new settlers were introduced and assigned to their companies, taxes were collected, the village song was sung, and speeches were made. Jean Usher, *William Duncan of Metlakatla: A*

Victorian Missionary in British Columbia, National Museum of Man Publications in History, No. 5 (Ottawa: National Museum of Man, 1974), 85.

25 These events are covered in Clah's Diary from 14 December 1873 to 24 January 1874. See Peggy Brock, "'Building Bridges': Politics and Religion in a First Nations Community," *Canadian Historical Review* 24, 2 (2000): 67-96, for a detailed discussion of these events.

26 Clah Diary, 25 December 1873.

27 Ibid., 28 December 1873.

28 Ibid., 4 January 1874.

29 Ibid., 9 January 1874.

30 Ibid., 23 January 1874. Dudoward claimed that someone else had been advocating the end of the potlatch system. In his diary entry, Clah, annoyed by these comments, wrote that he had indeed advocated ending the feasts and giving away property four years earlier. William Beynon, "The Tsimshian of Metlakatla, Alaska," *American Anthropologist* 43, 1 (1941): 86.

31 Clah Diary, 12 January 1874.

32 Ibid., 23 February 1874.

33 Ibid., 28 February 1874. Murray's discussion of these events gives a slightly different chronology but, because he does not reference his sources, this cannot be verified. It is likely that Clah's daily record is more accurate. Murray, *The Devil and Mr. Duncan,* 113.

34 Although some Anglicans blamed Duncan for allowing the religious vacuum at Fort Simpson to develop, Bishop Hills, with whom Duncan had a fractious relationship, pointed out that, had Duncan accepted ordination, the Methodists would not have set up a mission in such close proximity to Metlakatla. E.J. Hamblet to W. Duncan, 31 March 1874 and Bishop Hills to W. Duncan, 14 April 1874, University of British Columbia Library, William Duncan Papers, Correspondence – Letters received, 1874; Murray, *The Devil and Mr. Duncan,* 113.

35 Clah Diary, 12 October 1874.

36 Ibid., 28 June 1874. Jan Hare and Jean Barman, eds., *Good Intentions Gone Awry: Emma Crosby and the Methodist Mission on the Northwest Coast* (Vancouver: UBC Press, 2006), 43.

37 Hare and Barman, *Good Intentions,* 43, Emma Crosby to her mother, 1 July 1874.

38 Ibid., 45-46.

39 Clah Diary, 5 October 1874.

40 Clarence Bolt suggests class meetings were sober affairs called to ensure members were abiding by Methodist rules of conduct. See Bolt, *Thomas Crosby and the Tsimshian: Small Shoes for Too Large Feet* (Vancouver: UBC Press, 1992), 29.

41 Clah Diary, 5, 10, 24, and 31 January 1874.

42 Hare and Barman, *Good Intentions,* 8.

43   Quoted in ibid., 233.

44   Clah Diary, 25 March 1875.

45   Susan Neylan, *The Heavens Are Changing: Nineteenth-Century Protestant Missions and Tsimshian Christianity* (Montreal and Kingston: McGill Queen's University Press, 2003), 165-66.

46   Clah Diary, 30 December 1886.

47   See, for instance, Norman Etherington, *Preachers, Peasants and Politics in Southeast Africa, 1835-1880* (London: Royal Historical Society, 1978), 156; Robert Edgar, "New Religious Movements," in *Missions and Empire,* ed. N. Etherington (Oxford: Oxford University Press, 2005), 226.

48   For references to Nebuchadnezzar, see Clah Diary, 29 December 1882, 20 December 1884, 17 November 1885, 23 December 1885, 28 December 1887, 25 January 1889, and 26 December 1892. For references to King Saul, see 10 October 1886, 8 December 1889, 27 April 1890, and 19 January 1896.

49   See, for example, Clah Diary, 23 January and 18 February 1890, 23 January 1894, 10 November 1895, 5 January 1896, and 4 August 1901.

50   Ibid., 18 November 1866.

51   Franz Boas noted how accessible the Nisga'a were to religious ecstasy and that the drum of the Salvation Army had an important influence "because in their own beliefs the drum is supposed to attract supernatural help." See Franz Boas, *The Ethnography of Franz Boas,* compiled and edited by Ronald P. Rohner (Chicago: University of Chicago Press, 1969), 158. Clah, however, noted that the "heathen" were repulsed rather than attracted by the Salvation Army drum. Clah Diary, 24 November 1895.

52   See, for example, Clah Diary, 6 September 1881.

53   Jay Miller, *Tsimshian Culture: A Light through the Ages* (Lincoln: University of Nebraska Press, 1997), 63-65. Clah Diary, 31 October 1879. This is an interesting passage about Nebuchadnezzar that ends, "Since the days of the flood which confused the languages." This could apply to the Tsimshian as well as to the people of the Old Testament. Clah Diary, 17 January 1885 and 10 July 1898.

54   Miller, *Tsimshian Culture,* 34.

55   Marjorie Halpin, "'Seeing' in Stone: Tsimshian Masking and the Twin Stone Masks," in *The Tsimshian: Images of the Past, Views for the Present,* ed. Margaret Seguin (Vancouver/Seattle: UBC Press/University of Washington Press, 1993), 285.

56   Clah Diary, 25 December 1893.

57   Ibid., 19 January 1876.

58   Ibid., 24 December 1900.

59   M.-F. Guedon, "An Introduction to Tsimshian Worldview and Its Practitioners," in *The Tsimshian: Images of the Past, Views for the Present,* ed. Margaret Seguin (Vancouver/Seattle: UBC Press/University of Washington Press, 1993), 153; Miller, *Tsimshian Culture,* 3.

60 Neylan, *The Heavens*, 181-86; Miller, *Tsimshian Culture,* 169n5.

61 Beynon to Barbeau, 27 March 1923, BCA, Marius Barbeau Northwest Coast Files, MS-2101, Reel A1418, file 197.6.

62 Clah Diary, 17 January 1885. Clah made a similar claim in December 1900.

63 Ibid., 30 June 1883. One wonders whether Clah agreed with this observation, for he would have been familiar with the behaviour of whales.

64 The diary for 1875 begins with "First year 1875 Journal of Arthur Wellington writ this Book" and, on 25 March 1875, Clah wrote, "I say I am Arthur Wellington. God give me a New name." See also, 23 January 1881.

65 Ibid., 4, 14, and 21 March 1880 and 23 January 1881. Clah's wife, who was known by the Christian name Catherine, was baptized Dorcas.

66 Ibid., 5 February 1880.

67 Ibid., 15 January 1885.

68 Ibid., 28 November 1875.

69 Neylan, *The Heavens,* 187.

70 Bolt, *Thomas Crosby,* 44-45.

71 Neylan discusses the Metlakatla revival in some detail in *The Heavens Are Changing,* 192-200.

72 Bolt, *Thomas Crosby,* 43-44.

73 Usher, *William Duncan,* 96.

74 Clah Diary, 31 December 1876.

75 Ibid., 30 October 1877.

76 Ibid., 3, 5 November 1877.

77 Ibid., 20 December 1886. Bolt makes the observation, which is supported by Clah's diary, that in the winters when there were no revivals there was often a resurgence of Tsimshian winter ceremonial activity. Bolt, *Thomas Crosby,* 50. Also see Neylan, *The Heavens,* 187.

CHAPTER 8: PARADING AND PREACHING

1 Peter Murray, *The Devil and Mr. Duncan: The History of the Two Metlakatlas* (Victoria: Sono Nis Press, 1985); Jean Usher, *William Duncan of Metlakatla: A Victorian Missionary in British Columbia,* National Museum of Man Publications in History, No. 5 (Ottawa: National Museum of Man, 1974); Henry Wellcome, *The Story of Metlakahtla* (New York: Saxon and Co., 1887); John W. Arctander, *The Apostle of Alaska: The Story of William Duncan of Metlakahtla* (New York: Fleming H. Revell, 1909).

2 Susan Neylan, *The Heavens Are Changing: Nineteenth-Century Protestant Missions and Tsimshian Christianity* (Montreal and Kingston: McGill-Queen's University Press, 2003), 61. There is no record of which Tsimshian brought the Salvation Army to Port Simpson.

3 Arthur Wellington Clah, Diary, 16 November 1888, Wellcome Library, WMS Amer 140, 1-72 (hereafter Clah Diary). See also 13 and 14 November 1888.

4   Ibid., 21 November 1888. Clarence Bolt and Susan Neylan give later dates for the advent of the Salvation Army on the Coast, suggesting that the early years of its operation were not well documented. Clarence Bolt, *Thomas Crosby and the Tsimshian: Small Shoes for Too Large Feet* (Vancouver: UBC Press, 1992), 53, and Neylan, *The Heavens*, 61.

5   Clah heard Eva Booth (the daughter of the founder of the Salvation Army, William Booth, who became head of the organization in the United States and Canada) in Victoria in 1902. Clah Diary, 30 April 1902.

6   Neylan, *The Heavens*, 62.

7   Clah Diary, 9 December 1894. When Crosby refused to do so, the Anglican priest Fred Stephenson stepped in to bury Salvation Army children who had died. Ibid., 18 January 1895.

8   Ibid., 21 February 1880. In 1886, they nailed up the Anglican church and joined the Methodists. Ibid., 25 April 1886.

9   Susan Neylan, "'Here Comes the Band': Cultural Collaboration, Connective Traditions, and Aboriginal Brass Bands on British Columbia's North Coast, 1875-1964," *BC Studies* 152 (2006-7): 35-66.

10 Jay Miller, *Tsimshian Culture: A Light through the Ages* (Lincoln: University of Nebraska Press, 1997), 61, 108. William Beynon claims that William Duncan banned the drum from ceremonies at Metlakatla because of its association with Aboriginal ceremonies. See William Beynon, "The Tsimshians of Metlakatla, Alaska," *American Anthropologist* 43, 1 (1941): 86.

11 Usher, *William Duncan*, 85; Neylan, "Here Comes the Band," 18n22.

12 William Henry Collison, *In the Wake of the War Canoe*, edited by Charles Lillard (Victoria: Sono Nis Press, 1981), 178-79.

13 Clah Diary, 31 December 1862.

14 Ibid., 21 August and 31 December 1870.

15 Ibid., 26 August 1871.

16 Ibid., 27 and 29 February 1883.

17 Viola Garfield, *Tsimshian Clan and Society*, Publications in Anthropology, Vol. 7, No. 3 (Seattle: University of Washington, 1939), 319.

18 Bolt, *Thomas Crosby*, 50, 70. William Beynon refers to the Riflemen as "Volunteers." Beynon, "The Tsimshians," 87. See also Thomas Crosby, *Up and Down the North Pacific Coast* (Toronto: Missionary Society of the Methodist Church, 1914), 77.

19 Neylan, "Here Comes the Band," 3.

20 George Chismore, "From the Nass to the Skeena," *Overland Monthly* 6, 35 (1885): 452-53. See Chapter 3 (this volume) for a discussion of Chismore's journey, which was guided by Clah.

21 Clah Diary, 1 January 1900.

22 Neylan, "Here Comes the Band," 3.

23 William Beynon and Thomas Crosby suggest that the Band of Christian Workers was set up before the Salvation Army was introduced to the Coast. See Beynon, "The Tsimshians," 86, and Crosby, *Up and Down,* 61.

24 Crosby, *Up and Down,* 56, 61.

25 Ibid., 57.

26 J.B. McCullagh, *The Aiyansh Mission, Naas River, British Columbia* (London: Church Missionary Society, 1907).

27 Beynon, "The Tsimshians," 86. Anonymous, "Notes on Indian Work in BC by Methodists, 1859-92," University of British Columbia Library, Thomas Crosby Fonds, Box 1-20. This document states that the Band of Christian Workers was established at Port Simpson in 1888.

28 Bolt, *Thomas Crosby,* 52-53.

29 Bolt claims that the league was introduced at the end of the 1890s, but Clah mentions them as early as 1896. Bolt, *Thomas Crosby,* 53; Clah Diary, 15 November 1896. Both Viola Garfield and Susan Neylan suggest that the Epworth League became the dominant group of these two offshoots of the Methodist Church. During Clah's life time, however, the Band of Workers consistently attracted a large following. See Neylan, *The Heavens,* 201-2; Garfield, *Tsimshian Clan,* 320.

30 Clah Diary, 27 November 1892

31 Ibid., 3 and 6 December 1892.

32 Ibid., 26 December 1892.

33 Ibid., 6 December 1892.

34 Ibid., 30 December 1892.

35 Ibid., 28-30 December 1892.

36 Ibid., 4 January 1893.

37 Ibid., 16-25 December 1893.

38 Ibid., 17, 18 June 1893.

39 Ibid., December 1893.

40 Garfield, *Tsimshian Clan and Society,* 186. I thank Christopher Roth for pointing me to this reference and explaining its significance. The Salvation Army anti-chief movement is discussed in Chapters 10 and 11.

41 Clah Diary, 11 and 12 December 1892.

42 Ibid., 4 January 1893.

43 Ibid., 23 December 1892.

44 Ibid., 29 April 1887.

45 Ibid., 24 November 1895.

46 Ibid., 16 November 1896.

47 Ibid., 11 April 1897; Neylan, *The Heavens,* 62.

48 Ibid., 7 and 18 May and 4 June 1897.

49 Ibid., 11 and 21 December 1900.

50   Ibid., 2 January 1906.

51   Ibid., 18 January and 1 February 1874.

52   Ibid., 15 February 1874.

53   Ibid., 4 January 1893.

54   Ibid., 23 May 1875.

55   Ibid., 28 July 1875.

56   See, for example, ibid., 8 August 1875.

57   Ibid., 20 September 1880 and 18 February 1882.

58   Ibid., 2 February 1883.

59   Ibid., January-February 1883.

CHAPTER 9: CLAH AND THE MISSIONARIES

1   E. Palmer Patterson, *Mission on the Nass: The Evangelization of the Nishga, 1860-1887* (Waterloo, ON: Eulachon Press, 1982).

2   E. Palmer Patterson, "Nishga Perceptions of Their First Resident Missionary, the Reverend R.R.A. Doolan, 1864-1867," *Anthropologica* 30 (1988): 119-35.

3   William Henry Collison, *In the Wake of the War Canoe,* edited by Charles Lillard (Victoria: Sono Nis Press, 1981).

4   Arthur Wellington Clah, Diary, 10 June 1878, Wellcome Library, WMS Amer 140, 1-72 (hereafter Clah Diary).

5   Jan Hare and Jean Barman, *Good Intentions Gone Awry: Emma Crosby and the Methodist Mission on the Northwest Coast* (Vancouver: UBC Press, 2006), 224.

6   University of Washington Libraries, Manuscripts and University Archives, Garfield Papers, Box 9, Book 56-57.

7   William Henry Pierce, *From Potlatch to Pulpit: Being the Autobiography of the Rev. William Henry Pierce* (Vancouver: Vancouver Bindery, 1933).

8   William Duncan Journal, 20 November 1857 and 17 May and 9 June 1858, British Columbia Archives (BCA), William Duncan Papers, MS-2758.

9   Ibid., 2 June 1859.

10 Clah Diary, 6 December 1881. Peter Murray claims the confrontation between Duncan and Ridley, which resulted in Duncan's expulsion from the Church Missionary Society, occurred in early 1882, but rumours must have been circulating earlier if Clah heard about it in December 1881. See Peter Murray, *The Devil and Mr. Duncan: A History of the Two Metlakatlas* (Victoria: Sono Nis Press, 1985), 144-47.

11 Clah Diary, 5 September 1882.

12 See, for example, Clah Diary, 4 December 1886.

13 Ibid., 23-25 February 1888. Rev. William Henry Collison does not mention Ridley in his account of Sheldon's death. He claimed he encouraged the search for Sheldon to continue until the body was found and buried near the church Sheldon had built at Port Essington. Collison, *In the Wake of the War Canoe,* 203.

14 Clah Diary, 7 December 1889; Murray, *The Devil and Mr. Duncan,* 167.

15 Clah Diary, February–March 1874.

16 Ibid., 2 December 1874.

17 Ibid., 3 December 1874.

18 William Duncan, *Metlahkatlah: Ten Years' Work among the Tsimshean Indians* (London: Church Missionary Society, 1869); M.E. Johnson, *Dayspring in the Far West: Sketches of Mission-Work in North-West America* (London: Seeley, Jackson and Halliday, 1875), Chap. 12. I.W. Powell to Thomas Crosby, 16 Sept 1881, BCA, GR-0123, RG 10, Reel B0290, Vol. 3699, File 16682.

19 Peggy Brock, "Missionaries as Newcomers: A Comparative Study of the Northwest Pacific Coast and Central Australia," *Journal of the Canadian Historical Association,* n.s., 19, 2, (2008): 111.

20 Clah Diary, 24 October 1874.

21 Robert Galois argues that Clah left because he fell out with Crosby. R.M. Galois, "Colonial Encounters: The Worlds of Arthur Wellington Clah," *BC Studies* 115-16 (1997-98): 142

22 Clah Diary, 19 January 1876.

23 Ibid., 22-25 February 1876.

24 Ibid., 1 March 1876.

25 Ibid., 1 January 1887.

26 Ibid., 16 January 1887.

27 Ibid., 3 November 1889, 30 November 1891, 3 January 1892, and 24 and 27 August 1892.

28 Ibid., 27 August 1892.

29 Ibid., 2 September 1892.

30 Ibid., 11 February 1895; Clarence R. Bolt, *Thomas Crosby and the Tsimshian: Small Shoes for Too Large Feet* (Vancouver: UBC Press, 1992), 92.

31 Bolt, *Thomas Crosby,* 48, Appendix, Table 3.

32 Ibid., 45-46.

33 Clah Diary, 16 December 1894.

34 Bolt, *Thomas Crosby,* 88.

35 Clah Diary, 5 February 1890.

36 Hare and Harman, *Good Intentions,* 224.

37 Albert Edward Bolton, Diary, BCA, Albert Edward Bolton Fonds, E/C/B63.

38 Clah Diary, 9 November 1891; Bolton, Diary, 15 November 1890 and 23 January 1891. Bolton drained fluid from her distended abdomen.

39 Susan Neylan, *The Heavens Are Changing: Nineteenth-Century Protestant Missions and Tsimshian Christianity* (Montreal and Kingston: McGill-Queen's University Press, 2003), 220.

40 Clah Diary, 5, 17, and 19 November 1891.

41 Ibid., 7 December 1891.

42 Ibid., 16 and 25 February 1894.

43   Ibid., 2 January 1896.

44   Ibid., 16 November 1902.

45   Ibid., 5-8 March 1900 and 15 August 1903.

46   Ibid., Foreword, 1901. Note that the Psalm number should be XC-12.

47   Ibid., 3 December 1889.

48   Murray, *The Devil and Mr. Duncan*, 140, 148.

49   E. Palmer Patterson, "Kincolith's First Decade (1867-1878)," *Canadian Journal of Native Studies* 12, 2 (1992): 230-50.

50   Clah Diary, 6 and 11 March 1874.

51   Ibid., 15 and 18 January 1875.

52   Ibid., 22 January 1875 and 4 April 1876.

53   Ibid., 18-25 January 1879.

54   Ibid., 23 December 1879.

55   Ibid., 24-25 January 1880.

56   Ibid., 7 September 1869.

57   Ibid., 18-21 November 1894; 2, 11, 18, and 26 December 1894; and 7, 18, 22, and 23 January 1895.

58   E. Palmer Patterson, "Native Missionaries of the North Pacific Coast: Philip McKay and Others," *Pacific Historian* 30, 4 (1986): 22-37; Neylan, *The Heavens*, Chap. 5.

59   Clah Diary, 6 March 1866.

60   Ibid., 17 January 1869.

61   Ibid., 7 February 1895.

62   Ibid., 20 and 23 February 1869.

63   Ibid., 4 January 1872.

64   Frantz Fanon, *The Wretched of the Earth* (Harmondsworth: Penguin Books, 1967), 40.

CHAPTER 10: THE CHANGING WORLD OF FEASTING

1   Helen Codere, *Fighting with Property: A Study of Kwakiutl Potlatching and Warfare, 1792-1930* (Seattle: University of Washington Press, 1950).

2   Ibid., 97.

3   Codere was pleased if she had one or two reports of potlatches per year, indicating that most went unrecorded.

4   Christopher F. Roth, "'The Names Spread in All Directions': Hereditary Titles in Tsimshian Social and Political Life," *BC Studies* 130 (2001): 74.

5   Ibid., 75.

6   Jay Miller, *Tsimshian Culture: A Light through the Ages* (Lincoln: University of Nebraska Press, 85). Tsimshian painted their faces black for sad mourning feasts and red for happy completion feasts.

7   Christopher F. Roth, *Becoming Tsimshian: The Social Life of Names* (Seattle: University of Washington Press, 2008), 102.

8   Arthur Wellington Clah, Diary, 3 November 1863, Wellcome Library, WMS Amer 140, 1-72 (hereafter Clah Diary).

9   Ibid., 11 November 1863.

10   Ibid., 19 January 1865.

11   Ibid., 24 December 1866.

12   For an explanation of the use of *Ligeex*, see Chapter 1, note 50.

13   Clah Diary, 23 and 24 November 1870.

14   Viola Garfield, *Tsimshian Clan and Society,* Publications in Anthropology, Vol. 7, No. 3 (Washington: University of Washington, 1939), 208; Miller, *Tsimshian Culture,* 85.

15   Clah Diary, 1 January 1871. Christopher Roth suggests that Clah's children were being established as a "split off" Tsimshian house with a replicated set of names, including Gwisk'aayn from Dorcas' Nisga'a house. Christopher Roth, personal communication with author, December 2007.

16   Clah Diary, 25 January 1871.

17   Ibid., 1, 3 and 5 December 1870, and 17 and 25 February 1871.

18   Ibid., 5 December 1870

19   Ibid., 16 February 1872.

20   Ibid., 20 February 1871. The goods returned were as follows:

$200 worth of skins
100 plates and $20
He also returned $87 worth of goods:

2 bandana silk handkerchiefs	2.00
1 big meerschaum pipe	10.00
1 powder flask	2.00
1 empty case	2.00
1 canoe	20.00
1 comperty [?]	2.00
1 long comperty	1.25
20 fathoms cotton (for women)	10.00
1 peaty [?] coat	3.00
2 iron pots	2.00
2 washing basins	3.00
15 blankets worth	30.00

for chiefs who had bought whiskey.

21   Ibid., 20, 21, 22, and 28 February 1871. He also paid the four men who saved him from drowning two American flags worth sixteen dollars and two bandana silk handkerchiefs worth three dollars (he had already paid Chief Niisyaganaat).

22   Roth, *Becoming Tsimshian,* 105.

23   Clah Diary, 15, 16, 17, 18, and 22 November 1871.

24   Ibid., 29 December 1871 and 12 January 1872.

25   Clah observed in 1883 that that decision had been taken ten years beforehand. See ibid., 6 February 1883.

26   Ibid., 25 December 1877.

27   Ibid., 10-12 June 1880.

28   Ibid., 14-15 December 1880.

29   Clarence Bolt, *Thomas Crosby and the Tsimshian: Small Shoes for Too Large Feet* (Vancouver: UBC Press, 1992), 44.

30   Clah Diary, 29 December 1880–1 January 1881; Bolt, *Thomas Crosby,* 44.

31   Clah Diary, 4-5 January 1881.

32   Ibid., 17 February 1881.

33   Ibid., 26 December 1881 and 26 January 1882.

34   Ibid., 25, 30 January 1882. These may be the chiefs Duncan referred to as "would-be-chiefs" and malcontents who were jealous and humiliated about the influence of his church elders. Peter Murray, *The Devil and Mr. Duncan: A History of the Two Metlakatlas* (Victoria: Sono Nis Press, 1985), 148.

35   Clah Diary, 3 November 1883. 'Alamlaxha was held, along with 'Wiiseeks, by Albert McMillan.

36   Ibid., 26 and 28 October and 3-9 November 1883. Bolt, *Thomas Crosby,* 75-76. Clarence Bolt suggests that O'Reilly had deliberately excluded land from the reserve that might have been of interest to land speculators ahead of the decision on the route of the Canadian Pacific Railway. Two of these speculators had bought land in April 1883. An Indian agent, J.W. McKay, was forced on the Tsimshian at this time, even though they had explicitly rejected such an appointment.

37   Clah Diary, 20-24 November 1883.

38   Ibid., 29 November 1883.

39   Ibid., 4-5 December 1884.

40   Bolt, *Thomas Crosby,* 66; Amelia Susman, Viola E. Garfield, and William Beynon, "Process of Change from Matrilineal to Patrilineal Inheritance as Illustrated in Building, Ownership and Transmission of Houses and House Sites in a Tsimshian Village," *Völkerkundliche Arbeitsgemeinschaft* 26 (1979): 6; Andrew Martindale, "Tsimshian Houses and Households through the Contact Period," in *Household Archaeology on the Northwest Coast,* ed. E. Sobel, A. Trieu Gahr, and K.M. Ames (Ann Arbor: International Monographs in Prehistory, 2006), 140-58.

41   Garfield, *Tsimshian Clan and Society,* 276.

42   Clah Diary, 8 December 1885.

43   Ibid., 11 January 1886.

44   Ibid., 10 December 1885. Paul Legaic II was also warned by the HBC that he was building on its land.

45   Ronald William Hawker, "In the Way of the White Man's Totem Pole: Tsimshian Gravestones, 1879-1930" (Master's thesis, University of Victoria, 1988), 13.

46 Marjorie Halpin and Margaret Seguin, "Tsimshian Peoples: Southern Tsimshian, Coast Tsimshian, Nishga, and Gitksan," in *Handbook of North American Indians,* vol. 7, *Northwest Coast,* ed. Wayne Suttles (Washington: Smithsonian Institution, 1990), 275.

47 Garfield, *Tsimshian Clan and Society,* 209-10.

48 Clah Diary, 11 December 1885. A stone had been ordered in Victoria the previous year for Moses McDonald's grave. It cost one hundred dollars. There are several anthropological works that discuss the introduction of gravestones, including Garfield, *Tsimshian Clan and Society,* 212-14; Hawker, "In the Way," 104-16; and Margaret B. Blackman, "Totems to Tombstones: Culture Change as Viewed through the Haida Mortuary Complex, 1877-1971," *Ethnology* 12, 1 (1973): 47-56. These gravestones and memorials might have first appeared in coastal communities a few years earlier, but Clah first mentions them in 1886.

49 Clah Diary, 4 January 1887.

50 Ibid.

51 Ibid., 28 November 1887.

52 Ibid., 30 November 1887.

53 Ibid., 10 December 1887.

54 Ibid., 13-17 December 1887.

55 Ibid., 25-26 December 1887.

56 Ibid., 13 March 1887; Viola Garfield Papers, Box 7, Book 4, p. 37, University of Washington Libraries, Manuscripts and University Archives Division.

57 Clah Diary, 27 December 1887.

58 Ibid., 15-18 April 1889.

59 Ibid., 16 December 1888. It is likely that the anti-chief Salvationists were not taking a totally altruistic stand. Viola Garfield notes that there was a secessionist movement among the Eagle Gispaxlo'ots. See *Tsimshian Clan and Society,* 184-86. Christopher Roth suggests Brentzen was part of this movement. Christopher F. Roth, personal communication with author, December 2007.

60 Clah Diary, 18 December 1888.

61 Ibid., 4 December 1892.

62 Ibid., 26 December 1892. Clah names the main chiefs aligned against the Salvation Army as Alfred Dudoward, David Swanson, Albert McMillan, and Herbert Wallace (Niisyaganaat, Gits'iis chief).

63 Ibid., 25 December 1893.

64 Ibid., 16 December 1893.

65 Ibid., 27 December 1893.

66 Ibid., 23 January 1894.

67 Ibid., 28 January 1889. "[C]ity me[e]ting wanted put alfred out all together. because he sign his name to Be citizen in our Book[,] and he sign his Name to be whit citizens." See 13 January 1890.

68 Ibid., 21 December 1888. There might well have been some anti-Nisga'a feeling because the Nisga'a were trying to exclude the Tsimshian from the Nass eulachon fisheries.
69 Christopher Bracken, *The Potlatch Papers: A Colonial Case History* (Chicago: University of Chicago Press, 1997), 90-94.
70 Robin Fisher, *Contact and Conflict: Indian-European Relations in British Columbia, 1774-1890*, 2nd ed. (Vancouver: UBC Press, 1992), 206-8.
71 Clah Diary, 3-4 January 1891; Albert Edward Bolton, Diary, 4 January 1891, British Columbia Archives (BCA), Albert Edward Bolton Fonds, E/C/B63.
72 Clah Diary, 3 January 1891.
73 Garfield, *Tsimshian Clan and Society*, 169. Matthew Johnson told Garfield he was a great admirer of the Ligeex lineage, which might explain his antipathy to Xpi'lk, although Clah presents plenty of evidence that he was also antagonistic towards Ligeex at this time.
74 Clah Diary, 5 January 1891.
75 Ibid., 15-16 March 1891.
76 Douglas Cole and Ira Chaikin, *An Iron Hand upon the People: The Law against the Potlatch on the Northwest Coast* (Vancouver: Douglas and McIntyre, 1990), 46.
77 Mountain to I.W. Powell, 27 February 1886, University of British Columbia Library, Thomas Crosby Fonds, Box 1-8. Elliot, a magistrate, temporarily replaced J.W. McKay as Indian agent when McKay was relocated after the Metlakatlans refused to accept him. See Cole and Chaikin, *An Iron Hand*, 45.
78 James McCullagh to Attorney General, 19 April 1897, BCA, Attorney General Correspondence, GR-0429, Reel B09319, Box 4; "Nes Les Yan" to H.D. Helmken, 9 April 1898, BCA, Attorney General Correspondence, GR-0429, Reel B09319, Box 3. As McCullagh was trying to stamp out feasting, he wrote an ethnographic study of the potlatch, "Indian Potlatch," which he presented to the CMS's annual conference at Metlakatla in 1899. See also Cole and Chaikin, *An Iron Hand*, 46-47.
79 Clah Diary, 31 July 1891.
80 Ibid., 12 December 1891.
81 Ibid., 2-3 January 1892.
82 Ibid., 11-14 November 1903.
83 Garfield, *Tsimshian Clan and Society*, 205-6. There are aspects of Beynon's feast that were probably not found at Albert's because Beynon, who had grown up in Victoria, was a relative newcomer to the village and had been humiliated prior to taking the Gwisk'aayn title. He therefore had to humiliate guests in retaliation. He served them more ice cream than they could eat, while the crest women went about the village in wolf skins and headdresses, rounding up guests who had tried to avoid becoming the butt of the Wolf Clan's taunts.
84 Roth, *Becoming Tsimshian*.
85 See Garfield's *Tsimshian Clan and Society* and Roth's *Becoming Tsimshian* for detailed discussions of these issues.

Chapter 11: Ligeex, Chief of the Gispaxlo'ots

1 Susan Marsden and Robert Galois, "The Tsimshian, the Hudson's Bay Company, and the Geopolitics of the Northwest Coast Fur Trade, 1787-1840," *Canadian Geographer* 39, 2 (1995): 170-72.

2 For an explanation of the use of *Ligeex*, see Chapter 1, note 50.

3 See, for example, Viola Garfield, *Tsimshian Clan and Society*, Publications in Anthropology, vol. 7, no. 3 (Washington: University of Washington, 1939), 167-340; Marsden and Galois, "The Tsimshian"; Jay Miller, *Tsimshian Culture: A Light through the Ages* (Lincoln: University of Nebraska Press, 1997); Susan Neylan, *The Heavens Are Changing: Nineteenth-Century Protestant Missions and Tsimshian Christianity* (Montreal and Kingston: McGill-Queen's University Press, 2003); Marius Barbeau and William Beynon, *Tsimshian Narratives 1: Tricksters, Shamans and Heroes*, edited by George F. MacDonald and John Cove (Ottawa: Canadian Museum of Civilization, 1987); Marius Barbeau and William Beynon, *Tsimshian Narratives 2: Trade and Warfare*, edited by George F. MacDonald and John Cove (Ottawa: Canadian Museum of Civilization, 1987); H.G. Barnett, "Personal Conflicts and Cultural Change," *Social Forces* 20, 2 (1941): 160-71; Jonathon R. Dean, "'Those Rascally Spackaloids': The Rise of the Gispaxlots Hegemony at Fort Simpson, 1832-1840," *BC Studies* 101 (1994): 41-78; Michael Robinson, *Sea Otter Chiefs* (Calgary: Bayeux Arts Incorporated, 1996).

4 John W. Arctander, *The Apostle of Alaska: The Story of William Duncan of Metlakahtla* (New York: Fleming H. Revell, 1909); Henry S. Wellcome, *The Story of Metlakahtla*, 2nd ed. (London: Saxon and Co., 1887); William Duncan, *Metlahkatlah: Ten Years' Work among the Tsimsheean Indians* (London: Church Missionary House, 1869).

5 Arthur Wellington Clah, Diary, 8 February 1892, Wellcome Library, WMS Amer 140, 1-72 (hereafter Clah Diary). Paul Legaic I died at Fort Simpson but was buried at Metlakatla.

6 Ibid., 20 February 1889. The caption on a photograph of the painting in Barbeau's *Tsimshian Narratives 2*, 65, gives the location of the painting as the Skeena River, but Clah and Susan Marsden and Robert Galois, "The Tsimshian," 171, give it as the Nass River, which accords with the adawx of the events surrounding its creation. However, Beynon wrote that he saw the painting in 1920 at the mouth of the Skeena River. Draft copy of William Beynon "Ethnical and Geographical Study of the Tsimsiyaen Nation," 49, British Columbia Archives (BCA), Philip Drucker, Field Notes, MS-870, Box 6. See also Miller, *Tsimshian Culture*, 180n9n15.

7 Barbeau and Beynon, *Tsimshian Narratives 2*, 64-65; Marsden and Galois, "The Tsimshian." This article gives the history of Ligeex to 1840.

8 Viola Garfield Papers, Box 7, Book 3, p. 156, University of Washington Libraries, Manuscripts and University Archives Division. The four men were Matthew Johnson, Patrick Russ, William Pierce, and Philip Fanner.

9   Clah Diary, 7 May 1869. Clah describes Paul Legaic's death as follows: "[A]bout died[.] my dear Paul Legaic was laying death [dead] yesterday morning[.] died cough speed [spit] blood" in the HBC's fort.

10   Barnett, "Personal Conflicts and Cultural Change," 165.

11   William Duncan Journal, 5, 7, and 21 July 1862 and 20 April 1863, BCA, William Duncan Papers, MS-2758.

12   Ibid., 10 September 1862, and Clah Diary, Monday, September 1862.

13   William Duncan Journal, 13 October and 2 December 1862.

14   Ibid., 26 December 1862.

15   Ibid., January 29 and 14 February 1863.

16   Ibid., 21 March 1863.

17   Ibid., 20 April 1863.

18   Clah Diary, 14 October 1869.

19   Ibid., 20-24 October and 11-12 November 1869.

20   Ibid., 1-5 December 1870.

21   Ibid., 28 and 31 January and 1, 2, and 10 February 1871.

22   Garfield, *Tsimshian Clan and Society*, 201-4. The following winter, the Gispaxlo'ots hosted feasts for the Gitxaala and the Ginax'angiik. This was the season that Reserve Commissioner O'Reilly was on the Coast surveying reserves.

23   Clah Diary, February 1872.

24   Ibid., 3-4 February 1874 and 30 November and 1 December 1876.

25   Ibid., 2 January 1882.

26   Ibid., 30 December 1882. Paul Legaic II had brought a complaint against Ridley, who he claimed had knocked him down, to magistrate Hall in 1882.

27   Ibid., 29 November 1883.

28   Ibid., 10 April 1886.

29   Ibid., 17 April, 25 and 29 November, and 12 December 1886.

30   Ibid., 14 December 1887.

31   Ibid., 15 October 1889. Patrick Russ was Spooxs, a Gixpaxlo'ots titleholder.

32   Ibid., 8 January 1891; Albert Edward Bolton, Diary, 9 January 1891, BCA, Alberta Edward Bolton Fonds, E/C/B63. Bolton recorded that he had been called out at 3 a.m., when Paul Legaic's body was found in the water where he had drowned during a fit.

33   William Beynon, "Totem Poles," UBC Library, manuscript, Reel 2, No. 119.

34   Clah Diary, 9 January 1891.

35   Beynon, "Totem Poles," Reel 2, No. 119, pp. 19-49.

36   Clah Diary, 10 January 1891.

37   Beynon, "Totem Poles," Reel 2, No. 119, pp. 41-49.

38   Clah Diary, 16 January 1891; Albert Edward Bolton, Diary, 15 January 1891.

39   Clah Diary, 5 December 1891. Clah describes this as a berry feast, although it had originally been planned that bread, jam, butter, and meat would be offered. The

plan changed, however, when Matthew Johnson's wife sold them two boxes of dried berries.

40   Ibid., 17 January 1891.

41   Ibid., 4 December 1891.

42   Ibid., 8 January 1892.

43   Beynon, "Totem Poles," Reel 2, No. 119.

44   Clah Diary, 11 January 1891. Ronald William Hawker, "In the Way of the White Man's Totem Pole: Tsimshian Gravestones, 1879-1930" (Master's thesis, University of Victoria, 1988), 114-15. Hawker claims that this monument has been attributed to another stone mason, George Rudge, but it is clear from Clah's diary that James Fisher was responsible for it.

45   Hawker, "In the Way," 104.

46   William Beynon gave her previous name as Gadelbam Haiyeisk. See Beynon, "Totem Poles, Reel 2, No. 119, p. 29.

47   Clah Diary, 4 February and 13 November 1891. It is possible that Martha was then taken into Clah's T'amks house, although the text is a little ambiguous. See also ibid., 14 December 1897: "Better people take legaic out the house where I stay." Ligeex should have belonged to the Eagle Clan (Laxsgiik), but Clah's house was Killer Whale (Gispwudwada). However, George Kelly told Viola Garfield that Martha was the daughter of Simon Wallace, head of the Gitselas, and that she was Gispwudwada. Viola Garfield Papers, Box 7, Book 3, p. 159, University of Washington Libraries, Manuscripts and University Archives Division.

48   Clah Diary, 21 November and 1-10 December 1898.

49   Ibid., 16 November 1896.

50   Ibid., 6-24 December 1899.

51   Ibid., 6 January and 18 May 1902. She had a son in 1897 who died in 1900, ibid., 14 December 1897 and 26 August 1900.

52   Ibid., 20 August, 28 November, and 1, 4, 5, 15, 17, and 24 December 1902.

53   Ibid., 1907. Christopher Roth suggests that Kelly's accession might have been announced at his mother's memorial feast after her death in 1903 and not affirmed until 1907. Christopher Roth, personal communication with the author, December 2007.

54   Garfield, *Tsimshian Clan and Society,* 185.

55   Ibid., 186; Christopher F. Roth, *Becoming Tsimshian: The Social Life of Names* (Seattle: University of Washington Press, 2008), 102.

CHAPTER 12: OLD AGE

1   Arthur Wellington Clah, Diary, 30 November 1889, Wellcome Library, WMS Amer 140, 1-72 (hereafter Clah Diary).

2   Ibid., 28 March 1894.

3   Ibid., 21 November 1895.

4   Ibid., 28 and 30 September 1909.

5   Ibid., 1 October 1901.

6   Ibid., 22 January 1898.

7   Ibid., 15 April 1894.

8   Arthur Wellington Clah, Diary and Notes, British Columbia Archives (BCA), George Henry Raley Papers, 98208-50, H/D/R13/C52 (Volume 70 in the Clah Diaries, Wellcome Library).

9   Clah Diary, 21 January 1902.

10   Ibid., 3 December 1900 and 17 June 1897.

11   1911 Report, Department of Indian Affairs Fonds, Nass Agency, Correspondence and Agents' Reports, 1910-15, BCA, Department of Indian Affairs, GR-2043, RG 10, Reel B01920.

12   Rolf Knight makes the point that Aboriginal workers were defined by their wage labour, not their traditional cultural values. See *Indians at Work: An Informal History of Native Labour in British Columbia, 1858-1930,* 2nd ed. (Vancouver: New Star Books, 1996).

13   James A. McDonald, "Social Change and the Creation of Underdevelopment: Northwest Coast Case," *American Ethnologist* 21, 1 (1994): 168.

14   Clah Diary, 25 July 1896.

15   Ibid., 20 September 1997.

16   Ibid., 10 March 1894.

17   Ibid., 23 September–9 November 1895.

18   Ibid., 24 December 1895.

19   Ibid., 23 July 1907.

20   Ibid., 28 July 1907.

21   Ibid., 20 April 1895.

22   Ibid., 16 and 25 March and 8 April 1895.

23   Ibid., June 1894.

24   Ibid., 19 June 1895.

25   Ibid., 22 April 1906.

26   Peter Murray, *The Devil and Mr. Duncan: The History of the Two Metlakatlas* (Victoria: Sono Nis Press, 1985), 314-15.

27   Clah Diary, 29 December 1906.

28   See Murray, *The Devil and Mr. Duncan,* for a detailed account of the move to Alaska.

29   Clah Diary, 24 November and 6 December 1907.

30   Ibid., 18 November–7 December 2007.

31   Ibid., 13 May 1898.

32   Ibid., 12 July 1901.

33   See, for example, ibid., 1 August 1898, 28 August 1902, and 1 September 1904.

34   Ibid., 10 October 1907.

35   Ibid., 25 December 1900.

36 Ibid., 28-29 September 1905.

37 Ibid., 11 March 1895.

38 Ibid., 21 May 1898.

39 Ibid., 20-26 March 1894.

40 Ibid., 19-20 March 1894.

41 Ibid., 21 November 1908.

42 See R.M. Galois, "Colonial Encounters: The Worlds of Arthur Wellington Clah, 1855-1881," *BC Studies* 115-16 (1997-98): 106, 147. The Canadian census of 1911 states that the Wellington household comprised Clah, aged eighty, and a wife, aged seventy. The name of the wife is almost illegible, but it is neither Dorcas nor Catherine. I thank Christopher Roth for alerting me to the census data.

Conclusion

1 Orville Bertley, "Port Simpson," *Westward Ho* (1909): 313, 315-16, University of British Columbia Library. Clah spells Flewins name *Plewings*. The terminus of the Grand Trunk Pacific Railway was built at Prince Rupert.

2 The HBC did make a compensation offer to Clah that he did not think was adequate. It is not clear whether he received any money from the HBC.

3 Arthur Wellington Clah, Diary, 5 January 1897, Wellcome Library, WMS Amer 140, 1-72.

Bibliography

ARCHIVAL SOURCES

British Columbia Archives (BCA), Victoria, BC
Attorney-General Correspondence, GR-0429.
Marius Barbeau Northwest Coast Files, MS-2101.
BC Commission on Disturbances at Metlakatla, 1884, Port Simpson Enquiry, 1884, GR-0351.
Beynon, William. "Ethnical and Geographical Study of the Tsimsiyaen Nation." In Philip Drucker Field Notes, MS-870, Box 6.
Albert Edward Bolton Fonds, E/C/B63.
British Columbia Lands Branch. Correspondence Files Relating to the Administration, Management, and Development of Crown Lands and Natural Resources, GR-1440.
British Columbia Sessional Papers. Microfilm.
Department of Indian Affairs, RG 10
    GR-0123, McKenna-McBride Royal Commission on Indian Affairs, 1913-16
    GR-0933, Records of Joint Reserve Commission
    GR-2043, Records with regard to British Columbia
James Douglas to the Secretary of State for the Colonies, Letters, Secretary of State, 10 December 1855–6 June 1859, C/AA/10.1/3.
Philip Drucker Field Notes, MS-870.
Wilson Duff Papers, GR-2809.
William Duncan Papers, MS-2758.
Letter to A.W. Clah from A.P. Swineford, 23 September 1887, MS-0271.
McNeill et al. v. McNeill et al., Papers from Intestate Estates, GR-485, Box 17, File 1.
George Henry Raley Papers, 98208-50, H/D/R13/C52, Arthur Wellington Clah, Diary and Notes.

Stephen Redgrave, Journals and Sundry Papers, 1852-75, E/B/R24A.
Victoria Supreme Court Probate/Estate Files, GR-1304.

Canadian Museum of Civilization, Hull, QC
Barbeau Northwest Coast Files, B-F-24.5.

Church of England Archives, Vancouver, BC
Proceedings of the Church Missionary Society, 1893-94.

Hudson's Bay Company Archives, Winnipeg, MN
Biographical Sheets. http://www.gov.mb.ca/chc/archives/hbca/biographical.
Fort Simpson (Nass) Post Journal, B.201/a/8.

United Church of Canada, BC Conference, Bob Stewart Archives, Vancouver, BC

University of British Columbia Library, Rare Books and Special Collections and Microform Collection
Bertley, Orville. "Port Simpson," *Westward Ho* (1909): 313, 315-16.
Beynon, William. "Totem Poles." Manuscript. Microfilm.
Thomas Crosby Fonds.
William Duncan Papers. Correspondence – Letters received. MG 29 H 15. Microfilm.
McCullagh, J.B. *The Indian Potlatch*. Toronto: Women's Missionary Society of the Methodist Church, n.d. Microfilm.
Methodist Church (Canada) Missionary Society. Microform CIHM 15637.
Report from Gold Commissioner on Omineca District, BC Sessional Papers, No. 5, 1872. Microfilm D-24, Reel 1.
Seymour, Governor Frederick. "Report and Journal of Visit of Governor Seymour to the North West Coast in HMS *Sparrowhawk*, 1869."

University of Washington Libraries, Manuscripts and University Archives Division, Seattle
Viola Garfield Papers.

Wellcome Library, London
Arthur Wellington Clah. Diary and Papers, WMS Amer 140, 1-72.
Wellington, Albert. Memoranda and Accounts, 1901, WMS 141.

OTHER SOURCES
Akrigg, G.P.V., and Helen B. Akrigg. *British Columbia Chronicle, 1847-1871: Gold and Colonists*. Vancouver: Discovery Press, 1977.

Arctander, John W. *The Apostle of Alaska: The Story of William Duncan of Metlakahtla.* New York: Fleming H. Revell, 1909.

Barbeau, C.M., "Review of *Tsimshian Mythology* in *American Anthropologist.*" 19, 4 (1917): 548-63.

Barbeau, Marius, and William Beynon. *Tsimshian Narratives 1: Tricksters, Shamans and Heroes.* Edited by George F. MacDonald and John Cove. Ottawa: Canadian Museum of Civilization, 1987.

–. *Tsimshian Narratives 2: Trade and Warfare.* Edited by George F. MacDonald and John Cove. Ottawa: Canadian Museum of Civilization, 1987.

Barber, Karin, ed. *African Hidden Histories.* Bloomington: Indiana University Press, 2006.

Barman, Jean. *The West beyond the West: A History of British Columbia.* Toronto: University of Toronto Press, 1996.

Barnett, H.G. "Personal Conflicts and Cultural Change." *Social Forces* 20, 2 (1941): 160-71.

Baskerville, Peter A. *Beyond the Island: An Illustrated History of Victoria.* Burlington, ON: Windsor Publications, 1986.

Beynon, William. *Potlatch at Gitsegukla: William Beynon's 1945 Field Notebooks.* Edited by Margaret Anderson and Marjorie Halpin. Vancouver: UBC Press, 2000.

–. "The Tsimshians of Metlakatla, Alaska." *American Anthropologist* 43, 1 (1941): 83-88.

Blackman, Margaret B. "Totems to Tombstones: Culture Change as Viewed through the Haida Mortuary Complex, 1877-1971." *Ethnology* 12, 1 (1973): 47-56.

Boas, Franz. *The Ethnography of Franz Boas.* Compiled and edited by Ronald P. Rohner. Chicago: University of Chicago Press, 1969.

–. *Tsimshian Mythology.* Based on texts recorded by Henry W. Tate. 31st Annual Report of the Bureau of American Ethnology, 1916.

Bolt, Clarence R. "The Conversion of the Port Simpson Tsimshian: Indian Control or Missionary Manipulation?" In *Out of the Background: Readings on Canadian Native History,* edited by Robin Fisher and Kenneth Coates, 219-36. Toronto: Copp Clark Pitman, 1988.

–. *Thomas Crosby and the Tsimshian: Small Shoes for Too Large Feet.* Vancouver: UBC Press, 1992.

Boyd, Robert. *The Coming of the Spirit of Pestilence: Introduced Infectious Diseases and Population Decline among the Northwest Coast Indians, 1774-1874.* Seattle: University of Washington Press, 1999.

Bracken, Christopher. *The Potlatch Papers: A Colonial Case History.* Chicago: University of Chicago Press, 1997.

Brealey, Kenneth. "Travels from Point Ellice: Peter O'Reilly and the Indian Reserve System in British Columbia." *BC Studies,* 115-116 (1997-98): 180-236.

Brock, Peggy. "'Building Bridges': Politics and Religion in a First Nations Community." *Canadian Historical Review* 24, 2 (2000): 67-96.

–. "The Historical Dispossession of Indigenous Lands in Western Australia and British Columbia." *Studies in Western Australian History* 23 (2003): 157-65.

–. "Missionaries as Newcomers: A Comparative Study of the Northwest Pacific Coast and Central Australia." *Journal of the Canadian Historical Association,* n.s., 19, 2 (2008): 105-24.

–. "New Christians as Evangelists." In *Missions and Empire,* edited by N. Etherington, 132-52. Oxford: Oxford University Press, 2005.

–. "Setting the Record Straight." In *Indigenous Peoples and Religious Change,* edited by Peggy Brock, 107-28. Leiden: Brill, 2005.

–. "Two Indigenous Evangelists: Moses Tjalkabota and Arthur Wellington Clah." *Journal of Religious History* 27, 3 (2003): 348-66.

Butler, Caroline F., and Charles R. Menzies. "First Nations and the Natural Resource Economy: A View from the Tsimshian Nation." *Labour/Le Travail* 61 (Spring 2008): 133-49.

Carsten, Peter. *The Queen's People: A Study of Hegemony, Coercion, and Accommodation among the Okanagan of Canada.* Toronto: University of Toronto Press, 1991.

Chismore, George. "From the Nass to the Skeena." *Overland Monthly* 6, 35 (1885): 449-458.

Clark, Cecil. *The Best of Victoria: Yesterday and Today.* Victoria: Victorian Weekly, 1973.

Codere, Helen. *Fighting with Property: A Study of Kwakiutl Potlatching and Warfare, 1792-1930.* Seattle: University of Washington Press, 1950.

Cole, Douglas, and Ira Chaikin. *An Iron Hand upon the People: The Law against the Potlatch on the Northwest Coast.* Vancouver: Douglas and McIntyre, 1990.

Collison, William Henry. *In the Wake of the War Canoe: A Stirring Record of Forty Years' Successful Labour, Peril and Adventure amongst the Savage Indian Tribes of the Pacific Coast, and the Piratical Head-Hunting Haida of the Queen Charlotte Islands, British Columbia.* Edited by Charles Lillard. Victoria: Sono Nis Press, 1981.

Crosby, Alfred. *Ecological Imperialism: The Biological Expansion of Europe, 900-1900.* Cambridge: Cambridge University Press, 2004.

Crosby, Thomas. *Up and Down the North Pacific Coast.* Toronto: Missionary Society of the Methodist Church, 1914.

Cross, Peter G. "Persistence and Change: The Demographic and Cultural Reasons for Acceptance and Rejection of Economic Development on the Skeena and Nass Rivers of BC, 1831-1916." Master's thesis, University of Victoria, 1991.

Darling, John Davidson. "The Effects of Culture Contact on the Tsimshian System of Land Tenure during the Nineteenth Century." Master's thesis, University of British Columbia, 1955.

Davis, George T.B. *Metlakatla: A True Narrative of the Red Man.* Chicago: Ram's Horn Company, 1904.

Dean, Jonathon R. "'Those Rascally Spackaloids': The Rise of Gispaxlots Hegemony at Fort Simpson, 1832-40." *BC Studies* 101 (1994): 41-78.

Donald, Leland. *Aboriginal Slavery on the Northwest Coast of North America.* Berkeley: University of California Press, 1997.

Drucker, Philip. *Indians of the Northwest Coast.* New York: McGraw-Hill, 1955.

Duncan, William. *Metlahkatlah: Ten Years' Work among the Tsimsheean Indians.* London: Church Missionary House, 1869.

Edgar, Robert. "New Religious Movements." In *Missions and Empire,* edited by N. Etherington, 216-37. Oxford: Oxford University Press, 2005.

Etherington, Norman. *Preachers, Peasants and Politics in Southeast Africa, 1835-1880.* London: Royal Historical Society, 1978.

Fanon, Frantz. *The Wretched of the Earth.* Harmondsworth: Penguin Books, 1967.

Fisher, Robin. *Contact and Conflict: Indian-European Relations in British Columbia, 1774-1890.* 2nd ed. Vancouver: UBC Press, 1992.

Fiske, Jo-Anne. "Colonization and the Decline of Women's Status: The Tsimshian Case." *Feminist Studies* 17, 3 (1991): 509-35.

Fothergill, Robert. *Private Chronicles: A Study of English Diaries* London: Oxford University Press, 1974.

Galois, R.M. "Colonial Encounters: The Worlds of Arthur Wellington Clah, 1855-1881." *BC Studies* 115-16 (1997-98): 105-47.

Garfield, Viola. "The Tsimshian and Their Neighbours." In *The Tsimshian Indians and Their Arts,* edited by Viola E. Garfield and Paul S. Wingert, 5-72. Seattle: University of Washington Press, 1966.

–. *Tsimshian Clan and Society.* Publications in Anthropology, Vol. 7, No. 3. Washington: University of Washington, 1939.

Garfield, Viola E., and Paul S. Wingert. *The Tsimshian and Their Arts.* Seattle: University of Washington Press, 1966.

Gough, Barry M. *Gunboat Frontier: British Maritime Authority and the Northwest Coast Indians, 1846-1890.* Vancouver: UBC Press, 1984.

Grumet, Robert Steven. "Changes in Coast Tsimshian Redistributive Activities in the Fort Simpson Region of British Columbia, 1788-1862." *Ethnohistory* 22, 4 (1975): 295-318.

Guedon, M.-F. "An Introduction to Tsimshian World View and Its Practitioners." In *The Tsimshian: Images of the Past, Views for the Present,* edited by Margaret Seguin, 149-53. Vancouver/Seattle: UBC Press/University of Washington Press, 1993.

Halpin, Marjorie. "'Seeing' in Stone: Tsimshian Masking and the Twin Stone Masks." In *The Tsimshian: Images of the Past, Views for the Present,* edited by Margaret Seguin, 281-307. Vancouver/Seattle: UBC Press/University of Washington Press, 1993.

–. "William Beynon, Ethnographer: Tsimshian, 1888-1958." In *American Indian Intellectuals,* edited by Liberty Mercer, 141-56. Proceedings of the American Ethnological Society. St. Paul, MN: West Publishing, 1976.

Halpin, Marjorie, and Margaret Seguin. "Tsimshian Peoples: Southern Tsimshian, Coast Tsimshian, Nishga, and Gitksan." In *Handbook of North American Indians.* Vol. 7, *Northwest Coast,* edited by Wayne Suttles, 267-84. Washington, DC: Smithsonian Institution, 1990.

Hare, Jan, and Jean Barman. *Good Intentions Gone Awry: Emma Crosby and the Methodist Mission on the Northwest Coast.* Vancouver: UBC Press, 2006.

Harris, Cole. *Making Native Space: Colonialism, Resistance, and Reserves in British Columbia.* Vancouver: UBC Press, 2002.

–. "Voices of Disaster: Smallpox around the Strait of Georgia in 1782." *Ethnohistory* 41, 4 (1994): 591-621.

Harris, Douglas. *Fish, Law, and Colonialism: The Legal Capture of Salmon in British Columbia.* Toronto: University of Toronto Press, 2001.

Hawker, Ronald William. "In the Way of the White Man's Totem Pole: Tsimshian Gravestones, 1879-1930." Master's thesis, University of Victoria, 1988.

Hopwood, Victor G. "Thomas McMicking." *Dictionary of Canadian Biography Online.* http://www.biographi.ca.

Howay, F.W. "Potatoes: Records of Some Early Transactions at Fort Simpson, B.C." *The Beaver,* Outfit 259 (March 1929): 155-56.

Inglis, Gordon B., Douglas R. Hudson, Barbara R. Rigsby, and Bruce Rigsby. "Tsimshian of British Columbia since 1900." In *Handbook of North American Indians.* Vol. 7, *Northwest Coast,* edited by Wayne Suttles, 285-94. Washington, DC: Smithsonian Institution, 1990.

Johnson, M.E. *Dayspring in the Far West: Sketches of Mission-Work in North-West America.* London: Seeley, Jackson and Halliday, 1875.

Keddie, Grant. *Songhees Pictorial: A History of the Songhees People as Seen by Outsiders, 1790-1912.* Victoria: Royal BC Museum, 2003.

Knight, Rolf. *Indians at Work: An Informal History of Native Labour in British Columbia, 1858-1930.* 2nd ed. Vancouver: New Star Books, 1996.

Large, R. Geddes. *The Skeena River of Destiny.* Vancouver: Mitchell Press, 1958.

Lillard, Charles. *Seven Shillings a Year: The History of Vancouver Island.* Ganges, BC: Horsdal and Schubart, 1986.

Mackie, Richard Somerset. *Trading beyond the Mountains: The British Fur Trade on the Pacific, 1793-1843.* Vancouver: UBC Press, 1997.

Mallon, Thomas. *A Book of One's Own: People and Their Diaries.* New York: Tickner and Fields, 1984.

Marsden, Susan. "Adawx, Spanaxnox, and the Geopolitics of the Tsimshian." *BC Studies* 135 (2002): 101-35.

–, ed. *Na Amwaaltga Ts'msiyeen: The Tsimshian, Trade, and the Northwest Coast Economy.* Prince Rupert, BC: School District No. 52, 1992.

Marsden, Susan, and Robert Galois. "The Tsimshian, the Hudson's Bay Company, and the Geopolitics of the Northwest Coast Fur Trade, 1787-1840." *Canadian Geographer* 39, 2 (1995): 169-83.

Martindale, Andrew. "Tsimshian Houses and Households through the Contact Period." In *Household Archaeology on the Northwest Coast,* edited by E. Sobel, A. Trieu Gahr, and K.M. Ames, 140-58. Ann Arbor: International Monographs in Prehistory, 2006.

Martindale, Andrew, and Irena Jurakic. "Northern Tsimshian Elderberry Use in the Late Pre-Contact to Post-Contact Era." *Canadian Journal of Archaeology* 28, 2 (2004): 254-80.

Martindale, Andrew R.C., and Susan Marsden. "Defining the Middle Period (3,500 to 1,500 BP) in Tsimshian History through Comparison of Archaeological and Oral Records." *BC Studies* 138 (2005): 13-50.

Maud, Ralph. *Transmission Difficulties: Franz Boas and Tsimshian Mythology.* Burnaby: Talonbooks, 2000.

May, Nicholas Paul. "Making Conversation: Opening Dialogues of the Nisga'a Encounter with the Church Missionary Society, 1864-67." Master's thesis, University of Victoria, 2003.

McCarthy, Molly. "A Pocketful of Days: Pocket Diaries and Daily Record Keeping among Nineteenth-Century New England Women." *New England Quarterly* 73, 2 (2000): 274-96.

McCullagh, J.B. *The Aiyansh Mission, Naas River, British Columbia.* London: Church Missionary Society, 1907.

McDonald, James A. "Social Change and the Creation of Underdevelopment: A Northwest Coast Case." *American Ethnologist* 21, 1 (1994): 152-75.

McHarg, Sandra, and Maureen Cassidy. *Before Roads and Rails: Pack Trails and Packing in the Upper Skeena Area.* Hazelton: Northwest Community College, 1980.

–. *Early Days on the Skeena River.* Hazelton: Northwest Community College, 1980.

Meilleur, Helen. *A Pour of Rain: Stories from the West Coast Fort.* Vancouver: Raincoast Books, 2001.

Methodist Missionary Society. *Letter from the Methodist Missionary Society to the Superintendent General of Indian Affairs respecting British Columbia Troubles.* Toronto: Methodist Missionary Society, 1889.

Miescher, Stephan F. "'My Own Life': A.K. Boakye Yiadom's Autobiography – The Writing and Subjectivity of a Ghanian Teacher-Catechist." In *African Hidden Histories,* edited by Karin Barber, 27-51. Bloomington: Indiana University Press, 2006.

Miller, Jay. *Tsimshian Culture: A Light through the Ages.* Lincoln: University of Nebraska Press, 1997.

Murray, Peter. *The Devil and Mr. Duncan: The History of the Two Metlakatlas.* Victoria: Sono Nis Press, 1985.

Newell, Dianne. *Tangled Webs of History: Indians and the Law in Canada's Pacific Coast Fisheries.* Toronto: University of Toronto Press, 1993.

Newell, G.R. "William Henry McNeill." *Dictionary of Canadian Biography Online.* http://www.biographi.ca/EN/ShowBio.asp?BioId=39274&query=mcneill.

Neylan, Susan. "'Eating the Angels' Food': Arthur Wellington Clah – An Aboriginal Perspective on Being Christian, 1857-1909." In *Canadian Missionaries, Indigenous Peoples: Representing Religion at Home and Abroad,* edited by Alvyn Austin and Jamie S. Scott, 88-110. Toronto: University of Toronto Press, 2005.

–. *The Heavens Are Changing: Nineteenth-Century Protestant Missions and Tsimshian Christianity.* Montreal and Kingston: McGill-Queen's University Press, 2003.

–. "'Here Comes the Band': Cultural Collaboration, Connective Traditions, and Aboriginal Brass Bands on British Columbia's North Coast, 1875-1964." *BC Studies* 152 (2006-7): 35-66.

Ormsby, Margaret A. *British Columbia: A History.* Vancouver: Macmillan, 1958.

Patterson, E. Palmer. "Kincolith's First Decade (1867-1878)." *Canadian Journal of Native Studies* 12, 2 (1992): 230-50.

–. *Mission on the Nass: The Evangelization of the Nishga, 1860-1887.* Waterloo, ON: Euchalon Press, 1982.

–. "Native Missionaries of the North Pacific Coast: Philip McKay and Others." *Pacific Historian* 30, 4 (1986): 22-37.

–. "Neshaki: Kinfolk and Trade." *Culture* 10, 2 (1990): 13-24.

–. "Nishga Perceptions of Their First Resident Missionary, the Reverend R.R.A. Doolan, 1864-1867." *Anthropologica* 30 (1988): 119-35.

Pierce, W.H. *From Potlatch to Pulpit: Being the Autobiography of the Rev. William Henry Pierce, Native Missionary to the Indian Tribes of the Northwest Coast of British Columbia.* Edited by J.P. Hicks. Vancouver: Vancouver Bindery, 1933.

–. *Thirteen Years of Travel and Exploration in Alaska.* Edited by Professor and Mrs. H. Carruth. Lawrence, KS: Journal Publishing Company, 1890.

Raibmon, Paige. *Authentic Indians: Episodes of Encounter from the Late-Nineteenth-Century Northwest Coast.* Durham: Duke University Press, 2005.

Robinson, Michael. "Great Men in Northwest Coast Small Societies: Legaik, Cuneah and Maqunna." Bachelor's essay, University of British Columbia, 1973.

–. *Sea Otter Chiefs.* Calgary: Bayeux Arts Incorporated, 1996.

Roth, Christopher F. *Becoming Tsimshian: The Social Life of Names.* Seattle: University of Washington Press, 2008.

–. "'The Names Spread in All Directions': Hereditary Titles in Tsimshian Social and Political Life." *BC Studies* 130 (2001): 69-92.

Ross, W.M. "Salmon Cannery Distribution on the Nass and Skeena Rivers of British Columbia, 1877-1926." Bachelor's essay, University of British Columbia, 1967.

Rudolph, Lloyd. "Self as Other: Amar Singh's Diary as Reflexive 'Native' Ethnography." *Modern Asian Studies* 31 (1997): 143-75.

Rudolph, Susanne, and Lloyd Rudolph. "Becoming a Diarist: The Making of an Indian Personal Document." *Indian Social and Economic History Review* 25, 2 (1988): 113-32.

–, eds., with Mohan Singh Kanota. *Reversing the Gaze: Amar Singh's Diary – A Colonial Subject's Narrative of Imperial India.* Boulder, CO: Westview Press, 2002.

Scott, Jamie S., and Gareth Griffith, eds. *Mixed Messages: Materiality, Texuality, Missions.* New York: Palgrave Macmillan, 2005.

Seguin, Margaret. *Interpretive Contexts for Traditional and Current Coast Tsimshian Feasts.* Ottawa: National Museum of Man, 1985.

–. "Introduction: Tsimshian Society and Culture." In *The Tsimshian: Images of the Past, Views for the Present,* edited by Margaret Seguin, ix-xx. 2nd ed. Vancouver: UBC Press, 1993.

–. "Lest There Be No Salmon: Symbols in Traditional Tsimshian Potlatch." In *The Tsimshian: Images of the Past, Views for the Present,* edited by Margaret Seguin, 110-36. 2nd ed. Vancouver: UBC Press, 1993.

Sherman, Stuart. *Telling Time: Clocks and English Diurnal Form, 1660-1785.* Chicago: University of Chicago Press, 1996.

Soga, Tiyo. *The Journal and Selected Writings of Rev. Tiyo Soga.* Edited by Donovan Williams. Cape Town: A.A. Balkema, 1983.

Sterritt, Neil J., Susan Marsden, Robert Galois, Peter R. Grant, and Richard Overstall. *Tribal Boundaries in the Nass Watershed.* Vancouver: UBC Press, 1998.

Stewart, Hilary. *Cedar: Tree of Life to the Northwest Coast Indians.* Vancouver: Douglas and McIntyre, 1984.

–. *Indian Fishing: Early Methods on the Northwest Coast.* Vancouver: J.J. Douglas, 1977.

Stuckey, Naneen E. "Tsimshian Testimony before the Royal Commission on Indian Affairs for the Province of BC (1913-1916)." Master's thesis, University of Victoria, 1981.

Susman, Amelia, Viola E. Garfield, and William Beynon. "Process of Change from Matrilineal to Patrilineal Inheritance as Illustrated in Building, Ownership and Transmission of Houses and House Sites in a Tsimshian Village." *Völkerkundliche Arbeitsgemeinschaft* 26 (1979): 1-19.

Tennant, Paul. *Aboriginal Peoples and Politics: The Indian Land Question in British Columbia, 1849-1989.* Vancouver: UBC Press, 1995.

Thomann, G. *American Beer: Glimpses of Its History and Description of Its Manufacture.* New York: US Brewers' Association, 1909.

Tolmie, William Fraser. *The Journals of William Fraser Tolmie: Physician and Fur Trader.* Vancouver: Mitchell Press, 1963.

Tsimshian Chiefs. *The Tsimshian Trade and the Northwest Coast Economy.* Prince Rupert: Prince Rupert School District 52, 1992.

Turner, Nancy J. *Food Plants of British Columbian Indians.* Part 1, *Coastal Peoples.* Victoria: BC Provincial Museum, 1975.

Usher, Jean. *William Duncan of Metlakatla: A Victorian Missionary in British Columbia.* National Museum of Man Publications in History, No. 5. Ottawa: National Museum of Man, 1974.

Van Kirk, Sylvia. "Tracing the Fortunes of Five Founding Families in Victoria." *BC Studies* 115-16 (1997-98): 148-79.

Vaughan, J.D. "Tsimshian Potlatch and Society: Examining a Structural Analysis." In *The Tsimshian and Their Neighbours of the North Pacific Coast,* edited by Jay Miller and Carol M. Eastman, 58-68. Seattle: University of Washington Press, 1984.

Watson, Ruth. "'What Is Our Intelligence, Our School Going and Our Reading of Books without Getting Money?' Akinpelu Obiseasan and His Diary." In *African Hidden Histories,* edited by Karin Barber, 52-77. Bloomington: Indiana University Press, 2006.

Wellcome, Henry S. *The Story of Metlahkahtla.* 2nd ed. New York: Saxon and Co., 1887.

Williams, David Riccardo. "Peter O'Reilly." *Dictionary of Canadian Biography Online.* http://www.biographi.ca/.

Winter, Barbara J. "William Beynon and the Anthropologists." *Canadian Journal of Native Studies* 4, 2 (1984): 279-92.

Index

Note: Tsimshian and Nisga'a people and places are listed both by their Aboriginal and European names where these are known. Page numbers in *italics* refer to illustrations.

Printed and bound in Canada by Friesens

Set in Minion Pro and Garamond by Artegraphica Design Co. Ltd.

Copy editor: Lesley Erickson

Proofreader: Theresa Best

Indexer: Annette Lorek

Cartographer: Eric Leinberger